No 20

LUND'S BRISTOL AND EARLY WORCESTER PORCELAIN 1750-58

The A. J. Smith Collection

SIMON SPERO

(with a contribution by Richard Burt)

ISBN 10: 0-9551221-0-4
ISBN 13: 978-0-9551221-0-1

British Library Cataloguing-in-Publication Data.
A catalogue record for this book is available from the British Library.

Published by C and J Smith
Printed in England by Sealprint Ltd. London

CONTENTS

ACKNOWLEDGEMENTS

John and Clive Smith have been unwavering in their support, patience and enthusiasm for this project and their encouragement and material contribution have been crucial. Richard Burt has written two chapters which have added a fresh dimension to this study, aided by the researches of the local historian Ray Jones. It has been both a pleasure and a privilege to work alongside Richard and to discuss with him the progress of the book. David Birley and his team at Sealprint, especially Brian Adams, have worked tirelessly and with steadfast good humour to create this volume and my photographer Alf Barnes has provided a wonderful set of images, generated in difficult circumstances, all with his unfailing cheerfulness and conscientious attention to detail.

Hugh Roberts, representing the Friends of the Bristol Art Gallery, has been a constant source of encouragement and it was his original suggestion which sowed the seeds for this volume. Karin Walton, Curator of Applied Art at the Bristol Museum and Art Gallery has given generously of her time and energy and has been an enthusiastic supporter throughout this project. I would also like to express my gratitude to Rodney Dowling, Geoffrey Godden, Robert McPherson, Errol Manners and John Sandon, and to Sally Ball and Jane Holdsworth who have typed out my manuscript and transferred it on to disks. The exacting task of proof reading the manuscript was undertaken with meticulous accuracy by Clive and John Smith and my wife Diane.

My memories of A. J. Smith, his collection and the china-collecting spirit of the 1960s and 1970s have been augmented by the recollections of many friends of his and mine, including Andrew Dando and Gordon Dando, Anton Gabszewicz, the late Joseph and Elizabeth Handley, David March, Eric Manson, Tony Martin, Ron and Pam Sparrow, Robert Williams, and of course John, Clive and Jill Smith.

Simon Spero   June 2005

I would like to express my gratitude to the following people without whose help and support chapters 2 and 3 could not have been written; to the Headmaster and Governors of the Royal Grammar School, Worcester for allowing me to have a sabbatical term in which to complete much of the research; to the Cumming Ceramic Foundation in Canada for a grant toward the cost of that sabbatical term; to the Master and Fellows of St Hugh's College, Oxford for the welcome and support I received during the time that I was a Schoolmaster Fellow of the College in the summer of 2004. I would also like to acknowledge the helpful conversations and practical assistance I have enjoyed in the company of Harry Frost and Wendy Cook, curators past and present of the Dyson Perrins Museum of Worcester Porcelain. Robin Whittaker and his team at the Worcestershire County Record Office and the staff of the Worcester History Centre were of enormous help in guiding my initial research. I am also greatly indebted to local historians David Everett, Rodney Dowling and Ray Jones whose endeavours I have incorporated in order to bolster my own findings and to encourage them to publish in their own right. I would also like to thank principal author Simon Spero for his invitation to present some of my findings in such a magnificent volume. Finally, I must appreciate the forbearance shown by my wife and two daughters in neglecting familial duties in order to pursue what has been a very personal and extremely pleasurable quest. They may not have always appreciated or understood its nature but they have supported me nonetheless.

Richard Burt   April 2005

AUTHOR'S PREFACE

The original purpose of this book, when first discussed with John and Clive Smith, was to create a record of the Collection which was so skillfully assembled during the 1960s and 1970s by their father A. J. Smith. As so often in the making of books, the subject assumed a life of its own, expanding during the process. How did A. J. Smith set about forming his collection? How did the collection evolve? In what way did porcelain collecting forty years ago differ from today? The short-lived Bristol factory was the first outside London to produce domestic wares. Why was Bristol chosen for the site of this endeavour, so fraught with commercial hazards, and what was the character of the city at that time? This naturally awakened curiosity about mid eighteenth century Worcester, its inhabitants, its economy, and its social and political structure. And what was the motivation to establish a porcelain factory in this location, lacking any deep-rooted ceramic tradition, and how was this achieved?

The social, cultural, commercial and economic background to the English porcelain industry, as it developed during the 1740s and 1750s is gradually being accorded more prominence by writers on ceramics and the establishment of the various factories is being examined more closely within its socio-economic context. Richard Burt has addressed the issue, contributing two chapters to this volume concerned with this aspect of the interconnected development of the porcelain industry in Bristol and Worcester during the early 1750s.

It is helpful when considering a specific porcelain factory to place it within the context of the industry as a whole. After all, the output of a factory, its marketing strategies, its preferred decorative idioms and its perceived market would all have been principally determined by an awareness of developments and competition from elsewhere: other porcelain factories, oriental importations and perhaps even delftware and stoneware potworks. In studying the establishment of a factory and its initial years of production when its marketing strategies were being formulated, it is beneficial to be acquainted with the wider context of the ceramic industry. For this reason I have tried to relate the pieces in this collection whenever possible to contemporary models and decorative idioms from other factories, especially Bow, the largest English porcelain factory of the 1750s.

The distribution of the 150 pieces in the Collection into ten chapters created a dilemma. A chronological disposition was impracticable as the Collection is principally concerned with a narrow span of no more than six years, 1750-56. The Lund's Bristol, blue and white Worcester, together with the small section devoted to the post 1756 wares all fall comfortably into place. So too do the *kakiemon* style, the "pencilled" and printed components, and the tiny section devoted to European themes. Yet the main emphasis of the A. J. Smith Collection is concerned with the distinctive and innovative *chinoiserie* and *indianische Blumen* styles and it was this large portion which required separation into several chapters. Ultimately I chose to divide up this decorative idiom into four related segments (Chapters 6 to 9). This distribution was of necessity somewhat arbitrary and there is inevitably a measure of overlapping material. Similarly, I have felt it necessary to stress the decorative influences relating to the overall idiom in each of these four chapters. This crucial facet of the Collection is of course thematically coherent. Yet to have incorporated all 76 pieces into a single chapter would have been unwieldy and would have compromised the balance of the entire book.

John Smith in his Foreword has traced the family background and shared his memories of his parents and the germination of the Collection. In Chapter 1 I have tried to depict the character of A. J. Smith, his foibles and the methods through which he assembled his collection. I have also endeavoured to convey a flavour of the 1960s and 1970s from the specific perspective of the porcelain collector, a terrain now barely recognisable to his contemporary counterpart. In Chapters 2 and 3, Richard Burt places the Collection in its historical and socio-economic background within the contrasting mid eighteenth century cities of Bristol and Worcester, drawing together the threads which led to the establishment of the two interrelated porcelain factories. Much is still not known and many facts are open to interpretation. It is not clear at what point the decision was taken to "unite" the two factories, nor whether the establishment of the Worcester factory was dependent on securing access to the soapstone formula. Here Richard has had to tread the margins between verifiable evidence and informed conjecture.

The catalogue itself begins with the blue and white Lund's Bristol. Although comprising only 14 pieces, this is one of the most comprehensive collections devoted to this small class of surviving wares ever assembled. Infused by the innovative moulded shapes and models devised at Limehouse in the 1740s, the Bristol output and many of its decorative idioms provided a template for the subsequent production at Worcester. The following chapter flows on from these tentative beginnings, the output broadening until, within three years or so, it had expanded into the most sophisticated class of English blue and white porcelain, unmatched elsewhere for the excellence of its potting, the subtlety and detail of its moulded ornamentation and the *chinoiserie* panache of its painted idioms. Chapters 6 to 9 embody the central core of the Collection which is devoted to the *chinoiserie* style, short-lived, multi-faceted and expressing several layers of decorative and thematic influences. The sheer novelty of this innovative style, utterly different from any other in English porcelain, must have created a startlingly effective inauguration to the production at Worcester. Comparisons with the *famille rose* idiom at Bow are intriguing in both artistic and commercial terms and suggest a measure of foresight and enterprise without parallel in the English porcelain industry of the 1750s. Nothing of this kind had been seen before; nor was it to be seen again. The *kakiemon* idiom in Chapter 10 incorporates motifs from the related *indianische Blumen* style, yet differs in its decorative impact. A. J. Smith was very drawn to the European landscape designs of the middle 1750s (Chapter 11), inhabited by diminutive figures redolent in their costume and gesture of their time and place. Paradoxically, although extremely rare, this idiom lacked the spirit of inventiveness which characterises so much decoration of the period. Alongside a brief representation of the techniques of "pencilled" and transfer-printed decoration is a fleeting glimpse in Chapter 13 of the decorative idioms from the later 1750s and beyond. These few examples serve to underline the originality and resourcefulness of those who designed the earlier *chinoiserie* idiom, one of the most individual ever devised on English porcelain.

FOREWORD by John Smith

FAMILY HISTORY

My Father's family was settled in Bristol by the early l9th century and his grandfather Alfred John Smith was born in Bedminster in 1843. He became an accountant and was subsequently employed in the coal merchant's business of R.C.Ring with whom he later went into partnership.

In 1884 Alfred John Smith dissolved his partnership with R.C.Ring and set up in business on his own at 47 Queen Square as a coal merchant and a shipper of coal. He later moved to 9 Queen Square and at some later date incorporated the business in the name 'Alfred J. Smith Limited'. This business prospered and he became a typical successful Victorian businessman. He was very involved in public life and became Lord Mayor of Bristol in 1905 and again in 1906. After his death in 1920 the business was run by his son A.S.L. Smith (my grandfather and another accountant).

From the 1890s and throughout its existence Alfred J. Smith Limited owned a sizeable fleet of steamships and sailing vessels which carried coal from South Wales to Bristol and up and down the coast. The Severn Trow 'Spry' can still be seen at the Ironbridge Industrial Museum in Shropshire.

In 1943 my grandfather died and Father took over running the family business. Previously he had qualified as a Chartered Accountant and became Secretary of a very old established brush company called Greenslade's. During the war Alfred J. Smith Limited continued in business and the old steamships plied their trade round the south west coast.

By the late 1940s shipping coal was a dying business having been succeeded by rail and road haulage. Factories were converting to oil and Alfred J. Smith Limited went into voluntary liquidation in 1949. All but three of the remaining ships were sold for scrap and the last trow was given to the Chepstow Yacht Club. The coal business continued until 1959 in the name of Coal Agencies (Bristol) Limited in which year it was taken over by Renwick Wilton and Dobson.

All in all the story is very much the rise and fall of a small Victorian family business. I recollect meeting in London a contemporary of mine whose family had supplied pit props to the mines in Wales - a similar story.

My Mother's family was also closely associated with Bristol but not for such a long period. In the mid nineteenth century the family had been in Bradford-on-Avon. Mother's father tried his hand at farming unsuccessfully and for a time they lived in Bath. They then settled in Clifton, Bristol where grandfather had a butcher's shop in the Mall for many years.

THE COLLECTION

The origins of the collection stem from our family holidays at Treyarnon Bay near Padstow in North Cornwall. Mother had always been artistic and interested in silver and furniture. She collected bits and pieces mainly on her weekly trips by bus to Bath. One of the families we met on holiday each year was the Morris family from Leicester. Mrs Morris was discussing collecting with Mother and mentioned that Mother ought to be collecting Bristol porcelain because of the Bristol connection.

I do not think Mother knew anything about Bristol porcelain at this stage. She subsequently purchased a Champion's Bristol saucer from Elson a well known dealer who had a shop on Christmas Steps in Bristol. Once Mother started to buy something connected with Bristol, Father took an interest. Having retired and having only a part time business interest, he had time as well as energy still. He was also fortunate enough to have some moderate funds from the sale of the old family business.

Mother and Father enjoyed trips by car into the countryside and they began to buy a variety of pieces of porcelain. Some of the items purchased were sold on the same day, hopefully at a small profit, which would help towards the cost of petrol and lunch. By buying and selling in this way knowledge was gradually accumulated and likes and dislikes established.

The emphasis was soon on Cookworthy's Plymouth and Bristol and Champion's Bristol porcelain. At some stage the Worcester factory made its appearance probably because of the local connection again.

The main influence in the early years (the first half of the 1960s) was Jack West who ran an antique shop in Dawlish. It was from him that Father learned about early Worcester which he began to concentrate on. Other dealers who Father met and got on well with were Gordon Dando of Bath and Reg Andrade of Plymouth.

Once Father got the bug and started to buy in the London market the picture changed. Jack West generously told Father that if he wanted the best pieces he would have to get one of the London dealers to bid for him as they would outbid Jack West. Father therefore went to Leslie Perkins and later John Perkins of Albert Amor who acted for him for some years. It must have been very difficult for Amor trying to keep their various clients happy and steering them in different directions as they had to. Perhaps the availability of more pieces and the frequency of auction sales made it easier in those days.

During the 1960s Father met Simon Spero who then had a shop in Kentish Town. Simon's father had also been a well known dealer. They soon hit it off and in due course Simon became Father's main adviser.

Father was careful not to let it be known what he was buying and kept his activities quite secret for some years. He never joined any societies. When Robert Williams of Winifred Williams came to visit our home in Bristol he was astonished. He was under the impression that Father collected only Plymouth and Bristol and when shown the early Worcester upstairs exclaimed "Where have I been!"

Father did not believe in a static collection and enjoyed buying and selling equally. Although he started with a reasonably good financial basis, he did not have unlimited funds. A collection of Plymouth blue and white was sold to help finance further acquisitions and he was always trying to improve the quality of the collections.

This was a time (the 1960s and 1970s) when rare pieces could still be bought from provincial and country dealers. Many pieces still came from such dealers as Jack West and Gordon Dando. On one occasion Gordon Dando produced two very unusual Worcester cups with feet saying that he had never seen anything like them before to which Father instinctively replied that he had one already. Having purchased the two cups it was not until he got home that he realised what he had said as the one he already had was believed to be the only one.

Another source of purchases was the Antique Fairs particularly Grosvenor House and Bath. It was following one of the Grosvenor House Fairs that Father purchased the beautiful large dish which caused Mother sleepless nights because of the price Father had paid - well worth every penny!

This collection like many others was formed over a period of about fifteen years. Many collectors like Father start when their children have grown up and when they still have time, energy and some available funds. After a period of great activity additions to the collection gradually tail off and, while the interest is still there, caution sets in and age takes its toll.

Eventually the problems of insurance became too much. The house on the edge of the Downs in Bristol was detached and vulnerable to burglary. Father had always had good relations with the Bristol Museum and Art Gallery to which Mother was a regular visitor. He had loaned pieces to various exhibitions. It was natural therefore that the solution was to put the whole collection on long term loan with the Museum. The whole exercise gave Father a new interest.

The forming of the Collection occupied much of my parents time in their sixties and early seventies. Mother told us that they were the happiest years of her life and I suspect that they were for Father.

CHAPTER 1 A. J. SMITH AND HIS COLLECTION

I first met A. J. Smith in the autumn of 1964, soon after I had opened my first shop, tiny premises in Kentish Town. He, affable, unassuming, yet shrewdly perceptive and I, enthusiastic, beginning to learn about porcelain, but lacking any business experience or training. Despite an age difference of over thirty years, we warmed to one another immediately. This was the start of a friendship which was to endure until Mr Smith's death in 1989. For my part, he was a good customer, a staunch supporter and an unfailing repository of wisdom. We gradually established an active business relationship, buying and selling to one another and exchanging ideas and strategies for the development of his burgeoning collection. I became a regular visitor to his house in Westbury-on-Trym, always warmly welcomed by his wife, equally self-effacing yet no less astute. She rarely commented on the Collection but when she did so, she revealed an artistic insight which contributed so much to the formulation of the Collection, especially in the early days.

Eagerly anticipated on my part, visits to The Lodge, Cote Drive, followed a reassuringly predictable course. A glass of sherry would be followed by a tour around the superb collection of Champion's Bristol, displayed in two cabinets in the generously proportioned sitting room. We would then repair upstairs to the larger of the two spare bedrooms, housing the collection of early polychrome Worcester, together with the blue and white Lund's Bristol and Worcester. The smaller spare bedroom contained cabinets of more Worcester, interspersed with unusual pieces from other factories. It was from these cabinets that pieces were regularly "weeded out" in order to accommodate and subsidise fresh purchases. These were moments of great excitement, for there was no knowing which familiar piece might unexpectedly become available. Tantalisingly, the more fresh pieces that appeared in the main spare bedroom, the more would have to be culled from the smaller room. Mr Smith always set the prices and, even when unrealistically modest, he would never respond to a higher offer. Exhortations that the price was too low would invariably result in the piece being returned to its cabinet. The lesson was swiftly learned and Mr Smith's kindness much appreciated. His innate sense of fairness was unwavering. At precisely one o'clock, our deliberations were interrupted and we were summoned for lunch. The dining room, oak-panelled like so much of the house, was set about with still more porcelain, mainly Plymouth, together with plaques and pictures associated with the city of Bristol. On my initial visit, Mrs Smith had discovered my liking for steak and kidney pie and this became an immutable and always welcome component of my day in Bristol. A pudding and coffee were followed by a much needed walk. On our return, Mrs Smith would invariably be sitting reading. Her love of books was equalled only by her enjoyment of the English countryside. This was partly reflected in her garden, a shared enthusiasm which took up a great deal of time and energy and was Mr Smith's main hobby aside from his porcelain collecting. It was immaculately kept and their pride in it was always evident during our afternoon stroll around its perimeter. Afterwards, I was always keen for a second inspection of the early coloured Worcester upstairs. No other such collection, that I knew of, was so varied nor so extensive. Tea consisted of cucumber and fish paste sandwiches and cakes, served from a trolley. If I seldom did justice to this feast, it was a measure of my regard for Mrs Smith's steak and kidney pie. The day would end with the packing of my purchases and a leisurely drive to Temple Meads station.

Through these years of our friendship, either in Bristol or on his excursions to my shop in London, I grew to value Mr Smith's wisdom and advice. His business ethics and the principles by which he lived became the most fundamental single influence on my own business methods and philosophy. Modest, discreet and entirely lacking in pretension, his beliefs were firmly held, rooted in a combination of fairness and common sense. One characteristic aphorism which I still hold dear personifies the man and his pragmatic approach to life: "Always recognise and appreciate the good times; you may never know how good they are until they are over." He had a dry, almost impish, sense of humour and a deadpan delivery. Eric Manson recalls him listening to several fellow collectors bemoaning the lack of interesting porcelain on the market, and observing nonchalantly, "Someone has to die …." Startled at the prospect of so drastic a solution, they awaited amplification of this radical expedient. Pausing for a moment, a twinkle in his eye, he added by way of clarification, "There are not enough collectors dying."

The 150 or so pieces in this catalogue represent little more than 5% of Mr Smith's purchases through a span of just over 20 years. In this period between 1959 and his final purchase in 1981, his meticulously preserved account books itemise just under 2,500 acquisitions, although he probably never owned more than about 300 pieces at any one time. Aside from his ongoing purchases of Worcester, he formed a fine collection of blue and white Plymouth which he sacrificed in the middle 1960s in order to concentrate his resources on early polychrome Worcester. He was also unable to resist a rarity or an outstanding piece, regardless of its factory, when the opportunity arose: a beautiful triangle period Chelsea white basket with a gilt-metal swing handle; a superb early Lowestoft tankard bought at a furniture shop in Worcester in 1967; and a Plymouth sauceboat inscribed upon the base in red *Mr Wm Cookworthys Factory Plymouth 1770*. He and I spoke on the 'phone at least once a week, yet I would have no inkling of these extramural purchases until they were revealed on a subsequent visit to Westbury-on-Trym. In the eyes of most collectors and dealers, he was associated principally with Champion's Bristol. Whilst he did indeed assemble an outstanding collection of Bristol, notable for its wide range of shapes, he used this reputation as a camouflage for what became his primary focus: early polychrome Worcester. Thus he was able unobtrusively to assemble his Worcester collection whilst not creating a market against himself. With characteristic perception, he sensed the benefits of anonymity. By these means he was able to assemble one of the outstanding collections of its kind, unknown to all but a handful of dealer and collector friends. Although genial and friendly, he was essentially a very private man and this oblique method of collecting would have been second nature.

In 1957, at the age of 52, Mr Smith finally retired having sold his business. Still comparatively young and full of energy, he had little to occupy himself apart from his garden. He had been a keen tennis player, one of four left-handers who regularly played together, but he had ceased playing some years earlier. On the first full day of his retirement, he had enquired over breakfast what his wife's plans were for the day. She replied that she was having several friends in for coffee as was her custom on a Monday. Delighted to have such company, he said that he was looking forward to meeting these ladies. "Oh no you won't, Jock," she responded firmly, "I have my own routine and I don't want you cluttering up the house." Accordingly, Mr Smith spent a disconsolate morning wandering aimlessly on The Downs, returning for lunch determined to find a specific occupation for his time. His wife had always enjoyed looking around bookshops and antique shops and had recently taken to returning home from Bath with small packages containing pieces of china. Perhaps this was something which they could do together.

So began one of the most contented periods of their lives, travelling around the West Country, visiting antiques shops. At first Mr Smith's purchases were random, connected only by their associations with the city of Bristol: paintings, prints, porcelain plaques and even odd pieces of pottery. But Mrs Smith was drawn to porcelain, especially teawares with flower painting and garlands in the neo-classical style: Chelsea-Derby and particularly Champion's Bristol were her favourites. Her love of this decorative idiom had a practical application. She would buy undecorated plates and paint them with flowers, subsequently having the plates refired. It was her artistic eye and her taste which drew Mr Smith's attention towards Bristol porcelain. Initially, he knew little about it, but he reasoned the best way to discover more would be to visit antiques shops, talk to dealers and build up a picture of the availability of Bristol, its cost and range of shapes and decoration. He would enjoy the planning of routes and the driving and his wife would be able to indulge her pleasure in the

English countryside. Thus, his method of collecting, envisaged as a retirement hobby, gradually evolved into a way of life. Collecting forays were carefully planned with the aid of maps and guide books so as to incorporate as many antiques shops as possible within a predetermined area.

These days in the 1960s were not as we know them now. Every town and many villages would have their antiques shops. Among these would be some with constantly changing stocks of early English porcelain, nourished by regular accretions from provincial salerooms and private sources. The antiques business was far less centralised than today and lacking in the instant communication of information which we now take for granted. The London auction houses had a lower profile and the provincial salerooms were still largely the domain of the dealer, with collectors generally preferring to buy in the more congenial atmosphere of the antiques shop. There were a small number of established provincial antiques Fairs held annually at such places as Brighton, Cheltenham, Buxton, Kenilworth, Bath and Harrogate. With scarcely one such Fair per month, these were awaited with eager anticipation and viewed as prestigious events by collectors and dealers alike. The days of a proliferation of small two-day Fairs lay many years ahead. Mr Smith attended the opening day of most of these Fairs, but his principal source of porcelain sprang from his travels around the country.

These were still the golden days of the country antiques shop. A West Country porcelain trip for example, with a prompt start, might encompass Bath, Bradford on Avon, Trowbridge, Warminster, Wilton, Salisbury, Stockbridge, Wimborne Minster, Castle Cary, Honiton and back home via Wells. Further west lay excellent porcelain specialists in Exeter, Budleigh Salterton, Dawlish, Torquay, Plympton, Plymouth and Looe. It was in Dawlish Warren that Mr Smith first encountered Jack West and began to focus more clearly on the elements which were eventually to constitute his final collection. Jack's small shop was divided into two sections, one for china gifts for the tourists who comprised his main summer trade, and the other for his antique porcelain, of which blue and white was a great speciality. He had a sound knowledge of early porcelain, excellent contacts and transparent honesty. Straightforward, yet unassuming, he wore his expertise lightly and Mr Smith immediately warmed to his gentle manner. They became great friends and for several years until his untimely death in the late 1960s, Jack West was the guiding influence in the creation of the Collection. Indeed, he was unique among Mr Smith's ceramic friends and acquaintances in using his christian name.

Anonymity was a deliberate tactical device for Mr Smith and in this endeavour, he was born with a priceless asset. On entering an antiques shop for the first time, he would effortlessly sidestep questions about what he collected and on being asked his name, he would pause as if considering an appropriate rejoinder. Then reflectively, as if proposing a feasible suggestion, he would reply, "……Smith." Naturally, no-one ever believed him.

Essentially a very private and reserved man, Mr Smith's reticence was rooted in his Methodist background, the hardships of the harsh economic climate in the early years of his marriage in the 1930s and also perhaps as a reaction to the extrovert personality of his grandfather, a prominent Bristol businessman and public figure. He disliked parties and social gatherings, although once there, he would chat readily in his affable and genial manner. Unsurprisingly, for so self-effacing a character, he had a particular aversion to having his photograph taken. Yet paradoxically, in the days of his retirement, he relished the companionship of fellow china collectors and dealers, though he would never join collecting societies and avoided seminars and lecture evenings. He was a source of practical wisdom, delivered in a deadpan manner and infused with his dry humour. Joseph Handley, a Californian collector who came to admire Mr Smith immensely, never forgot the firmly stated stricture, "Never step out of the market place Mr Handley." He never did. Another collector elicited the characteristic recommendation that, "A secret is no longer a secret if you tell anyone at all. Even your wife." His wisdom and his philosophy towards collecting was shaped by the experiences of his

No 85 (reverse)

working life and especially of those austere years in the 1930s. Gordon Dando, then an antiques dealer in Bath, remembers some typically pragmatic advice about purchasing porcelain cups and saucers: "Always start off by saying to yourself 'They don't match', and then try to prove to yourself that they do." Yet alongside this sense of caution, even wariness, lay an innate kindness and generosity of spirit. It was almost as if his interest in collecting porcelain and the companionship which it engendered released some inhibitions and allowed the evolution of new friendships, warm yet safe within the parameters chosen by himself. Certainly, he is still remembered with great affection and respect by the small band of collectors and dealers whose lives he touched in the 1970s and early 1980s.

Warm-hearted and generous, he was embarrassed by any gestures of affection or emotion and would go to great lengths to avoid expressions of gratitude. From the time when we first met in 1964, he would call into my shop on each of his regular visits to London. We would chat about possible future purchases, price levels, forthcoming auctions, new research and all the other matters and gossip of the ceramics world, interspersed with his enquiries about my family and particularly my younger sister Philippa, of whom he was fond. In later years, with declining mobility and the conclusion of his term as an active collector, he travelled to London more infrequently. On one of his last visits to my shop, he carried a small parcel which he handed to me, with the terse injunction not to unwrap it until he was gone. He would say no more. On unwrapping the parcel later on, it proved to contain an early Worcester hexagonal teapot and cover, similar to no. 85. I was dumbstruck. It was a piece which I had admired since I first saw the Collection, twenty years earlier. I wrote to him immediately but he never thereafter referred to it, nor wished me to do so.

Those days from the middle 1960s until the early 1980s were a golden era for collecting early English porcelain. Aside from the plethora of country antiques shops, provincial salerooms and well-established antiques Fairs, there were at least a dozen specialist dealers in London. Sotheby's alone had seven or eight auctions each year, packed with early English porcelain and there were also frequent sales at Christie's, Phillips' and Bonham's. Mr Smith visited London regularly, going around all the shops and viewing the major auctions. He thought nothing of walking from Paddington Station to Bond Street, on to Knightsbridge and then to Kensington Church Street. He also attended all the major auctions, although rather than bid himself, he would commission a dealer to act on his behalf, primarily to preserve his anonymity. Most London dealers, as those elsewhere, regarded him as a collector of Champion's Bristol who occasionally purchased pieces from other factories. They would have been as amazed as Robert Williams, many years later, to see the superb collection of early Worcester displayed in those two bedrooms in Westbury-on-Trym. For his part, Mr Smith relished the success of his anonymity and the camouflage of his principal collecting field, quite apart from the benefits which it afforded.

When he began collecting in the early 1960s, Champion's Bristol was comparatively expensive. Yet the earliest coloured Worcester, often referred to as "Lund's Bristol" or "Bristol-Worcester", though far rarer and earlier in date, was relatively undervalued. Many collectors or dealers made little distinction in price between a simple unmoulded creamjug, such as no. 66, and a "sparrow beak" jug of 20 years later in date. One of the beautiful quatrefoil lobed beaker cups, no. 89, could be purchased for under £30 and at least eight would have passed through Mr Smith's hands. We now have the advantage of a rich and comprehensive literature of up-to-date books on early Worcester porcelain, comprising over a dozen volumes. In the early 1960s, of the few books devoted to Worcester porcelain, only three were of recent vintage and only one, by Franklin Barrett, paid much attention to the early coloured wares. Thus, it was fertile ground for a collector with energy, determination, a good eye and adequate resources. Worcester porcelain was strongly collected as a whole, but only a handful of collectors, among them Sarah and Jack Cohen and H.E. Marshall, concentrated exclusively on the wares of the early and middle 1750s. The most active period of

Mr Smith's collecting, therefore, coincided with the 1960s, when he had relatively little competition from the other specialist collectors and when prices were comparatively modest. By the 1970s, tastes were changing and these allusive and innovative early wares were becoming far more widely collected.

A. J. Smith's collecting of Lund's Bristol and early Worcester spanned a period of just over 20 years, from the first purchase to be represented in his ultimate collection, the blue and white Worcester conical bowl, no. 39, acquired in 1960, appropriately from Jack West in Dawlish, to his last, the Lund's Bristol tankard, no. 8, purchased in 1981 from myself. The 150 or so pieces illustrated in this volume represent only a small proportion of his total purchases over this period. Collecting had become Mr Smith's main source of interest in his retirement and he devoted most of his time and energy to it. He came to enjoy *la chasse*, the planning of buying expeditions and the *camaraderie* and companionship of a small group of dealers with whom he became friendly as he bought and sold his porcelain. These included Jack West, John Perkins and Ann George of Albert Amor, Gordon Dando, Robert Williams and myself. Generally speaking, pieces were kept for several years before being sacrificed in order to subsidise further purchases. With these constant accretions, the Collection was perpetually changing and through these changes, a gradual process of refinement and a narrowing of focus was taking place. A regular visitor to the Bristol Museum and Art Gallery, he had noted two small cabinets of Champion's Bristol porcelain, bequeathed by E. MacGregor Duncan in 1963. Though small in size, this group of pieces representing the very finest of Bristol decoration became a touchstone for Mr Smith, a yardstick to which to aspire.

Early on, purchases came principally from London and provincial antiques shops, and occasionally from Fairs. But as he began to concentrate more specifically on the earliest Worcester, he was obliged increasingly to buy at auction, almost invariably commissioning a dealer to act on his behalf. Through the 1960s, he was able to acquire an average of a dozen or so pieces each year towards what became his ultimate collection, together with many others which he later disposed of. Then, in January 1969, he had the opportunity to purchase the collection formed by H.E. Marshall, a retired Bank Manager from Chippenham.

Assembled principally through the 1940s and 1950s on a limited budget, yet with great discernment and knowledge, this was a collection abounding with rarities, even though some were in a damaged condition. The financial outlay was daunting and Mr Smith felt it necessary immediately to dispose of approximately half the collection, retaining about 20 items for himself. These made a significant contribution to his own burgeoning collection. Among these accessions were several important additions, including two pieces of blue and white Lund's Bristol: a cream pail, no. 9, and a creamboat bearing the embossed *BRISTOL* mark, no. 2. The polychrome pieces included a pair of fine pedestal sauceboats, no. 43, together with two exceptional teapots, nos. 83 and 85. Mr Smith later regretted his somewhat precipitous decision to sell so many of the Marshall items, but his accountancy training, his memories of the hardships of the 1930s and his philosophy of life nourished a deep-seated prerequisite to balance the books.

The blue and white Lund's Bristol in Chapter 4 represents one of the most substantial holdings of this rare class of English porcelain ever assembled. The superb spirally flared bowl, no. 14, with its rippling contours redolent of George II silver, seems to be the only one of its kind. So too is the small beaker vase, no. 13. The acquisition of this piece in May 1968 displayed Mr Smith's persistence and collecting instincts at their most acute. He had driven to the South Coast to visit the annual Bournemouth Antiques Fair. In the queue outside, he had chatted amiably with Mrs Hoff, a redoubtable London dealer with a good eye and quick reactions. At the entrance to the Fair, Mr Smith turned towards the stands on the left whilst Mrs Hoff hastened determinedly to the right. Arriving some minutes later at the stand of Mary Wise, Mr Smith was confronted by a fine display of blue and white porcelain recently acquired from the collection of Dr and Mrs Statham. His eye immediately alighted on the small beaker-shaped vase labelled "early Worcester". Alas, it had already been sold. Still more frustratingly, he was unable to elicit the identity of the buyer. Driving back to Bristol that afternoon he pondered the problem, "Who was he? Or she?!" He recalled Mrs Hoff presciently turning right at the entrance to the Fair. Might she have had foreknowledge of the pieces from the Statham Collection? She would certainly have been able to reach Mary Wise's stand ahead of him. The following morning he travelled up to London, hot on the trail, and was in Mrs Hoff's shop by mid morning. Yes, she admitted to buying the "pretty little Worcester vase" …. but it was now sold. Once again, no clue was offered as to the identity of the latest purchaser. Undeterred, Mr Smith set off to do the rounds of the London porcelain shops, arriving at Albert Amor in Bury Street midway through the afternoon. There, the kindly John Perkins reached into a cupboard and drew out a recent purchase which he felt might possibly be of interest. The elusive vase had finally been snared. Whilst the price had risen by several unwelcome notches within less than 36 hours, it proved on close inspection to be Lund's Bristol rather than early Worcester, the only such example of its kind.

The section devoted to blue and white Worcester in Chapter 5 represents only a tiny proportion of the many fine pieces purchased by A. J. Smith over a span of some 20 years. He had gradually realised that it was not practicable to concentrate on *both* the polychrome and blue and white wares of the 1750s. Consequently, the blue and white became subordinate to the main Collection. Nevertheless, this aspect of the Collection includes several outstanding pieces amongst which are the bottle or guglet, no. 19, an early plate, no. 21, and a fine baluster mug, no. 16. Perhaps the *tour de force* is the massive vase and cover from the Lord Chandos Collection, no. 20, purchased at Sotheby's in 1975. For an example of so early a date, this is an extraordinarily ambitious achievement in both its substantial proportions and its decorative idiom. It affords an intriguing and revealing insight into the priorities and objectives of the Worcester factory during its initial two years of production, and to the relationship between its polychrome and underglaze blue output. Yet perhaps the most challenging piece in the entire Collection is the simple globular teapot, no. 15, poorly painted, clumsily potted and lacking even the redeeming feature of a cover. But this teapot which has obstinately defied attribution for the 40 years since its purchase from Jack West in 1964, may have an important role in our understanding of the evolution of the first porcelain made at Worcester.

As the Collection evolved through the 1960s, it became increasingly clear that its main emphasis focused upon the polychrome wares from 1752-55, the initial phase of the factory's production. Mr Smith eventually assembled almost 100 pieces from this early period, one of the largest and most comprehensive such collections ever accumulated. At the time when he set out on this ceramic odyssey which he perceived as no more than a retirement activity, his purpose was to assemble ceramics associated with his home city of Bristol. These early Worcester wares, so different in character from those of the mainstream production of the later 1750s and beyond, nos. 148 and 151, were variously described in the reference books, auction catalogues and antiques shops as "Lowdins Bristol", "Lund's Bristol", "soft paste Bristol" or sometimes "Bristol-Worcester". It was not until the early 1970s that these distinctive wares were firmly classified as early Worcester, by which time the Collection had been created on the false premise that the components had been made in Bristol. Yet Mr Smith's initial motivation had long since developed into a deep appreciation of the porcelain itself, its shapes, palettes and its captivating decorative idiom. Its lack of Bristolian connections was no longer of consequence.

Reflecting on the superb array of early models and innovative decorative motifs laid out in Chapters 6 to 9, it is striking how dissimilar these pieces are from all other early Worcester porcelain. A comparison with the examples from the later 1750s illustrated in Chapter 13 is illuminating. Nowadays, it would be well nigh impossible to assemble so large and representative a collection of these early wares. Yet A. J. Smith probably disposed of as many of these early pieces as he retained, a revealing commentary both of their availability and of the prevailing tastes of the 1960s. At one time or another, he culled two hexagonal teapots, several creamjugs, both lobed and plain (nos. 87 and 108), five low moulded sauceboats and several pedestal sauceboats (nos. 71 and 88), octagonal teabowls, saucers and coffee cups (no. 56) and many more early pieces. He pursued E.MacGregor Duncan's example of constant refinement both with unwavering rigour and evident pleasure.

He had a particular affection for the wonderful fluted baluster vase from the Hughes Collection, no. 119, the rare helmet shaped jug, no. 46, and the beautiful globular vase, no. 67, from the Frank Arnold Collection. This had been the inside cover illustration in the Sotheby's catalogue for the first part of the Frank Arnold Sale in November 1963, the first I ever attended. Mr Smith was determined to secure the vase but to his chagrin, it was accidentally knocked over during viewing prior to the Sale, and subsequently withdrawn. Happily, through the agency of some adroit negotiations from the faithful John Perkins, together with sympathetic restoration, this rare and intriguing vase was added to the Collection. The purchase of the apparently unique large dish in 1967, no. 99, and that of the magnificent pair of early vases from Christie's in 1972, no. 47, both caused sleepless nights due to their high cost. By contrast, the pair of beaker cups on three feet, no. 130 were modestly priced, despite their extreme rarity. A dealer friend in Bath produced them from a cupboard, remarking that he had not seen their like before and adding, "And I don't suppose that you have either Mr Smith?" To this A. J. Smith responded, "Very likely. I have one like these at home. How much are you asking?" The wind entirely taken out of his sails, the dealer's price was reasonable and a sale was completed. Mr Smith did indeed have a similar one at home, no. 48, but he neglected to mention that these were the only three known examples. I have heard this story recounted by both parties. Mr Smith regretted his lack of candour and the dealer regretted his modest price, but they remained friends.

Unlike many collectors of Worcester and despite the example of MacGregor Duncan, A. J. Smith would accept a measure of damage if it was justified by extreme rarity of either form or decoration. Should an alternative example present itself in better condition, he would replace the damaged item. This pragmatic and shrewd approach added character to the Collection, permitting the retention of such idiosyncratically decorated pieces as the mustard pot, no. 96 and the delightful fluted baluster vase, no. 81.

For Mr and Mrs Smith, the twenty years during which the Collection developed and matured were amongst the happiest of their married lives, especially those in the 1960s when they would drive around the country on their buying expeditions, visiting country antiques shops and provincial salerooms. Mrs Smith had an enduring love of the countryside and enjoyed the companionship of her husband, relaxed yet animated by his collecting and the friendships which it generated. Indeed, like her husband, reserved and self-effacing yet also affectionate and sociable, she relished this new dimension to their lives. In 1973, the collection of Lund's Bristol and early Worcester was given on permanent loan to the Bristol Museum and Art Gallery, and A. J. Smith's career as an active collector gradually receded. Yet the friendships born of his collecting endured uninterrupted, nourished by mutual affection. Regular visitors to The Lodge at this time included fellow collectors such as Ron and Pam Sparrow and the Americans, Joseph and Elizabeth Handley from northern California, and Dewayne and Faith Perry from New Jersey. Talk of mutual friends, ceramic activities in both England and America and reminiscences of past collecting would be followed by tours of the garden and substantial high teas.

The A. J. Smith Collection is now accommodated in the Bristol Museum and Art Gallery, laid out in two substantial cabinets, the foresight and generosity of a very private man sharing with us the fruits of his retiring years.

No 96 (detail)

CHAPTER 2 **A TALE OF TWO CITIES:**
BRISTOL AND WORCESTER IN THE MID EIGHTEENTH CENTURY

Introduction

In his opening of his magisterial work, R L Hobson posed the question why Worcester should have been the English porcelain company with the longest unbroken tradition of production (and he might also have added the first to be firmly established outside of London) when other areas such as Staffordshire seemed better placed to pick up the mantle from the Limehouse, Bow and Chelsea factories. He pointed out that we need to[1]

"remember that porcelain was not discovered in England by a process of evolution from the native earthenware. It was, on the contrary, an exotic plant of eastern origin, naturalized and, one might say, hybridized on the Continent, and brought to England, as it were, in cuttings which were planted first in the neighbourhood of London and afterwards disseminated in more congenial soils".

Hobson then went on to assert

"That one of the earliest offshoots should have taken root at Worcester was, as we shall see, largely due to chance; but that once established, it should have outlived its fellows was due to natural law of the fittest".

I would contend that neither of these two conclusions is entirely sound or at least depend upon the interpretation of terms. The long term survival depended as much upon chance as any inherent superiority of the factory; it was the good fortune of Worcester that men like Thomas Flight and R W Binns intervened at crucial moments to rescue the firm from the doldrums nor should it be forgotten that the partnership was reconstituted following the deaths or defections of some of the original members such as occurred in 1754 and 1776. Moreover, the emphasis upon the longevity of the factory has perhaps distracted attention away from the favourable preconditions which were in place well before its establishment. Much of the argument in this chapter will try to refocus attention on the period prior to 1751 rather than the subsequent narrative of events.

Despite the "foreign and exotic" nature of porcelain, it was ultimately dependent upon internal rather than external capital, raw materials and labour. English soft paste porcelain factories, without the secret of the true porcelain formula and the backing of royalty, had to develop in a markedly different way to European factories like Meissen and Sevres. Lacking the financial support of the state enjoyed by the latter, the grim reality of commercial profit and loss underpinned the success and failure of English porcelain manufacture and the margin of error was small in the face of competition from cheaper and often superior Chinese imports. Given the nature of the product, the most important consideration of all was access to good transport links which needed to be able to bring in bulky ingredients and fuel from remote areas and to take the delicate finished product to households throughout the country. It was no accident that the first London factories at Bow, Chelsea, Limehouse and Vauxhall were conveniently positioned on the Thames. Indeed, Hobson himself, in the following chapter, acknowledged that Worcester was more favourably located than other provincial rivals such as Lowestoft since it was by no means

"remote from West Country clays, nor yet from the coal mines; and the river Severn affords the means of export and import".

It is upon this last observation that I wish to focus my initial attention by exploring the significance of the commerce of the river and its extended estuary in the Bristol Channel,[2] sometimes described as the Severn Sea. In doing so, I hope then to be able to re-evaluate the significance of the broader socio-economic and political context in which the factories of Benjamin Lund and Dr Wall were established in Bristol and Worcester respectively and in which the subsequent merger of the two companies took place in 1752. Although the former was but a short-lived affair, its demise not only made possible the survival of the Worcester Porcelain company but provides an object lesson in understanding the very fine line between success and failure in eighteenth century porcelain production. As so often is the case in business, the coincidence of time, place and individuals proved crucial in making the difference.

This essay will argue that

1) In the 18th century the Severn served as a vital artery of trade connecting Worcester and Bristol not only to one another but to inland raw materials and markets, both vital to the development of the porcelain industry and the tastes which fashioned it. Understanding the importance of river and coastal navigation in assembling such disparate elements as timber, coal, bricks, soapstone, clay not to mention access to skilled labour and markets - prior to the transport revolution of the second half of the century, is fundamental to explaining the initial competitive advantages enjoyed by both cities prior to the establishment of their porcelain works; and also why the Worcester factory, which benefited from later canal building and the industrial development of the Midlands in a way that Bristol did not, was better equipped to survive in the long term.

2) Prior to and during the 18th century the socio-economic development of Bristol and Worcester had much in common which made them two of the most important provincial cities and well placed to take up the torch of porcelain production once it had passed outside of London as polite and commercial societies developed outside the metropolis. However there were perhaps some subtle but important divergences. If contemporary accounts are to be believed, Bristol's abrasive entrepreneurs had not yet softened into a genteel society by the time of the establishment of Lund's factory. Bristol was unable to present itself as a place of fashion that could compete with Bath; arguably, Worcester, with closer and more deferential interaction with a local landed gentry, was perhaps better placed to do so in the second half of the century and through to the next. Moreover, although both cities were affected by economic crisis and transition in the middle decades of the century, Bristol was well placed to diversify and exploit its commercial hinterland in a way that Worcester was not. In Worcester, a new project like the porcelain works was more critical to the fortunes of the city than in Bristol and therefore more likely to attract the support of local investors.

3) Finally, with economic and political unpredictability in the 1730s and 40s both cities were plagued by anxieties and fears about the urban poor as well as remaining ever vigilant for a profitable opportunity. Unemployment, crime, apathy and the threat of France threatened to pull down the pillars of the nation's commerce. Moralists and entrepreneurs sought remedy in schools, hospitals, workhouses and new local industry, all of which could reinforce hierarchical values as well as stimulate the local and national economy. Moreover, as will be argued, the production and consumption of tea and porcelain were also intimately connected with these interests in the improvement of health, manners and morality. These concerns were expressed in Bristol in terms of philanthropic endeavour but disagreements over control and purpose caused the commercial elite to fragment along deep seated religious and political divisions. By contrast, the spirit of co-operation engendered by party political interest and various civic projects in Worcester proved a launch pad for the extraordinary partnership of 1751. Its composition and modus operandi was not only unique in the manufacture of early English porcelain but also reminds us of the prehistory of its members, a tale that is as noteworthy as the factory's unbroken tradition of production down to the present day.[3]

1) **THE ARTERY OF TRADE**

It is difficult to believe when surveying the peaceful scenery along the banks of the River Severn as it winds its way from its mountain source in Wales to its estuary in the Bristol Channel that it was once, with the possible exceptions of the Elbe and the Meuse, the foremost commercial waterway in Europe and that its uncertain current was the pulse beat of the early industrial revolution in England. From the fiery landscapes of Ironbridge down to the crowded dockyards at Bristol flowed much of the commercial lifeblood of the nation's burgeoning trade. The importance of this trade is made all the more remarkable when one considers the serious difficulties of navigating and fording this often treacherous river. Merely crossing the river by ferry was a fraught business as one contemporary noted in 1704 in the Ironbridge Gorge

"The river was in full flood and the wind did chill my bones. I paid the ferryman and he pulled away from the shore. The journey normally was no more than a ten minute episode but we were pushed hither and thither by the wind tossed waves. I clung to the sides as the little vessel was swept downstream...after a full three quarters of the hour we reached the shore".

These obstacles were compounded by the river's estuarial waters in the Bristol Channel, which has one of the highest tidal ranges in the world, meaning that the flood tides flow between three and six knots, sweeping along sediment and creating dangerous sandbanks. In March 1705, twenty Bristol Customs tidesmen and boatmen were drowned in "a most calamitous and fierce storm" in the Channel[4] despite its normally sheltered position. (This prompted a speculative project to construct a lighthouse on the island of Flat Holm which was to have some significance in this story which is addressed in Chapter 3.) A further hazard was the Severn Bore, a tidal wave which could roll back the waters of the river to a height of six feet.

It has also been observed that the great city which both served and was served by this estuary was also, in many senses an unlikely beneficiary of the development of commerce.

"Bristol is probably the unlikeliest site for a major port in the whole of the kingdom; not only does its entrance lie up a difficult and dangerous waterway with its menacing sandbanks and daunting tides, but the port itself is situated some seven miles from the sea reached by a long and winding journey up a muddy and treacherous river".[5]

The city lay at the confluence of two rivers, the Frome and the Avon, which offered almost negligible direct communication with the hinterland, even after the Avon became navigable to Bath in 1726. The dock facilities themselves were too small, overpriced and its location in the city centre restricted its subsequent development, not to mention making smuggling easier. As Alexander Pope observed in 1739 on a visit to the Hotwells

"From thence you come to a Key along the Old Wall with houses on both sides and in the middle of the street, as far as you can see, hundreds of ships, their masts as thick as they can stand by one another, which is the oddest and most surprising sight imaginable".[6]

This scene was captured in the iconic painting of the dockyard at the Broad Quay, formerly attributed to the artist Peter Monnamy, which is used in countless school textbooks to illustrate Bristol's involvement in the transatlantic sugar, tobacco and slave trade with which its eighteenth century prosperity is most closely associated. These same textbooks have always emphasized that the city's favourable location for the great Atlantic routes was the explanation for Bristol's ability to overcome the natural obstacles described above.

There is much to commend this line of argument and it is one which helps us understand why Lund and Miller may have considered Bristol to be a suitable base for the first porcelain factory to go into production outside London. From the Middle Ages onwards, the port was one of the key points of export for English woollens and the importation of French wine, great staple products of medieval trade. Stretching back to the voyages of the Cabots and the development of the Newfoundland fisheries in the late fifteenth century, Bristol had long associations with the colonies in the Americas and the Caribbean and this was largely responsible for the transformation of the city in the eighteenth century. By 1700 Bristol had become Britain's second largest town and port and even though it struggled to retain this honour as the pace of economic change increased after 1750, its population trebled in size growing from 20,000 to 60,000 in the course of the century. Much of this was stimulated by its Atlantic trade in the first third of the eighteenth century, especially after the opening up of the slave trade in 1698. Bristol's more favourable position allowed it to overtake London in the profits of the slave trade and ships exploited this most lucrative and cruel commerce at its peak in 1739. The total tonnage of ships entering the docks rose from 20,000 to 76,000 tons during the course of the century whilst the number of ships arriving from foreign ports doubled from 240 in 1700 to 485 in 1787. As Thomas Cox recorded in his "Magna Britannia et Hibernia" in the 1720s

"All are in a hurry, running up and down with cloudy looks and busy faces, loading carrying and unloading goods and merchandizes of all sorts from place to place: for the trade of many nations is drawn hither by the industry and opulency of the people".[7]

It was a major entrepot port for Britain's maritime commerce. The city retained its traditional domination of the Atlantic fishing industry with cod being brought direct from Newfoundland or exchanged en route home in Spain or Portugal for wine, oil, fruit and wool used increasingly in the later eighteenth century to service the West Country textile trade. From Ireland came the dairy, meat, leather and linen goods; from Virginia and South Carolina came tobacco, cotton, iron and skins; from North West Europe and the Baltic came paper, steel, brandy, linen, timber and naval stores; from the Caribbean came molasses, rum, dyewoods, coffee and, most important of all, sugar which fed the twenty or so sugar houses based in the city.[8]

In addition, the exotic nature of its foreign trade acted as a stimulus to smuggling in the Bristol Channel. The development of the fore and aft rigging helped vessels navigate strong tides, shallow rocks and treacherous coastlines. The prolonged wars with France from the late 17th century onwards also obliged governments to raise duties to pay for the armed forces and to impose restrictions upon the importation of luxury French goods such as wine, brandy, silk, gloves and lace. A consequence of this was a veritable epidemic of smuggling which often involved the Channel pilots, Irish entrepreneurs, cross channel traders, local peasantry and fishermen, Royal Navy officers and sometimes the customs and excise officials themselves.[9] It was largely due to the activities of the smugglers that a taste for tea and sugar, which would otherwise have been prohibitively expensive, developed at this time amongst the middle and lower classes, often to the chagrin of moralists and commentators like Jonas Hanway, Dr Johnson and Arthur Young. Duncan Forbes noted gloomily in Scotland in 1744

"When Sugar, the inseparable Companion of Tea, came to be in the Possession of the very poorest Housewife, where formerly it had been a great Rarity - and thereby was at hand to mix with water and Brandy, or Rum - and when tea and Punch became thus the diet and debauch of all the beer and Ale drinkers, the effects were suddenly and severely felt".[10]

Thus Bristol's maritime trade had a significant impact upon the development of the English porcelain industry. Not only did its products caused seismic shifts in taste and consumer demand but its profits generated capital for new ceramic ventures. Benjamin Lund, co-partner in the first Bristol soft-paste porcelain factory, would have profited from the demand by the slave traders for the brass and metal goods he produced. Fellow Quaker Richard Champion acquired through his shipping interests the capital that would later fund his interest in Cookworthy's porcelain manufactory which he transferred from Plymouth to Bristol in 1770.[11] Bristol had also gained an early prominence in supplying earthenware goods to the American colonies which, at least until the dispute with George III's government, shared the Mother Country's thirst for the new hot beverages. Many of the Delftware potteries that developed in the Bristol area thus encouraged by these transatlantic connections would later provide, in turn, a possible stimulus for Lund and Miller's enterprise.

Yet, even more crucial to an understanding of the origins of English provincial porcelain production is the importance of Bristol's internal commerce. Unlike its rival Liverpool, Bristol had a highly interdependent relationship with an extended hinterland in which the Severn played a vital role. Whereas 60% of Bristol's tobacco imports between 1680 and 1724 passed up the Severn via Gloucester (of which Worcester consumed one third!), most of Liverpool's tobacco was re-exported.[12] Liverpool inland trade was only equivalent to that of lesser Bristol Channel ports like Bridgwater and Minehead.[13] This, until the opening of the Midlands canal network in the second half of the eighteenth century remedied the defect, is explained by Liverpool's more limited access to navigable rivers. Despite the difficulties outlined above, Bristol's chief advantage - inherited by Worcester - was its access via the Severn and the Channel to inland raw materials and markets.

The Severn and the narrow waters of the Channel not only provide an opening to the great sea lanes of the Atlantic but they also, in the manner of an inland sea, connect a series of smaller waterways from the regional hinterlands of England and Wales to one another, a fact enhanced by improvements in the navigation of these rivers[14] and advances in the operational efficiency of coastal and river craft. Its sheltered waters were accessible to the trows and barges of the Severn and Wye and smaller vessels of the Usk and the Taff. The Channel and its numerous tributaries, of which the Severn, (navigable as far north as Welshpool) is the most prominent, opened a back door into the very heart of England and a variety of commerce.

This was a point echoed by contemporaries such as John Campbell who proclaimed

"for by the Avon she draws unto herself commodities from Warwickshire; by the help of the Teem, she receives those of Herefordshire and Shropshire; the Wye also brings her some part of the tribute of the former of those counties, and of Radnorshire; and if there be any thing yet left in Herefordshire and Shropshire, the Lugg drains them both; both Monmouthshire and the adjacent parts of Wales send their supplies by the Uske: and a great part of Somersetshire communicates both goods and manufactures by the Ivel, the Parrot and Tone; and Cornwall sends hither its tin and copper for the pewter and brass wire and copper company manufactories.".[15]

To this he might have added - and it was a peculiar oversight - that the Severn linked Bristol to the diverse agriculture of the Vale of Evesham and the Midland plain from whence it acquired its salt, hops and malt, and to the abundant iron and coal of the river gorge to the north. The economic significance of the area is revealed when one examines the construction of turnpike roads in 1740 which reveals how much the Severn dominated the inland trade and provided the spinal cord of a network of internal road and water communications.[16] The flurry (by eighteenth century standards!) of Parliamentary legislation - eleven acts relating to road improvement around Worcester were passed between 1725 and 1751 - resulted in Worcester being able to enjoy not only a favourable position on the river but also one at the heart of one of the country's most significant road networks, along with Bristol and Hereford, which thus provided additional tributaries to the Severn and the Channel.[17]

This axis also underpinned some of the first links between the medieval cities of Bristol and Worcester. The monastery of Worcester obtained a charter in the late 12th century which allowed it to purchase food and clothing from Bristol with payment of tolls. In 1277 Edward I ordered that the weirs should be opened up to 26 feet to allow ships and boats to pass up the river from Gloucester and Bristol and it was the men of Worcester who were ordered to do the work.[18] Fish, wine, wood and alabaster from Bristol, iron from the Forest of Dean and pottery from Hanley Castle was sent up to Worcester whence it was distributed by road to Coventry and other inland markets. Of particular note in the seventeenth and eighteenth centuries were the strong dynastic connections between the Quaker iron masters of Bristol and Coalbrookdale after Abraham Darby's move up the river. Bristol became, in effect, Worcester's window to the wider world making it a regional entrepot for the great port's commerce and this reached a peak in the early eighteenth century. Bristol merchants like Graffin Prankard not only imported colonial products like tobacco and traded it upstream along with the city's manufactures but also dealt in downriver shipments of Abraham Darby's iron, Droitwich salt and the agricultural products of the Vale of Evesham carried in Worcester trows. It is interesting to note in passing that a certain Edward Jackson, the name of one of the founding partners of Worcester porcelain in 1751, ran a salt carrying business down the Severn. If they are indeed one and the same person one could even speculate further, that he later became the distribution manager at the Worcester factory because of the knowledge he could bring to the business of transporting goods via the Severn and other navigable waterways, an area of expertise that would prove invaluable as the pace of economic change quickened and affected profit margins.

However it is important to stress that this was not a one-way relationship between the two cities. Although Bristol did indeed act as a stimulus to regional economies, there was by no means a colonial dependence of the hinterland upon the port.[19] It was, in fact, the very independence of these ports and the regions they served which allowed for such diversity and that Bristol was as much a beneficiary as a determinant of external entrepreneurialism. Thus, much of the shipping, especially Severn trows, noted by Pope and other contemporaries was not owned by Bristol merchants but by West Country and Welsh traders and that a good deal of cross Channel trade - particularly coal and culm from Newport and Swansea and clay and agricultural produce from Bridgwater - passed back and forth without reference to Bristol. The development of the Stourbridge glass industry effectively sealed the Severn Valley markets against the competition from the Bristol works because of cheaper transport costs, a factor which would play an important part in an economic shift of power northwards up the Severn. Local businessmen, as the Worcester partnership was to prove in 1751, may have needed Bristol to create an entrepreneurial culture in the region but they were quite prepared to seize for themselves the opportunities as and when they were presented.

The significance of re-emphasizing the importance of regional and coastal trade is fundamental to any explanation of why Bristol and then Worcester was able to take up porcelain production. Despite Hobson's reminder that porcelain was a foreign import, English soft paste porcelain had no dependence upon foreign raw materials. English porcelain production was largely a home grown affair using local products, notwithstanding some experimentation with the American clay unaker. It was the Severn and the Severn Sea that provided the vital link in the development of the early porcelain industry outside of London, connecting the works at Bristol, Worcester and, later, Caughley and Coalport. It was the fleet of Severn trows that brought up china clay and soaprock from Cornwall and timber and coal from the river valley for the furnaces. Without the axis of the river, it is less than likely that the above factories would have been able to emerge as the heirs and successors to the first factories established in London.

Yet, paradoxically, in the long run, Bristol's location in the Severn estuary proved ultimately to be vulnerable and overly dependent upon those vagaries of river transport outlined earlier. When the

No 19 (detail)

next generation of provincial entrepreneurs sought in the third quarter of the century to exploit the commercial advantages offered by the sprouting canal network they bypassed Bristol. From being at the centre of the country's best internal transport system at the beginning of the century, Bristol now found itself peripheral to the improvements in the 1760s and 1770s. The linking of the Stroudwater and the Thames, for example, provided a canal route for Welsh iron to London which did not pass through Bristol.[20] In particular, the development of canals in the north Midlands provided superior water-borne transport links and the manufactures of the region which had previously come south for export down the Severn were now diverted north to Liverpool. It was not only in transatlantic commerce that Liverpool gained the competitive edge over Bristol. Its access to the new canals also gave the Lancashire port an advantage in interior lines of communication and one cannot resist pointing out that this found a metaphor in porcelain production as the Liverpool factories were set up, like that of Worcester, in the wake of the passing of Lund and Miller's pioneer venture.

"Some of the principal commodities of the surrounding country, exported from Bristol, are, cheese, cider, and beer, a few coals, herrings taken in the Channel, salt from Droitwich, coarse woollens and stockings, hardware from Birmingham and Wolverhampton, and earthenware from Staffordshire. In the exportation of these last articles, however, Liverpool has gained upon Bristol, chiefly on account of the superiority of the canal navigations to that town, above the difficult and uncertain navigation of the Severn".[21]

Worcester, by contrast, with its more central location on the Severn, was able to re-orientate itself in order to take advantage of the Staffordshire and Worcestershire and Trent and Mersey canals giving it access to an improved network of waterways developing in the Midlands. It became a major distribution point for Shropshire coal with seven out of the eighteen river coal-tax collectors based in Worcester by the end of the century, more than any other town. The completion of Brindley's Grand Trunk canal link to the Thames at Oxford also allowed Worcester to look increasingly to London, rather than Bristol, as its main internal market. One might also add that Derby's position - which looked a little isolated in the late 1740s - was even more transformed by the completion of the canal system which certainly helps explain its comparable longevity. In short, there was no reason why a provincial city such as Worcester with access to this network of water-borne commerce - and its subsidiary road links - could not aspire to a porcelain industry provided that any enterprise was backed by shrewd business sense, sound finance and favourable market conditions. We should also remember that consumer culture was, thanks to this quickening pace of transport, not just restricted to the great cities and the mercantile elites. It was up the small rivers and creeks that household goods such as linen, table ware, pottery etc, reached the more peripheral and humbler households of the interior and in doing so created the taste for porcelain upon which the future growth of the industry would depend. It is to these changes in taste and society we must now turn.

2) A POLITE AND COMMERCIAL PEOPLE

From the Middle Ages to the late seventeenth century both Bristol and Worcester were able to enjoy an extended period of commercial prominence. Bristol was, as Eden noted, "not more a commercial than a manufacturing town";[22] access to a wide range of raw materials prompted local manufactures and a diversification of skills and trades. The cramped medieval city depicted in James Millerd's "Exact Delineation of the Famous Cittie of Bristol" in 1671 had changed considerably by the time Nathaniel and Samuel Buck produced two prospects of the city in 1734. Brass and copper works which were supplied by Cornish tin and Anglesey copper are already visible. During the eighteenth century production in the coal mines at Kingswood increased as did the manufacture of soap using wood ash and kelp from the Somerset ports. West Country wool fed the looms that produced its celebrated nightcaps. The imports of colonial tobacco and sugar fed new processing and refining works in the city. The opening of the spa in the Clifton Gorge also acted as a stimulus to bottling industry; as Defoe noted in 1724 there were 15 glass houses (also visible in the Buck's Prospect of 1734)

"which are more in London...and vast numbers of bottles are used for sending the water of the Hotwell not only over England but all over the world".

Production really took off when the growth of the London market rapidly accelerated demand. In 1718 500 baskets were sold, 311 of which were traded to London; by 1725 the figure was 5,075 baskets and London's share was 3,305.[23] Using kelp and clay from Stourbridge, this became Bristol's most important industry, producing also large quantities of window glass for urban rebuilding and the American colonies. It is traditionally held that it was at one such glassworks that Lund and Miller set up their short-lived porcelain works and it may have been Dr Wall's interest in glass-painting that alerted him to their enterprise. The combination of local glassworks and potteries certainly would have given this area a significant advantage in promoting the launch of their enterprise. The kiln technology and expertise of glassworkers seems to have provided a useful stepping stone for early porcelain pioneers such as Bristol merchant Edward Heyleyn, one of the Bow partners.[24] Lund and Miller were also doubtlessly confident that skilled potters and painters of local Delftware, trained by the likes of Joseph Flower, John Niglett, and John Bowen,[25] were available to call upon in setting up their factory and it is inconceivable that at least some of the employees with related skills in the area did not work briefly for Lund and Miller and perhaps also moved on to Worcester in 1752.

Worcester was also able to capitalize upon its natural advantages and in the later 17th century the city had enjoyed a real boom on the back of its luxury wool industry which was carried on in the houses of outworkers. The civil wars made Worcester one of the principal armaments manufacturing centres and the wars of the 1690s led to an embargo against salt from the Bay of Biscay which worked to the advantage of Cheshire and Droitwich salt; Worcester's domination of the latter was further enhanced by the success in 1695 of Robert Steynor in the Court of Chancery in breaking a restrictive production cartel and thus allowing the sinking of new brine pits in Droitwich to the detriment of Cheshire in the Severn trade.[26] A study of the electoral and occupational registers give a clear indication of Worcester's local importance in processing, redistributing and retailing agricultural produce, particularly the brewing and shipment of hops. There is also, bearing in mind the significant connections in Bristol between the glass and ceramics industries, evidence in the Worcester Journal that a local glass factory may have existed based on a report of the imprisonment for debt in 1729 of Edward Dixon "a glassmaker" of Worcester and another seven years later referring to some objects removed from the river "out of a meadow near the glasshouse, about half a mile above Worcester."[27]

However Worcester's prosperity, the woollen industry aside, was not based primarily upon its manufacturing prowess; unlike Bristol, its economy was based much more squarely upon distribution than manufacturing, making it potentially more vulnerable to the winds of economic misfortune. An examination of the map of Worcester in 1740 by John Doharty, another of the 1751 partners, reveals little evidence of any manufacturing and this also appears to be the case with Buck's engraving of the city (1732) and even Valentine Green's much later map of 1790. Indeed, the canvas showing a prospect of Worcester from the east attributed to John Harris (c 1750) depicts a rural idyll of golden cornfields, harvesters and the shooting of game. Even Paul Sandby's bustling water colour (1772) of the river front adjacent to the porcelain factory shortly before Dr Wall's retirement, showing busy river traffic, the unloading and loading of goods and the kilns belching smoke is balanced by the serenity of the Cathedral and unpolluted skies in the background. It is in sharp contrast to the contemporary depictions of Ironbridge, showing the river gorge overwhelmed by clouds of smog and highlighted by flame. The industrialization of Worcestershire would for the most part take place north of the county town with nail-making in Bromsgrove, glass works at Stourbridge and carpet weaving in Kidderminster. Perhaps even more surprisingly, there is little evidence of a city pottery in the eighteenth century; there was certainly nothing to compare with Bristol's delftware or Staffordshire earthenware. Worcester's ability to overcome this apparent handicap would seem to be further confirmation of the greater significance that needs to be attached to transportation, markets and the financial security of the partnership in explaining why some of the early works survived and others failed. Skilled labour would gravitate towards the successful factories rather than vice versa as events were to prove.

However, in the early eighteenth century at least, the prosperity described above led to the transformation of both cities as an aspiring commercial and professional class sought to convert their wealth into the tangible signs of gentility. The most overt symptom of this was the architectural redevelopment of private and public buildings. In Bristol, Queen Square and St James' Square were laid out as were elegant residential streets such as Park Street and Great George Street where the sugar magnates, the Pinneys took up residence. The heights of Clifton began to acquire its reputation as a desirable area for people of taste and fashion. Notable public buildings such as the Corn Exchange and St Thomas Church were erected. Significant urban rebuilding had also taken place in Worcester, gaining the admiration of most visitors. The impressive Guildhall had been completed by 1724 by the noted architect Thomas White whilst the rebuilding of exceptional baroque parish churches such as those of All Saints and St Nicholas, duly noted in the parliamentary legislation of 1738 and 1739 respectively,[28] was testament to the wealth and conventional piety of the citizens of Worcester. The wool merchant Robert Berkeley of Spetchley left in his will in 1697 £6,000 for the creation of the elegant almshouses and hospital in Foregate Street, which was, in its own right, considered one of the most elegant residential roads in the West Midlands.

This programme of building was indicative of the attempt by the local gentry and prosperous merchants to create the outward signs of gentility that they sought simultaneously to cultivate in their own behaviour.[29] A significant innovation in Bristol was the opening up of the Hotwells Spa in Clifton. Famous visitors like the Duchesses of Marlborough and Kent were portrayed in "Characters at the Hotwells" published in 1723 and the novelist Smollett set the opening chapters of "Humphrey Clinker" there. In 1729 the constant stream of leisured visitors helped bring about attractions such as evening balls and parties held in public rooms owned by the Pump Room and even the opening of a small theatre. Similarly in Worcester, we find Dr John Wall and William Davis, the chief instigators of the Worcester Porcelain manufactory, conducting experiments on spring water in 1743 and endorsing their own local spa in Malvern in the 1750s which was to develop as one of the attractions of the area. In both cases the draw of tourists was sufficient to promote entertainment in the area. Although opposed by more puritanical elements in Bristol, John Hippisley, the original Mr Peachum in *"The Beggar's Opera"*, took advantage of the fact that his theatre at Jacob's Well lay outside the city's jurisdiction and attracted every summer leading London players such as Woodward, Mrs. Pritchard and William Powell. This taste for dramatic productions would eventually lead to the opening of a new Theatre Royal in the city itself in 1766. It was here that Michael Edkins, a leading Bristol pottery decorator, painted not only the theatre building but also scenery and even trod the boards as an apparently talented singer. It is worth noting that the Theatre was funded by public subscription, one of the ways in which one could proclaim one's membership of polite society; the sum raised by 1767, in all some £5,000, was very considerable[30] and comparable to that raised by the Worcester partners for commencing their porcelain works some sixteen years previously, an observation to which I shall return later.

This search for identification with gentility was also reflected in the numerous entertainments to be found in Worcester. The emergence of the Three Choirs Festival was a major triennial event in Worcester which not only demonstrated the cultural aspirations of the city's commercial classes but also its music, with a strong emphasis on Handel, became a triumphalist celebration of the Hanoverian succession. Working from a selection of advertisements in the Worcester Journal, David Whitehead concluded

"It was a city of concerts, coffee houses, lectures, theatres, exhibitions, bowling greens, drawing schools and dancing academies. Frequent race meetings had been held there at least since 1700 and the Three Choirs Festival had been born there. There were public baths, public breakfasts, public gardens and public walks. If anyone wished to see a crocodile swimming, a bear baited, a cock fighting, an exhibition of ballooning or a solar microscope, he came to Worcester".[31]

In short, both were places of considerable prosperity in the first half of the eighteenth century and with developing markets for consumer goods and genteel recreation which would help sustain innovations such as a local porcelain works. Local records reveal that a taste for pottery and porcelain was already developing as the imports of tea and sugar became increasingly affordable, largely thanks to the efforts of the smugglers mentioned above. In 1716 Graffin Prankard had shipped from London to Bristol a "tea table, teapot, dishes & all things according the latest faision", an extravagance which he sought to conceal from his Quaker brethren by assigning it in the first instance to a linen draper on Bristol Bridge.[32] The poet, Thomas Chatterton, born near St Mary Redcliffe, asked a local potter who was a kinsman of his father to make him a cup depicting a winged figure of fame, bearing a trumpet, spreading the young man's greatness.[33] Tea dealers proliferated; by 1784 out of a total of 1769 shopkeepers in Bristol and Bath, well over a third were registered tea dealers.[34] A will of Joseph Watts "Chinaman" of the parish of St Michael's, Worcester drawn up in 1736 suggests that fifteen years before the formation of the Worcester partnership, there was already a taste for the exotic import or at least a cheaper earthenware substitute from Bristol or Staffordshire.[35]

However, not all visitors to Bristol were impressed by the city's claim to gentility. Walpole, Pope, Defoe and even the local protégé Chatterton[36] amongst many others were scathing in their criticisms. Bristol, it seems never quite succeeded in throwing off its country bumpkin image and rude ways in the eyes of the more "discerning" visitors to the city, who castigated its buildings, its refuse problems, the unsightly slurry visible at low tide of the river, the unmannerly behaviour of the local citizenry, the want of polite entertainment and the parsimony of its Corporation. Many of the merchants' homes still served as counting houses and warehouses rather than salons to the literati and fashionable. Unfavourable comparisons drawn not only with London but also neighbouring Bath reflected the view that the city was seen first and foremost as a place for making money rather than spending it. This was not altogether justified but the persistence and frequency of such comments cannot easily be ignored. The old deep-rooted Puritanism of the city, dovetailing with its eighteenth century manifestations in Quakerism, Presbyterianism and Wesleyanism,[37] had a tendency to regard the latest frippery and fashion with some distaste; to indulge in consumerism was seen in some quarters as sinful self-indulgence at best - remember the secrecy of Graffin Prankard's purchase of his tea ware - and at worst an invitation to Satan himself. There was much local hostility to the Hotwells and its theatre at Jacob's Well and John Wesley himself led the opposition to the new Theatre. In fact, reading contemporary comments one is struck by how polarized seem the views of "fashionable opinion" - (derived largely from outside visitors) - and those of local worthies representing the Corporation, commercial community and religious sects. For the former, the merchants and tradesmen of Bristol were little more than pirates still living out the rumbustuous days of Drake and Hawkins, an impression assisted by the high profile of the more unsavoury aspects of the slave trade in its dockyards and sordid holding rooms at the quay side. On the other hand, many of the visitors to the Hotwells and its theatre were seen as a moral threat to the values of work and godliness upon which the city's greatness had been built. It was not surprising then that local amenities serving the wells should commend themselves by emphasizing their detachment from the local inhabitants. The delay in the process of the gentrification of Bristol, which did not really get under way until the third quarter of the century, may have denied Lund's factory the advantage of a sufficiently strong local market that would have helped it consolidate its sales and profits in the crucial first years after its establishment. The works which had been visited by Pococke in 1750 had already - perhaps as a result of Worcester's takeover bid - closed its doors to locals and visitors alike by the following year.

Worcester, by contrast, seems to have received almost universal approbation from visitors to the city in the eighteenth century, with the notable exception of Defoe. From Celia Fiennes in 1696 to William Cobbett one hundred and thirty years later all commented upon its tidy streets, elegant buildings, the polite company and the range of activities suitable to the leisured and professional classes. The Worcester Journal felt entitled to brag in 1763 that the city had become famous for "entertaining company in the most agreeable gentle manner". Because it acted not just as county town but also a regional capital many of the landed gentry and aristocracy from the surrounding counties took up residence in the city, usually in St Michael's parish, adjacent to the Cathedral, or Foregate Street. They were also required by virtue of their status to frequently visit the city to attend the Assizes, military musters, the Three Choirs Music Festival and other county business. Here, unlike Bristol, the city economy was far more geared to the demands of its visiting polite society and the commercial and professional class increasingly shaped itself in their image.

Whilst this marked divergence in the social pretensions of the two cities is impossible to quantify and played no significant part in the initial establishment of either Lund or Wall's factories, it is worth speculating on the importance of a sound local market for the survival of newly created provincial porcelain factories in addition to quickly securing a niche in the predominant London market. For Bow, Chelsea and Limehouse this was never going to be a problem but for provincial factories it was perhaps an important consideration that had to be borne in mind; if, as will be argued, a considerable proportion of the initial *famille verte* output was aimed at connoisseurs and collectors[38] - even if not at the luxury end like Chelsea - rather than a mass market like that of Bow, then the social milieu of Worcester may well have been both a determinant of the factory's commercial strategy and, initially at least, an important factor in its survival in the first critical five years. It is indeed unfortunate that it is not possible to trace the records of early sales to see what proportion of goods were sold in Samuel Bradley's shop in Worcester or in the factory itself. It is, however, probably fair to say that given the number of potential customers already drawn to the city, its established reputation in retailing to the gentry and its lack of a London outlet until 1756 it was likely to have been an important corollary to its excellent transport links. The numerous recorded visits to the factory by dignitaries like the Royal Family and Nelson and less prominent individuals like Libby Powis in the later eighteenth and early nineteenth centuries suggests this was likely to have been a significant component of any visit to Worcester.

No 81 (reverse)

Another significant divergence between both cities prior to porcelain manufacture came in their responses to the need for economic reorientation in the middle decades of the century. Wars, shifts in demand, new competitors, weather and pure bad luck could overtake the unwary as Defoe's words, particularly apposite to Bristol and Worcester, made clear

"great towns decay, and small towns rise; new towns, new palaces, new seats are built every day; great rivers and good harbours dry up, and grow useless again; new ports are open'd, brooks are made rivers, small rivers navigable ports, and harbours are made where none were made before".[39]

Nothing could be taken for granted in a world of rapid change. We have already noted that the development of the canal and turnpike road network combined with the inherent navigational problems of the Severn meant that the new industries of the Midlands began to direct their products away from Bristol towards Liverpool. In addition, during the last two thirds of the eighteenth century, Bristol began to find its maritime position challenged in the short term by crop fluctuations in the colonies and also in the long term by its inability to compete with Liverpool and later Glasgow. The limitations of the Bristol docks and the slowness to improve them combined with growing Quaker hostility to the slave trade saw the West Country metropolis lose its predominant position in transatlantic commerce. There was a marked depression during the war of Austrian succession 1744-47 with the combined number of ships and tonnage of coastal and foreign trade indicating a marked decline. From 1737 to 1744 the number of ships at Bristol fell from 822 to 530 and tonnage fell from 20,030 to 13,962 and although there was a recovery in the later 1740s the writing was on the wall. Graffin Prankard, the Quaker iron merchant who had so surreptitiously bought a tea set from London in the latest fashion, would find himself bankrupted in the summer of 1740.

However, it is important to stress that Bristol's economic "decline" was relative rather than absolute and was by no means terminal. New businesses arose to replace those that had been lost, sometimes at the expense of traders and producers in Bristol's hinterland. The manufactures of Gloucester were gradually displaced by those of its larger neighbour according to one contemporary in 1780. However, more generally, the new opportunities presented in Bristol's hinterland encouraged its wealthy merchants to finance the products of the iron and coal industries outside of the city as the city's own labour and fuel costs increased to the detriment of local forgemasters and the mines of Kingswood Chase. Unlike the businessmen of Worcester, they were much more accustomed to a wider market view and investing beyond their immediate neighbourhood. They were prominent in financing the White Rock Copper Company (1737) and numerous ironworks and coalmines in South Wales not to mention the roles of Thomas Goldney and Richard Reynolds in the Coalbrookdale iron works of Abraham Darby. Other enterprises backed by Bristolians included glasshouses in Chepstow, Nailsea and Chelwood, tin mining in Cornwall and a network of banks and insurance offices was created following the establishment of the Bristol Old Bank (1750) and the Bristol Fire Office (1787).[40] The city continued to grow and diversify, even if at a slower rate, and one cannot but help feel that regional extraction and manufacturing businesses outside the city, new tertiary services and established industries within it like the sugar refineries, glassworks and soap works yielded sufficient profit to deter investors from backing more speculative projects like that of Lund and Miller. Indeed, given that Miller himself died leaving a reputed fortune of £190,000 from his trading and banking activities in 1781, he may well have been tempted by such opportunities to invest elsewhere,[41] leaving his impecunious partner in the lurch. Contemporaries and historians have noted the reticence of Bristol's mercantile elite to be as willing to speculate in their dock facilities as their counterparts in Liverpool which is difficult to reconcile with the obsession with profit noted by contemporaries above. The answer may lie in the fact that as the economic pendulum swung to favour investment in provincial rather than metropolitan enterprise, Bristolians looked to their hinterland instead. One is tempted to ask whether it was purely coincidental that the Lancashire port saw more whole-hearted, if not always successful efforts, to develop local porcelain industries in the city since it lacked the contacts and opportunities outside of it. Even more relevant to our present enquiry is why Worcester, with its much narrower economic base was able to promote and sustain its own ceramics industry and perhaps part of the answer lay in the fact that, facing a more serious crisis of trade, the burghers of Worcester were left with less comfortable options than those of Bristol, especially with the erosion of its staple business, the wool trade, upon which there was a dangerous dependence. In other words, even though early porcelain manufacture was a highly risky and speculative affair, it was easier to attract and retain the venture capital of local businessmen because outlets were closing and options were limited. In the case of Worcester, a virtue was born out of necessity as much as confidence.

From the 1690s onwards there was significant readjustment in England's staple industry, the wool trade, with the prosperity it had brought to traditional centres like Bristol and Worcester shifting outside to cheaper, less regulated rural areas. Gwen Talbut[42] has examined and explained in some depth the dramatic change in the quality wool trade in Worcester in an exemplary piece of local historical research. As late as 1727 Defoe described the city as "very full of People and the People generally esteemed as very rich, being full of Business, occasion'd chiefly by the Clothing Trade" and yet by 1790 when Treadway Nash was writing his "History of Worcestershire" the cloth trade was but a memory and had been replaced by the gloving industry.

This decline was brought about by a fatal combination of external and internal factors. The development of the Scottish linen industry had reduced English demand for continental imports which in turn led to diminished reciprocal demand for British wool, particularly that of the West Country. Similarly the Levant trade upon which Worcester depended so greatly was also affected by the emergence of new products and markets.[43] Internal factors included the lifting of restrictions on entering the trade, the disappearance of the local Ryeland sheep[44] which affected the quality of the wool and the problem of fending off the competition from the New Draperies of the southern counties. The plight of the woollen industry was such that the Society of Worcester People in London was busy trying to find apprenticeships for Worcester children and sending money for the poor weavers of their home town. In 1753 Jonas Hanway was to comment "our Turkey merchants, who some years since figured at the top of the commercial world, now bow their diminished heads". One might ponder upon the impact this change may have had upon the decision of two of the Worcester partners of 1751 with interests in the cloth trade - Richard and John Brodribb - to diversify into new products.

By the mayoralty of Joseph Withers in 1740-41 the number of glovers and butchers admitted as freemen outnumbered clothiers and the new tradesmen being admitted - building craftsmen, food trades, metalworkers, suppliers of luxury goods - revealed the extent to which Worcester was undergoing a period of economic and political transition.[45] Small wonder, then, that in the controversial city election of 1747, the cry was "Vote for Trade" as the influential citizens of Worcester sought to provide new sources of employment. Within four years, there would begin the energetic campaign to introduce porcelain manufacturing into the city and that it should be imported wholesale from Bristol does suggest a desire and unity of purpose behind the scheme that reflected the different perceptions and opportunities prevailing in the respective cities. It also, as will be argued in the final section, reflected a common social and political outlook that was forged in the battles for control of the city in the turbulent decade prior to the formation of the partnership in 1751.

3) A DECADE OF CRISIS; 1740-50

In order to understand the enterprise created by the Worcester partners we need to consider the calculations that underpinned their decision; in commercial terms it was not a straightforward step even if they had already been alerted to the opportunity of taking over the existing concern at Bristol. The nascent ceramics industry between 1745 and 1755 in many respects anticipated the higher risk strategies required by the rest of the manufacturing sector in the second half of the century as the Industrial Revolution proper took off. It required a high level of entry cost in capital equipment and premises; production processes were unpredictable, costly and experimental; skilled workmen were in short supply and management had to be learnt on the job;[46] it faced existing Chinese competition which was often superior and invariably cheaper; numerous but, as of yet, unknown domestic rivals were also planning to mark their entry on the scene with products that were still under wraps, making marketing strategy a matter of guesswork; without the limitless funding of the state or aristocratic patronage there was little apparent attraction for shrewd investors and market information was limited and contradictory. In so far as one could gain an insight into a market that was no more than six years old, the failures of Limehouse and Pomona should have countered the successes of Chelsea and Bow in the prognostications of Dr. Wall and his friends.

In addition, the socio-economic and political climate could hardly have looked worse, but paradoxically, it may well have been the sense of crisis forming the backdrop to the establishment of the Worcester factory that generated the determination to take on the commercial challenge. We need to see the Worcester partners as more than mere business associates; we need to see them as social and political animals with motives that were shaped by a much wider set of concerns than simply profit and loss and which had their origins over ten years prior to the establishment of the factory. Conjoined by party political interests, they had already been involved in civic projects designed to advance a shared vision of local and national renewal. Without a knowledge of these earlier activities, the partnership of 1751 seems an almost inexplicable venture.[47]

In the first place we need to understand why the partners were anxious to provide a new form of employment in the city. Mention has already been made of the fact that the Brodribbs perhaps needed to diversify as the cloth trade teetered towards oblivion and Worcester could not match the investment opportunities of Bristol. However, for the rest of the partners - including two physicians, two glovers, two clerics, an apothecary, an attorney, a goldsmith, a merchant, a draughtsman, a publisher and possibly a printer - there was no previous involvement with ceramics and it is difficult to see why they should be tempted into such a speculative project. To understand why they were willing to back the venture, one needs to see the partners in other guises, playing other roles. We need to remember that they were tax payers and members of the propertied classes who were alarmed by the consequences of increases in unemployment and the unwelcome pressure to a system of poor relief which contemporaries were already castigating as expensive and ineffectual. They had much to lose as the problems of the decade mounted. The rapid demobilisation of armies in 1749 caused massive disruption and lawlessness. In 1749 70,000 men were discharged and the crime rate rose dramatically; over 50% of those hanged for robbery in 1749 were servicemen and a disproportionate number continued to be implicated until a resumption of hostilities abroad in 1756.[48] The mob could, with the slightest provocation, threaten life and property and yet neither magistrate nor army officer felt confident to open fire in the face of possible prosecution, such was the legal ambiguity enshrouding the enforcement of the Riot Acts.[49] In a sermon preached in his parish church in Bristol in 1746 Josiah Tucker claimed

"our People are drunk with the cup of Liberty... Such brutality and insolence, such debauchery and extravagance, such idleness in religion, cursing, swearing and contempt of all rule and authority, Human and Divine, do not reign so triumphantly among the Poor in any country as ours".

It is not difficult to find evidence of this disorder in Bristol and Worcester. In 1727 and throughout the 1730s the unruly colliers of Kingswood broke down the new turnpikes since they objected to paying tolls on the carriage of coals out of the city. They delayed the successful operation of improved roads until 1749 when coals were excluded from tolls. In 1749 the *Gentleman's Magazine* reported the destruction of the Ashton Road and Dundry turnpikes by an armed mob of 400 Somerset rioters.[50] *The Worcester Journal* of January 9th 1744 reported some of the effects of soldiery in the city where five soldiers who had been committed for robbery attempted to escape and kill the turnkey and another two soldiers James Painter and William Armstrong were committed for robbing Joseph Bradley of his coat, two waistcoats and his hat. The same source was also to report that in November 1755 Dr Wall himself had a lucky escape and it was his travelling servant who was relieved of ten shillings by Edward Sheward, a deserter from a recruiting party in Kidderminster, although the good doctor was not so lucky two years later when he was robbed of four guineas by William Lissimore who, like Sheward, was swiftly apprehended and imprisoned.[51]

The restoration of gainful employment was seen as an essential complement to the vigorous application of the law if men of substance were to continue to enjoy their property and Worcester would follow Bristol's lead in creating a workhouse. In 1695 the Bristol merchant and economic pamphleteer John Cary wrote his "Essay on the State of England", thus starting the campaign for a workhouse in the city leading to an Act of Parliament the following year providing for the unification of all 17 city parishes into a Corporation of the Poor to collect a poor rate, build a workhouse and compel the poor to enter it. The money raised in Bristol was used to buy a building known locally as the Mint or St Peter's, for the purpose of educating 100 boys, 100 girls and later housing the infirm as well as acting as a house of correction for beggars and hawkers. This would be followed by similar measures in Worcester from 1703 onwards where the parishes combined in association with the Corporation to appoint a body of guardians and build a city workhouse. These proposals were intended to save on legal battles for resettlement between parishes and, with an emphasis on moral and vocational retraining of the young, would offer a long term solution to structural urban poverty. In the short term it would reduce poor rate expenditure and purge the streets of beggars and criminals. These were considerations which supplemented the profit motive in the creation of the partnership of 1751. Richard Brodribb was certainly involved in this earlier project as one of the Guardians of the Poor and it is tempting to note not only the desire to provide work but also the similarities between the regimes of workhouse and factory with the segregation of the sexes, the insistence upon moral behaviour and training of youth.

Secondly, in addition to this indirect material self-interest, we need also to remember that the partners shared a conventional piety and morality which endorsed the efficacy of charitable undertakings and acknowledged a duty to improve the physical, spiritual and educational welfare of those less fortunate than themselves. The sense of Christian duty that led a number of them into supporting the rebuilding of Worcester's churches also led them to look to a moral reformation of its citizenry. The encouragement provided by the 1690 Act to distilling, intended to boost the incomes of cereal farmers had led to a phenomenal explosion of gin shops and alcoholism.[52] The consequences for trade, sexual behaviour, child mortality and crime were all too graphically revealed in the engravings of Hogarth. This was exacerbated by the apparent negligence and decadence of government at national and local level. For the commercial classes of Bristol and Worcester who dominated city politics there was much grumbling against an aristocratic elite which seemed increasingly responsible for sexual libertinism, French manners and a proliferation of imported luxury goods.[53] By failing to set an appropriate example, the ruling elite encouraged social inferiors to behave in a way that belied their allotted station in life and contemporary observers like Defoe and Hanway constantly railed against servants, labourers and rude mechanics indulging in extravagant fashions, tea drinking and gambling. The governing classes were also seen to be shirking their civic obligations. In Worcester, the county gentry deliberately bought houses in St Michael's parish beyond the city's jurisdiction so that they were not eligible for poor rates or parish office. Bishop Isaac Maddox of Worcester, a prominent member of the Society for the Reformation of Manners, played a prominent part in calling for action. Maddox was an evangeliser par excellence and was not abashed at using his position to challenge the complacency of the establishment or to make some apparently unlikely alliances in his support for good causes. In his St Luke's Day sermon in 1748 to a well-to-do congregation he was not afraid to utilise fire and brimstone tactics to urge greater generosity

"How dreadful will your condition then be if any present Disregard and Cruelty to your Brethren shall treasure up Wrath against the day of Wrath; when those who have showed no Mercy shall have Judgement against Mercy?".[54]

Without doubt his passionate sermons and speeches were instrumental in shaping the moral tone of the city in the 1740s and in particular Maddox and Wall worked closely together to establish an Infirmary in Worcester, again following the lead given by Bristol in the interlinking of Christian charity, moral instruction and economic utilitarianism.

John Elbridge, Bristol's deputy Controller of Customs had launched an initiative for a hospital in the wake of Alured Clarke's example at Winchester in 1736. The new infirmary was opened in St James' churchyard in December 1737 and the following year Carew Reynell's sermon preached before the contributors to the Bristol Infirmary argued the need to cure the head of a family so that the whole family contributed to rather than drained the local economy. The Infirmary Quarterly Board of Governors' minutes for 7th March 1739 ordered that visitors should "give preference to the Laborious Industrious Poor". Patients attending the hospital were also to be exposed to daily prayers and forbidden to drink alcohol, swear or gamble, a moral reformation outlined by Josiah Tucker's explicit sermon of 1746 entitled "Hospitals and Infirmaries Considered as schools of Christian Education for the Adult Poor: and as a Means Conducive Towards a National Reformation in the Common Peoples". It was perhaps significant that when Dr Wall and Bishop Maddox sought to emulate Bristol and open Worcester's own Infirmary in 1746, the new Infirmary bought a copy of the regulations of Bristol Infirmary. Firstly, it suggests that Wall's medical contacts in Bristol might offer an explanation for his awareness of the Lund's porcelain factory some five years later. Secondly, there is clear evidence of wide ranging motives and purposes behind the scheme similar to those in Bristol, emphasizing moral discipline and industry, themes that are also later apparent in the regulations of the porcelain works suggesting that the creation of the Worcester factory may be seen as part of this series of measures combining self-interest and philanthropy. Finally, the raising of money by subscription and extending voting rights in the elections and running of the new hospital provided a new model of open government and accountability; it was a model that would have an echo in the deeds of partnership of 1751 with the insistence upon accessible accounts and the mutual obligations that were entailed, particularly in preserving the secrecy of the newly acquired porcelain recipe.[55] Moreover, it was deliberately in marked contrast to the corrupt practices of the recently deposed regime of Robert Walpole and the increasingly dominant Tory faction which was on the point of winning control of the Worcester Corporation, much to the alarm of Wall and his associates.

This brings me on to the third role of the Worcester partners, that of political activists. There were some intense political rivalries in mid century Worcester. Evidence from the poll books of 1741 and 1747 and the Vernon papers show that the partners were very closely connected to the Sandys[56] and Vernon "Country" Whig interest which was opposed to the "Court" Whig ministry of Walpole. In temporary alliance with local Tories the so-called Country or Patriot interest had successfully resisted the Excise Tax of 1733 and in 1734 brought about the electoral defeat of the ministry candidate for the city, Sir Richard Lane. Throughout the decade they attacked the jobbery and self-interest of the regime of Robert Walpole, particularly its foreign policy. The pursuit of Hanoverian interests on the continent appeared to jeopardize the commercial preoccupations of British merchants and tradesmen who favored a more aggressive maritime policy to protect colonial interests in the Americas from the incursions of France and Spain.[57] This dissatisfaction was best expressed in the widespread celebration of the triumphs of Admiral Edward Vernon[58] in 1739-40 which were used by Walpole's opponents in Bristol, Worcester and elsewhere to highlight the failings of the ministry in the 1741 election campaigns and bring about its removal in 1742.

In the short term, it appeared as if some of the antagonisms underlying the old Whig Ascendancy might be alleviated by Walpole's resignation. The formation of a more inclusive administration under Henry Pelham and Lord Hardwicke, perhaps prompted by the crime wave as well as the need to bolster resistance to the allure of Jacobitism, saw the restoration of proscribed Tory landowners to the commissions of the peace, despite the reservations of some local Whigs. At the same time, the growing prosperity and the electoral backing of the Dissenter community, particularly the Quakers, increased the pressure for the reduction of restrictions to their holding of office in local government. However this was anathema to Tories, resenting the encroachment into civic life of non-Anglicans who did not take oaths on entering office. They were also, with good justification, infuriated by the way in which local Whig grandees like Sandys, Rushout and Winnington deserted their Country Tory allies as soon as government posts became available.[59] For their part the Whigs, including Wall and his friends in the Sandys/Vernon interest, were becoming concerned by the way in which the Tories were beginning to win control of the Worcester Corporation and use their power to create new honorary freemen from the landowners in the surrounding counties, a move which dramatically increased the number of local Tory squires eligible to vote in city elections. This reached near panic proportions in the crisis of 1745-46 caused by Charles Stuart's invasion. The Tories, it was alleged, were slow to support Maddox's Infirmary and the Constitution Club - created to raise troops to defend against the Pretender - by refusing to pay subscriptions under the pretence that it was unconstitutional and in contempt of parliament's sole right to authorize any form of taxation.[60] The Whigs were quick to smear their opponents with charges of Jacobitism and lack of charity. This was to provide the volatile backdrop to the bitter election battle of 1747.

Herein lay a dilemma that could do much to sabotage the reforming impulses in urban politics. Whilst there was broad agreement, as we have seen, about the methods needed to restore order and economic prosperity, the real issue often became confused by the debate over who was best suited to provide the means by which it should be achieved. "Competitive philanthropy" often followed political and religious alignments as local businessmen sought to maintain order and exploit opportunities for social and political gain. These issues would take on an added resonance at election time in Bristol and Worcester which were already highly politicized cities with a well-established press, coffee house culture and political clubs; both were atypical boroughs with, by eighteenth century standards, large open franchises of over 4,000 and 2,000 voters respectively, and polls characterized by the very sort of unruly behaviour that alarmed the authorities so greatly. Although elections only took place every seven years, the undercurrent of conflict that would often erupt with spectacular effect on such occasions was constantly bubbling below the surface of civic government with arguably even more damaging consequences.

In Bristol the large Dissenter presence was a constant source of political disagreement over the administration of the poor laws, charity schools and other civic projects and in Worcester too we find local resentment of a Quaker presence in the turnpike trusts and a long running dispute between the City Corporation and the Guardians of the Poor, the latter represented by Richard Brodribb. Yet, these disputes, if anything, seemed to have created a bond between the future partners because their political association preceded the various proposed reforms with which they were connected and was indeed a *raison d'être* for the latter; the show of political unity and co-operation that was required to defend the party interest would also manifest itself in the desire to create the Constitution Club, an Infirmary and a porcelain factory in the city. Just as Maddox drove through the proposals to create the Infirmary at the apparently unpropitious time of the 1745 invasion, so the partners took a leap of faith in 1751 when it probably was not yet clear that it would be possible to take over Lund's factory. It was a leap of faith that was based not solely upon inflated and unrealistic notions of profit, but one which took into account civic, philanthropic and political interests.

To conclude, an analysis of the activities of the Worcester partners prior to the formation of the company shows the latter to be unique amongst the first porcelain factories. In the first instance, we find that many of them had associations which predated the factory. Wall, Doharty and Pritchett were at school together at King's School; there is good reason to believe from their illustrations that Wall and Doharty were fellow Masons; Wall and Davis had, as already been shown, long collaborated over analysing and promoting Malvern water in the previous decade; Wall and Brodribb were prominent members of the Whig Constitution Club formed in 1745 to counter the Jacobite menace; the two Holdships were Quakers; perhaps even more significantly from the evidence of the 1741 and 1747 city poll books and the Vernon Papers all of the nine partners who can be traced voted for the Whig interest - Wall, Davis, Richard and Josiah Holdship, Edward Jackson, Samuel Bradley, Richard Brodribb, John Berwick, John Thorneloe - and some even acted as political agents for Sir Thomas Vernon. No partner can be traced who voted for a Tory candidate in either of the two city elections. Significantly the only two with Tory connections, Edward Cave[61] and William Baylies[62] were not Worcester men and therefore not involved in the rough and tumble of city politics.

Secondly there is considerable evidence to suggest that the partners were united in their attempts during the 1740s to combat what appeared to them a number of threats to their city and their position within it. They were concerned to provide charitable support for schemes to contain the mounting social problems within the city such as the city workhouse and the Infirmary; they appear to have been influenced by the charismatic Bishop Maddox and his evangelical brand of Anglicanism; they were also prominent in their display of loyalty to the Hanoverian dynasty in the face of the Jacobite challenge in 1745; and in the controversial 1747 poll they were vigorous in their denunciation of the Tory gerrymandering preceding the election and in their celebration of the eventual victory of the Whig candidate Robert Tracy following the disqualification of his Tory rival. R W Binns even suggested that there was a political motive for the creation of the factory in that it was intended to bolster the Whig vote in the city.[63] This is difficult to substantiate one way or the other because of the lack of poll books in the third decade of the eighteenth century and because most of the new jobs created would have been, if Libby Powis' description of the factory is to be believed, performed by women and children who did not, of course, have the vote. Nevertheless, the so-called Tracy Mug celebrating the electoral victory of 1748 and the printed commemorative ware of the 1750s and 1760s suggest that there was a strong Whig ideology underpinning the partnership which supplemented their earlier personal connections and their common response to the crisis of the 1740s.[64] This, I believe, may well have strengthened the resolve to bring a porcelain factory to Worcester; philanthropic and political objectives could work, for the moment, if not for the long term, in harmony with the profit motive.

This should not, in fact, surprise us because as a great deal of recent research has shown, there are intriguing connections between the production and consumption of both tea and porcelain and the socio-economic revolution in eighteenth century society. Both products were seen as beneficial to the health of individuals and society at large. The drinking of tea underpinned the temperance movement and the campaign against gin drinking in which Maddox played such an important part, and medical men such as Wall would have shared this opinion. Certainly this could be suggested by his interest in Malvern water and his research into the effects of lead poisoning in cider drinking in

No 82 (reverse)

Herefordshire. The regulations at the Infirmary certainly did everything to restrict the consumption of alcohol leading to the dismissal of at least one nurse. The health of individuals was not just a matter of Christian charity, however. Contemporaries, imbued with mercantilist ideas, stressed the need for a bigger and healthier population in order to withstand the threat posed by France and to guarantee labour and markets for Britain's growing commerce. It has been argued that tea-drinking[65] was instrumental in triggering Britain's mid century population growth not only by replacing the consumption of alcohol and tainted water but also because the medical benefits of the tea leaf greatly reduced fatalities during child birth and infancy.

The drinking of tea also brought about a revolution in manners, changing society profoundly. Men of business could now gather and conduct their affairs in the more salubrious and sober atmosphere of the coffee house; ladies of leisure could demonstrate their wealth and status through the etiquette and equipage required by the afternoon tea party; even the sort of observers who initially objected to its conspicuous consumption among the lower classes came to see the social benefits of tea as the century progressed. The labourer was more likely to stay away from the tavern and, by sharing tea with his wife and children, fulfilled more satisfactorily his patriarchal role - which took on additional significance when society seemed beset by lawlessness and effeminacy. He was also more likely to work more effectively if he was sober and yet also refreshed by the stimulants contained in the leaf. In addition he was deemed to be safeguarded against a wide variety of ailments, especially those associated with waterborne diseases.

Similar benefits were associated with another magical product of the Orient, porcelain. At first, like tea, it was viewed with some ambiguity by the commercial and political classes. On the one hand, Lars Tharp's study of porcelain in Hogarth's art[66] has pointed out the emblematic role of porcelain early in the century when it is often used to deride vanity, excess and imported foreign taste. However mere possession of such objects could be taken as proof of aspiration, self-improvement and gentility as well as increasing prosperity, reflected in the prominence increasingly given to ceramics in eighteenth century portraits. Apart from the fact that it was the preferred choice of ware for the tea-drinking habit of the political and commercial classes, its use was interlinked with other values. It was seen as healthier and cleaner - like tea itself - because of its delicacy, colour and easiness to clean. This would lead to a wide range of ware such as spittoons, baby feeders and containers for pills and powders. Furthermore, the decoration of useful ware and the production of figures could be used to celebrate individuals, causes and events that served as an inspiration for patriotic behaviour. The Royal Family, the king of Prussia, successful generals, admirals and politicians and worthy charities such as the Marine Society were all thus commemorated. Thus, eventually - even within Hogarth's own work - it came to be used to symbolize domestic, social and political order and by the end of the century it was interwoven with an enduring sense of Britishness. This transformation would, moreover, be further assisted by the production of domestic British porcelain which could compete with the "exotic import" described by Hobson. Sarah Richards[67] has suggested that ceramics was one of the principal ways in which "entrepreneurial middle classes of Whig persuasion" like the Worcester partners could

"steer a path through the contradictory nature of the times which encouraged a relish for commercial enterprise and a desire for moral restraint".

It is difficult, therefore, to avoid the conclusion that the formation of the partnership of 1751 not only resembled an exercise in modern management team building but was also underpinned by a wider social and political agenda that would play a part in the initial success and survival of the factory. However, this management team had yet to focus its attention upon the questions of establishing a porcelain factory and developing a commercial strategy that would meet this agenda. Quite when and how this was achieved will be the subject of the following chapters.

NOTES

Chapter 2   A Tale of Two Cities: Bristol and Worcester in the Mid Eighteenth century

1. R. L. Hobson "Worcester Porcelain" (Bernard Quaritch 1910) p.1.

2. It is perhaps rather apposite that the family of A. J. Smith, the founder of the Collection, was involved in shipping Welsh coal across the Bristol Channel in the nineteenth century, principally to large consumers such as Bristol Corporation, the gas works, and Wills' tobacco factories. I am grateful to Mr. John Smith for sending me an article by R. M. Parsons "Mighty Miniatures of the Bristol Coal Trade".

3. Regrettably this proud boast would appear to be about to end with a small proportion of Royal Worcester now being made at the Seven Street works.

4. Graham Smith "Smuggling in the Bristol Channel" (Countryside Books 1994) p.72.

5. Smith (ibid) p68.

6. Peter Marcy "Eighteenth Century Views of Bristol and Bristolians" in "Bristol in the Eighteenth Century" ed Patrick McGrath (David and Charles 1972) p.20.

7. W. E. Minchinton "The Port of Bristol in the Eighteenth Century" in McGrath (ibid) p.129.

8. Sir Richard Lane, later MP and mayor of Worcester came from a family of Bristol sugar bakers before moving to Worcester where he began a salt carrying business on the Severn. See Romney Sedgwick "The House of Commons 1715-54" (Oxford University Press 1970) vol 2 p.197.

9. In 1685 the Collector at Bristol, John Dutton Cole, uncovered collusion between 22 merchants and customs officials, resulting in fines in excess of £2,700 and the pillorying of the officials. He also brought to justice two Bristol merchants who regularly supplied re-exported tobacco to France but who were also transferring large quantities -13,000 lbs on this occasion - to Chepstow having illegally claimed the duty refund. Yet even this supposed paragon of virtue was the subject of an enquiry after his retirement in 1700 which revealed that Cole himself owed the Crown £3,000 in unremitted duties! Smith (ibid) pp.71-72.

10. Jane Pettigrew " A Social History of Tea" (The National Trust 2001) p.52.

11. Although, of course, it was equally true that their outside business failings eventually sabotaged their efforts to sustain porcelain manufacture in Bristol.

12. David Hussey "Coastal and River Trade in Pre-Industrial England: Bristol and its region 1680-1730" (Regatta Press 2000) p.86.

13. Hussey (ibid) p.60.

14. According to Paul Langford the navigable mileage of inland waterways rose from almost 700 to 1,100 from 1660-1725 "A Polite and Commercial People England 1727-1783" (Clarendon Press 1999) p.416.

15. Quoted in W Barrett "The History and Antiquities of the city of Bristol" (Bristol 1789, reprint Gloucester 1984) p.168.

16. Paul Langford "A Polite and Commercial People" Clarendon Press 1998 p.393.

17. (ibid) pp 393-94.

18. David Whitehead "The Book of Worcester" Barracuda Books 1986 p.28.

19. Hussey (ibid) pp.196-97.

20. W E Minchinton "Bristol-Metropolis of the West in the Eighteenth Century" The Alexander Prize Essay Transactions of the Royal Historical Society 5th ser. 4 1954 p.88.

21. John Aikin "England Delineated " (1788) quoted by Marcy (ibid) p.15.

22. F. M. Eden "The State of the Poor" quoted by Minchinton "Metropolis" p.77.

23. Hussey (ibid) p.82.

24. Heyleyn's creditor in his bankruptcy proceedings in July 1737 was John Berrow esquire who was himself bankrupted in May 1760 where his occupation is described as "glassman and merchant" Minchinton "The trade of Bristol" pp.185-88.

25. W. J. Pountney "Old Bristol Potteries" EP Publishing reprint 1972 chs 10-14.

26. Whereas in 1696 84% of salt unloaded at Bridgwater came from the Cheshire or Merseyside, by 1698 Worcestershire was supplying 60% and salt shipped from Liverpool had fallen to about a third. Hussey (ibid) pp.156-63.

27   F. Buckley "The Glass Houses of Dudley and Worcester" (Transactions of the Society of Glass Technology 1927)reference quoted by W H McMenemey "History of Royal Worcester Infirmary" (Press Alliances Ltd 1947) p.86.

28   Tim Bridges "The Georgian Churches Of Worcester" (Transactions of Worcester Archaeological Society vol 13 1992 pp 211-222).

29   John Brewer "The Pleasures of the Imagination: English Culture in the Eighteenth Century" (Harper Collins 1997)

30   Katharine Barker "The Theatre Royal Bristol" in McGrath (ed) ibid pp.65-66.

31   David Whitehead "Urban Renewal and Suburban Growth: The Shaping of Georgian Worcester" p.6.

32   David Hussey (ibid) p.199.

33   Basil Cottle "Thomas Chatterton" in McGrath (ed) ibid p.91.

34   H-C & L Mui "Shopkeepers and Shopkeeping in Eighteenth Century England" (1989).

35   It is interesting to note that Watts himself was only able to afford pewter vessels and could not sign his name, perhaps suggesting that he was either a simple decorator or a small scale dealer. I am grateful to local historian David Everett for this reference.

36   Marcy (ibid) pp.20-38.

37   Nicholas Rogers "Whigs and Cities" p.269 In Bristol, with its additional Presbyterian, Wesleyan and Moravian connections, nonconformists made up 20% of the city's population, which was twice the national average. The Quaker community was the largest in England with an assembly of 1,700 and Lewin's Presbyterians numbered 1,400 in 1715. They also held a disproportionate share of the city's commercial wealth, the Quaker fortune estimated at over £500,000 and that of the Presbyterians valued at £400,000. In addition with 700 nonconformist votes in borough elections they were politically influential. An observer commented in the Bristol Gazette (31 October 1771) that "dissenters are numerous at Bristol; in one parish are 9 places of worship for different persuasions; in elections their votes chiefly preponderate, and those who canvass are not a little assiduous to gain their favour".

38   See chapter 6.

39   Quoted in Roy Porter "England in the Eighteenth Century (Folio Society 1998) p.199.

40   W. E. Minchinton "Metropolis" (ibid) p.85.

41   W E Minchinton "The Trade of Bristol" (ibid) footnote 89 p.188.

42   Gwen Talbut "Worcester as an Industrial and Commercial Centre 1660-1750" Transactions of the Worcestershire Archaeological Society vol 10 1986 pp.91-102.

43   In the 1720s 75% of all imported silk came from the Levant which in turn imported Worcester broadcloth. However Levant silk found itself undercut from two new sources in the 1730s, France and Bengal. By the 1760s Levant silk composed only 25% of the silk imports into Britain leading to a further blow to reciprocal Worcester broadcloth exports. Talbut (ibid).

44   The Ryeland sheep was the victim of brutal economics. Although its fleece fetched 30d for each 1lb of wool as against a mere 6d per lb for the larger breeds of sheep, a Romney fleece weighed 10lb whilst a Ryeland fleece was less than 2lb. Talbut (ibid).

45   The percentage of newly admitted city freemen connected to the wool trade fell from over 50% in the period 1669-1709 to a mere 3% by 1721-48. Talbut (ibid).

46   Even in 1800 factories were something of a rarity and it was not really until Josiah Wedgwood that a prominent entrepreneur in the ceramics industry got to grips with thorny issues such as the division of labour, economies of scale, advertising and lowering production costs. See Julian Hoppit "Risk and Failure in English Business 1700-1800 (Cambridge University Press 1987).

47   A considerable amount of recent scholarship on the eighteenth century has drawn attention to the interlinking of diverse elements in the pursuit of schemes for national renewal. Calls for philanthropic measures to aid and improve the poor, campaigns to promote naval and colonial expansion, protests against the importation of continental goods, cuisine and art, the formation of clubs to engage citizens in the political process were all part of the mobilization of men from the professions and trade to create a virile, Protestant patriotism that was in striking contrast to the alleged effete cosmopolitanism of the English aristocracy. The life and work of Hogarth may be regarded as one notable expression of this backlash to Walpole's regime. See especially Linda Colley "Britons: Forging the Nation 1707-1837" Yale University Press 1992 , Kathleen Wilson "The Sense of the People: Politics, Culture and Imperialism in England 1715-1785" (Cambridge University Press 1995) and Ben Rogers "Beef and Liberty: Roast Beef, John Bull and the English Nation" (Vintage 2003).

48   Nicholas Rogers " Confronting the Crime Wave; The Debate over Social Reform and Regulation 1749-53" in Davison, Hitchcock, Keirn and Shoemaker "Stilling the Grumbling Hive: The Response to social and economic Problems in England 1689-1750" Alan Sutton 1992 p.78.

49   Tony Hayter "The Army and the Crowd in Mid-Georgian England" Rowman and Littlefield 1978.

50   Porter ibid p.97.

51   W. H. McMenemey "History of Royal Worcester Infirmary" Press Alliances Ltd 1947 p.80.

52   Patrick Dillon "The Much-Lamented Death of Madam Geneva: the Eighteenth Century Gin Craze" Review 2002 ;Lee Davison "Experiments in the Social Regulation of Industry: Gin Legislation 1729-51" in Davison, Hitchcock, Keirn and Shoemaker (ibid).

53   This was highlighted by the formation of the Marine Society, the Anti-Gallican Society and the Society for the Encouragement of Arts. Manufactures and Commerce in the middle of the century. Wilson (ibid) p.191.

54   W. H. McMenemey (ibid) p.53.

55   It is also a unique survival in early ceramic history's documentation; it would be interesting to know whether any comparable deeds were ever drawn up by the other factories during this period. My presentiment, given the lack of other surviving deeds, and the more informal association of sleeping partners would be that this is unlikely.

56   Wall, in fact, had been "adopted" by Walpole's leading opponent Samuel Sandys after his own father's breakdown and had married his niece Katharine. His father-in-law, Martin Sandys, was a prominent Whig activist in the city.

57   Bristol MP Thomas Coster was one notable critic Sedgwick (ibid) vol2 p.479.

58   They also stimulated a range of commemorative pottery including a new and sophisticated form of design in a limited range of plates painted by Joseph Flower at Bristol which would foreshadow the propaganda use to which Worcester porcelain was later put in support of post Walpole Whig governments in the 1750s. Wilson (ibid) p.147

59   See the Corporation's protests to Winnington and Sandys in 1742 recorded in the *Gentleman's Magazine* 1742 quoted by Sedgwick (ibid) vol 1 p.357.

60   See Maddox's letter to Philip Doddridge letter dated Feb 25 1748 quoted by WH McMenemey (ibid) p.50 and Worcester Journal June 26-Jul 23 1747.

61   Colley "In Defiance of Oligarchy" describes him as a Tory entrepreneur.

62   Stood unsuccessfully as Tory candidate for Evesham before emigrating.

63   The election dispute of 1774 in which there was an attempt to prevent the porcelain factory workers exercising their right to vote - again commemorated by an important mug in the Museum of Worcester Porcelain - would lend weight to this supposition.

64   I have shown how the imagery of the Tracy Mug was drawn from a triumphal arch erected by the Constitution Club - in the face of an explicit prohibition by the Corporation - to greet their returning victorious candidate in the first two editions of "The Melting Pot", the Journal published by the Friends of the Worcester Porcelain Museum. A similar temporary structure was put up in 1749 to celebrate the Peace of Aix-la-Chapelle, replete with Hanoverian and Masonic symbols.

65   A. and I. Macfarlane "Green Gold: The Empire of Tea" Chapter 9 (Ebury Press 2004).

66   L. Tharp "Hogarth's China: Hogarth's Paintings and 18th Century Ceramics"(Merrell Holberton" 1997).

67   S. Richards "Eighteenth Century Ceramics: Products for a civilised society" (Manchester University Press 1999).

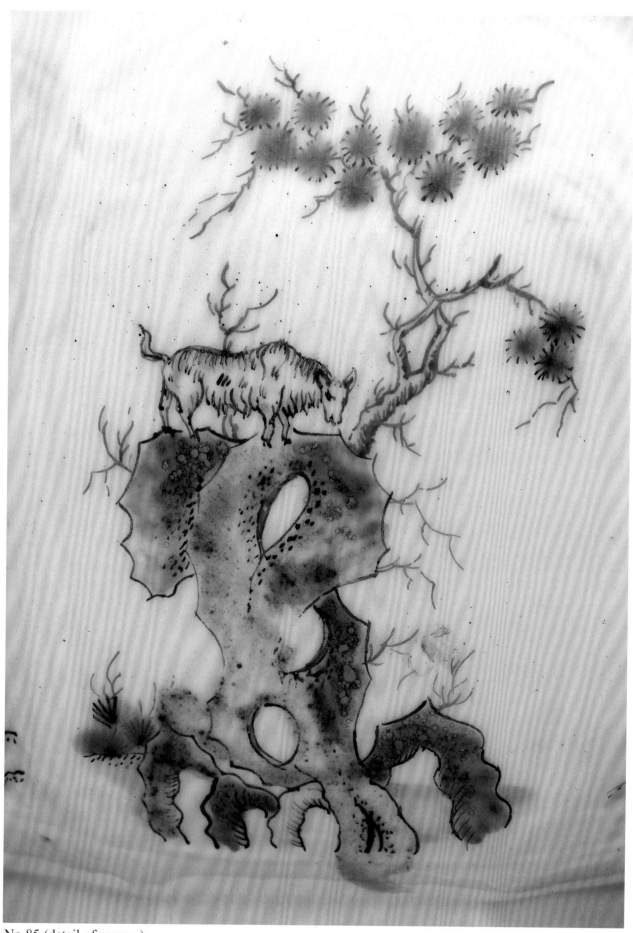

No 85 (detail of reverse)

THE FOUNDATION OF THE BRISTOL AND WORCESTER PORCELAIN FACTORIES: AN HISTORIOGRAPHICAL SURVEY

At first glance one could be forgiven for thinking that there is little need to review once again the sequence of events leading to the establishment of the two porcelain factories at Bristol and Worcester. They have been well rehearsed in numerous texts already and given that much of the evidence available is contentious, it may appear that there is nothing more to be said on the issue. It could be argued that it is difficult to see, unless dramatic new sources become available, how further analysis will, with any degree of certainty, advance our knowledge of the relationship between the two factories. However, it is an issue which a book of this nature could not ignore for numerous reasons.

Firstly, this narrative is directly related to the identification of many of the items illustrated in the plates; observation of the styles and shapes as shown in chapter 4 can have a bearing on the unravelling of the narrative and, in particular, chemical analysis of the porcelain body may in the near future be able to turn speculation into certainty. Secondly, a new or general reader may appreciate a summary of earlier monographs and articles which are not always easy to find and the key pieces of evidence upon which they are based; the method of presentation chosen here will at least alert them to the dangers of forming the opinion that any single account so far written has been able to give a full and unimpeachable record of what transpired in what proved to be a critical twenty four months in the history of eighteenth century porcelain production. Thirdly and most importantly, it does celebrate over a century of valuable research by historians of English ceramics and also points out the dangers of complacency; this is a story which we may never be able to complete beyond any reasonable doubt but which demands constant revision. There may have been until recently some reason to feel that the pioneering work done by some of the earliest contributors to the *Transactions of the English Porcelain Circle* - later the English Ceramic Circle - would represent the bulk of what we are likely to discover. However, one can never rule out the possibility of new discoveries coming to light. It is, therefore, especially exciting to put into print for the first time Ray Jones' research which has identified the likely location of Lund and Miller's Bristol factory. One can only hope that it will lead to an archaeological breakthrough that will emulate that of Bernard Watney and the Museum of London's dig at Limehouse.

This chapter will also, conversely, reveal how fresh evidence can muddy the waters and undermine an established opinion. What can advance our understanding of one aspect of Bristol and early Worcester porcelain can demolish the assumptions made about another. If there is anything to learn from this story it is that one should not commit oneself prematurely to any one interpretation but nor should one refrain altogether from speculation. One often needs to be aware of the possibilities before the actual facts to support them come to light in order to appreciate the true significance of the latter. Some of the earliest writers about the subject can, at times, appear to make unwarranted assertions because of the lack of information that was available to them. Yet even in questioning these assertions, it has been possible for later generations of researchers to move us nearer the truth.

It is, I think, particularly instructive to review the evidence that was available to the first great pioneer of the history of Worcester Porcelain, R W Binns, who as John Sandon says,[1] is one of the giants upon whose shoulders all subsequent analyses must rest. When he wrote his "*A Century of Potting in the City of Worcester*" in 1865 he was doing so before many crucial primary sources, both documentary and archaeological, were available; he knew nothing of the Limehouse or Bristol factories; he was under the impression that a "New Canton" inkwell dated 1750 was an early

Worcester piece; the only name of the Worcester partners he knew for sure was that of Dr Wall;[2] he believed that the Worcester factory had commenced with the taking out of the Warmstry House lease on May 16th 1751; he considered that the crescent mark superceded that of the script W and workman's marks; the first documentary evidence he had of the use of soaprock - although he was confident "it was largely used before this date," - was as late as January 1st 1770 when Wall, Davis and Blayney entered into an agreement with George Hunt Esq of Llanhydrock, Parish of Mullion.

However since then, a considerable amount of fresh evidence has come to light. In 1883 Binns himself published the original partnership deeds of June 1751 revealing the names of the fifteen partners, Wall and Davis' experiments in making porcelain, the names of the two workmen Podmore and Lyes who helped them and the financial and operational arrangements of the factory. A few years later in 1888 the Camden Society published the travel correspondence of Richard Pococke which related the connections between a porcelain factory at Bristol - which used Cornish soaprock- and an earlier factory at Limehouse and a contemporary works in Staffordshire. Before Hobson wrote the second great monograph *"Worcester Porcelain"* H Eccles FCS[3] had analysed the soaprock content in early Worcester pieces which were now seen to be distinct from Bow and Chelsea.[4] In addition to this information Hobson was able to bring forward the date of the use of soaprock at Worcester by reference to the departure of Richard Holdship from Worcester in 1760 and his subsequent offer of the soaprock formula to William Duesbury of Derby in 1764. Newspaper advertisements of July 1751 also alerted Hobson to the enlargement of the Bristol works, prompting him to speculate that Dr Wall had gained his secret of the soaprock formula from "Lowris China House" mentioned in Pococke's letter. In addition one should also note the significance of the publication of W J Pountney's research of Bristol potteries[5] which contained valuable, if occasionally misleading, research on the Redcliffe Backs and the life of Benjamin Lund. By 1923 when Hobson wrote his introduction to the *Frank Lloyd Collection of Early Worcester Porcelain* Pountney's discovery of an advertisement in the *Bristol Intelligencer* in July 24th 1752 of the merger between the Bristol and Worcester factories convinced him that his "conjecture is now turned to certainty".

There was then, as F Severne Mackenna in his *"Worcester Porcelain: The Wall Period and its Antecedents"* in 1950, noted, a forty year gap before the next monograph was published. However this did not mean to say research had not continued to add to our knowledge. In 1938 C W Dyson Perrins was able to produce a synopsis of the results in his lecture *"John Wall and the Worcester Porcelain Company"*.[6] Most of it came in the form of invaluable discoveries by members of the English Ceramic Circle, in particular the valuable evidence of newspaper advertisements relating to the mysterious Limehouse factory mentioned by Pococke and their connections with Bristol and Worcester.[7] Special mention should also be made of E Morton Nance's article on soaprock licences in 1935 which revealed the earliest use of steatitic porcelain dating back to Benjamin Lund's first licence of 1748/49.

Between the publication of Mackenna's work and that of Franklin Barrett in 1966 came the discovery of Aubrey Toppin in 1950 of the bankruptcy papers of Richard Holdship 1760/61 which at long last revealed the names of the two Bristol proprietors as Lund and Miller and the circumstances relating to the merger. Within three years came the first edition of Henry Sandon's *"The Illustrated Guide to Worcester Porcelain"* which although it had no fresh documentary evidence to add to the narrative could refer to the first archaeological excavations on the Warmstry House site. This was updated by John Sandon in a second edition and also in his *"Dictionary of Worcester Porcelain 1751-1851"* and his chapter in *"Worcester Porcelain 1751-90: The Zorensky Collection"*. Although the first dig had not been able to get access to the lowest levels of production, the subsequent discovery of poorly fired shards in 1979 did seem to indicate the very real, if yet unproven, possibility that Wall and Davis had developed a non-steatitic porcelain paste prior to the merger with Bristol and the acquisition of the Lund soaprock licence. Chapter 5 describes the discovery of a naively decorated plate in a private American collection which might just be a surviving example of this early body. Finally, the triumph of the discovery of the Limehouse factory, the apparent progenitor of Lund's Bristol, by Bernard Watney and a team from the Museum of London might appear to have filled in all the gaps in the incomplete jigsaw which Binns left us in 1865.

We can now tell then, with some confidence, the following story. Briefly, the Bristol factory was established by Benjamin Lund and William Miller, its location always held to be in the Redcliffe Backs area, but now open to question. There may also have been another partner involved, who according to the correspondence of Richard Pococke was formerly a principal of the factory at Limehouse that failed. Given that this latter establishment which we now know was in production between 1745 and 1748[8] and many of its shapes and decoration are related to Bristol and Worcester ware, it is quite reasonable to suppose that Limehouse was a common ancestor of both;[9] one a weakly progeny that died in infancy and the other an offshoot that survives today as the grand dame of English porcelain. There is evidence of production beginning in Bristol in 1749/50 and making use of Cornish soapstone in its porcelain body, a material which was heat resistant and therefore highly suitable for tea ware which often cracked on contact with hot water. At this point, as Pococke's visit reveals, the factory was obviously open to inspection by the public. By 1751 another enterprise was started by Dr Wall and William Davis who, by one means or another, had convinced a group of local businessmen to back their project and participate in the running of another provincial porcelain factory at Worcester. However, after an initially successful period of production, the Bristol works appears to have run into difficulties at about the same time that the Worcester factory was about to embark upon production. Dr Wall's company, or rather one member of his partnership, Richard Holdship a Quaker merchant, put up the money that was used to buy up the Bristol factory. More crucially still, Holdship bought up Lund's right to extract soaprock from the Cornish mines at Gew Graze which allowed Worcester to produce the soapstone porcelain which gave the factory a competitive edge in the production of tea wares. This union was - according to the Holdship bankruptcy proceedings - first promoted as a merger of a factory which favoured the production of Oriental style blue and white ware with a company which was set up to produce European style wares decorated in polychrome. Consequently, the Bristol factory stock and workmen were brought up the Severn and (possibly under the temporary guidance of Benjamin Lund) were absorbed by the complex established at Warmstry House by Wall's partnership at Worcester. However, the process seems to have been much more of a buy-out with the demise of the Bristol factory being covered up as hastily as the embossed "Bristoll" markings on Lund's remaining stock which was subsequently decorated at Worcester.

Yet, this account still contains a number of gaps and the accommodation of fresh evidence has added as many new problems as it has helped to answer old ones. The remainder of this chapter will examine a series of key questions which need to be resolved before we can be confident that we know the full story from the closure of the Limehouse factory to the full emergence of Dr Wall's factory by 1757, the period covered by the A. J. Smith collection.

WHO ESTABLISHED THE BRISTOL PARTNERSHIP?

The names of the Bristol proprietors were discovered by Aubrey Toppin in a file of papers relating to the 1760/1 bankruptcy of Richard Holdship[10] - one of the key partners at Worcester. These were named as William Miller who is known as a grocer[11] and banker in Bristol and Benjamin Lund a Quaker brass and copper merchant. Miller was a originally a grocer of St John's parish in Bristol who later used funds to finance mercantile and banking activities in Bristol's commercial hinterland and transatlantic trade. He had a counting house adjacent to his house in Taylor's Court where he lived for over twenty years. Unlike his partner, Miller was obviously more astute with money and bequeathed, on his death at the age of 82 in 1781, to his nephew the sum of £5000 and household goods including china ware. Miller's role in the Bristol factory is difficult to ascertain because he is not named in any of the advertisements or other documentation. However, it is most likely that he was a mere sleeping partner rather like Alderman George Arnold at Bow, and, as indicated in the previous chapter, probably found more lucrative outlets for his capital, the withdrawal of which precipitated the crisis at Bristol. Without doubt Lund was the active partner at Bristol; an advertisement in the Bristol Intelligencer which appeared between November 1750 and July 1751 invited would be apprentices to apply to him rather than Miller. Lund's career is better documented thanks to the work of Pountney and Toppin. He was born in Hammersmith on April 30th 1692 and the second son of four children of Benjamin Lund, a carpenter and his wife Mary Adams. His father died before 1706 when his mother remarried and in 1719 Lund married in Bristol Christobel Ingram, daughter of Robert Ingram, "late of London". It would be reasonable to suppose that Lund met his bride in London and had by the time of his marriage only recently moved to Bristol.

His personal life seems to have been a tragic tale with his wife and five children all predeceasing him and his wife dying just about the time that the Bristol factory was being set up. In 1728 he took out a patent to manufacture copper and extract silver from copper along with Francis Hawksbee of London which again locates him in Bristol where he had a home in the Parish of St Philip and Jacob between 1720 and 1752. Toppin also points out that because of the baptism and burial of two of his children in St Gregory's, London he was probably in the capital in between 1732 and 1737[12] and again in the 1740s judging by the apprenticeship of his son John to a butcher in London in 1741. The death of his wife Christobel in December 1749 in Bristol would appear to suggest he had moved back to his adopted city and, although he moved to Worcester in 1752/3, he was back in Bristol for a final time soon after until his death there in 1768. He appears to have been in constant financial difficulty as he was adjudged to have been a bankrupt on December 8th 1740, on August 1st 1745 and was either still, or again, in that condition in 1753.[13] The second of the named bankruptcies also implicated Edward Heyleyn of Bow in Lund's financial misfortune and this has given rise to a belief that the two men may have had business connections but nothing further has emerged to corroborate this. However, during his later spell in London, he may well have had the opportunity to investigate the mysteries of porcelain production. It would be extremely helpful to be able to resolve the lack of certainty concerning the use of soapstone at Limehouse. Although there is no unambiguous documentary or physical evidence of soapstone being used at Limehouse, it would be interesting to know how Lund, with all his financial difficulties, would have had such confidence in its qualities to apply for a licence to quarry it unless he had the opportunity to experiment with it prior to the establishment of his works in Bristol.

The most important things to bear in mind about Lund were that he seems to have been more of an unsuccessful backer of speculative projects rather than a practical manufacturer and that most of his business life was spent on the run from his creditors. Lund's documented financial difficulties stemmed from his involvement with William Crispe in trying to finance the building of a lighthouse on the island of Flat Holm in the Bristol Channel. Crispe's failure to settle his debt to Lund of £636 16s 8d occurred shortly before he took out the lease from the Hiscock family to begin brass and copper manufacture on St Philip's Plain in 1738 and triggered the bankruptcy of 1740. There is here a degree of similarity with the later career of Richard Holdship at Worcester but also a significant difference. Unlike Holdship - who appears to have embraced publicity - Lund does not really ever emerge from the shadows in Worcester when, as the man with supposedly the most hands-on experience, we might expect him to have played a more prominent part in establishing the new works. We believe that when one puts the personal problems of Benjamin Lund and his desire for anonymity at the heart of the investigation we begin to understand both the answer to many of the questions surrounding the Bristol factory and why those questions exist in the first place.

WHEN WAS THE BRISTOL FACTORY ESTABLISHED?

That great pioneer of ceramic history scholarship, Mr Dyson Perrins, was of the opinion that "The Bristol factory evidently commenced about 1745"[14] which would have given it a provenance coinciding with the earliest London factories at Bow, Chelsea and Limehouse. This, in turn, was based upon Pountney's dating of the sale of the lease of a property belonging to William Lowdin, long supposed to be a glass house, to the brewer John Tandy who kept part of the site for his own use but surrendered the part including a kiln to a mason James Davies. This information came, according to Pountney, from "an old Bristol newspaper appearing in 1745", which was later confirmed by Toppin as "The Bristol Oracle" of June 23rd 1745. However, our greater knowledge about the Limehouse factory and the discovery of leases and licences associated with the Bristol enterprise would challenge such an early starting date. It does not seem to corroborate Pococke's comment in 1750 that the works in Bristol were "lately established here by one of the principal manufacturers at Limehouse which failed". The word "lately" suggests a date closer to 1750 whilst the reference to the failure of Limehouse would appear to confirm a post 1748 date.

Further support for a later date comes from the discovery of the licence to quarry for twenty one years the soap rock at Gew Graze, near the Lizard[15] granted to Lund on March 7th 1748. Although Pococke's correspondence does suggest that two types of ware were being produced simultaneously, and one of these was seemingly non-steatitic earthenware, it would be difficult to conceive of Bristol being able to go into production without the crucial raw material which his letter so clearly identified with the Bristol factory. His letter of October 13th 1750 certainly confirms that production was under way when he told his mother that he had been "to see the Soapy Rock which is mostly valued for the manufacture of porcelane, and they get five pounds a ton for it, for the manufacture of porcelane now carrying on at Bristol". With the first recorded advertisement for apprentices in November 1750 and the first known sales advertisement in July 1751 it would appear much more realistic to assert that the production must have begun at the earliest in the second half of 1748 or at the latest by the first half of 1750. Moreover Pountney's identification of the sale of Lowdin's premises as the origins of Lund and Miller's factory is open to debate and perhaps based upon a misreading of Pococke's original manuscript. This will be discussed in greater depth in the following section.

WHERE WAS THE BRISTOL WORKS ESTABLISHED?

There was some initial confusion relating to the owner of the Bristol factory which was caused by some errors of transcription in Pococke's original letters which, in the Camden Society's publication, spoke of Lowris' China House. Pountney[16] however showed that the original document referred to Low—ns and that the word Glass House has been altered by a second hand to refer instead to China House. His research produced only one glassmaker whose name appeared to fit the bill, that of William Lowdin and this identification was confirmed by his discovery of the 1745 lease described above. From this Pountney claimed to have discovered the lost site

"It was immediately below the Shot Tower on Redcliff Hill, on a site that afterwards became Alfred's Wharf, and is now part of the Midland Railway Company's Wharf. It was a glass house as a rule, but on occasions a pottery, for many generations before 1750".[17]

He goes on to say that the caves under Adder Cliff on which Redcliffe Parade now stands were used for quarrying the sandstone used by the glass works and that

"all traces of the works and of the ground upon which they stood have long since disappeared".[18]

However, subsequent research by J C Whitting[19] - much of it later endorsed by the Jacksons and Price[20] - went some way to discrediting the association of this lease with the site of the Lund and Miller factory, thus demonstrating that sometimes new evidence can mislead as much as help. Of the four glasshouses in Redcliffe parish marked on Millerd's map of 1710, the three premises with cones can all be eliminated from the investigation because two were owned and occupied by Richard Warren and Co (and one was demolished in 1718) and the other by Benjamin Perrot beyond the time of Lund and Miller. Lowdin's lease of 108 Redcliffe Street from the Dean and Chapter of Bristol in 1733 does not seem to tally with the site of the remaining glasshouse shown on Millerd's map without a cone which Pountney believed to be the site of the soapstone porcelain factory. However, the Redcliffe Pit glassworks shown on Millerd's map is also known from a notice in the *Bristol Weekly Intelligencer* of August 1750 to have been occupied by the white enamelled glass-makers Cross and Berrow at the time that Lund and Miller were supposedly producing porcelain.[21] The kiln used for making one, was entirely unsuitable for producing the other. The reference to the lease of the Lowdin property being known by "the sign of the Glass House" must, Stilling inferred, refer to the fact that it was a showroom or a shop rather than a factory.

Secondly, and even more importantly, he cast doubt on the identification of any glasshouse belonging to the Lowdin family at this period. Without Pountney's extrapolation of the Pococke manuscript there is no documentary evidence of Lowdin owning a glasshouse after 1699; there is no record of him taking in apprentices after this date and indeed by 1750, he is recorded as being too impoverished to pay his Poor Rate, which one would not expect if he had until recently been the owner of an active glasshouse. Surely, if this was the case, it is difficult to believe that the premises would have still been known by this name in 1750. However, Whitting then failed himself to escape the lure of Redcliffe parish and continued to seek the factory amongst other pottery sites in the area, believing it instead to have been located on the works owned by Thomas Franks, whom Pountney - working before Toppin's discovery of the names of the two proprietors - believed was one of the original partners of the Bristol soft-paste porcelain factory.

Author and researcher Ray Jones[22] has, however, opened a new and much more convincing alternative explanation. If, as has been argued above, the name of Lowdin should be discounted from the equation, we should look more carefully at the name of Benjamin Lund, whose role in the factory had already been identified by Pountney through an advertisement of 1750 requesting apprentices to report to him in St Philip's Plain. Pountney, however, discounted his significance regarding him as the agent for the proprietors or, at best, a minor subscriber whose occupation as a brass and stay maker and whose residence outside Redcliffe would have precluded his active involvement in the factory.[23] Yet even after Toppin had been able to establish that Lund was indeed a key figure at Bristol, it was only at the end of his seminal article that he offered the throwaway comment "we should, I think, definitely call the factory 'LUND'S CHINA HOUSE'.[24] Now, by this, we understand him to refer to the practice at the time of calling early Bristol ware "Lowdin's China" rather than suggesting that we should read the transcription of Pococke's letter differently but Jones suggests that this may well be exactly what we should do. If, as has been argued, we may no longer rely upon the name Lowdin, what is the alternative interpretation of Pococke, especially since the name written as *Lowdns* or *Loudns* could, given the vagaries of eighteenth century spelling and an unfamiliar name, represent Lunds? It is also worth bearing in mind that it is less easy to understand why Pococke would have had any reason to conceal the name of the partner if he knew it, given that his private correspondence to his mother was not intended for publication to a wider audience.

Even if this is not the case, Watney's discovery of the Lund bankruptcy papers of 1753 revealed other more important information the full significance of which was not noted at the time. Jones points out that Lund had not revealed the full extent of his assets in earlier proceedings in 1741 and that he had two properties in St Philip's Plain; one was his residence and the other premises adjoining

Hooper's glasshouse which he had held since 1738 had a "workhouse for the making of brass" and which he still held *without interruption* until 1752-53. He presumably then was obliged to sell up to settle his debts before moving to Worcester. If we accept that Lund was already in possession of commercial premises when he returned to Bristol after his sojourn in London in the 1730s, where he may have picked up some inside knowledge of porcelain manufacture, it would make sense, especially given his lack of funds, to start his soft-paste porcelain factory on this site.

Further circumstantial evidence is provided by the strong likelihood that these premises in Avon Street were also occupied by the potter Paul Townsend, who is described as a gallypot maker in the parish of St Philip and St Jacob in 1739, shortly after Lund had taken out the lease on his brass works. At all events Townsend was certainly taking in his two sons as apprentices in 1748 and 1753 but was declared bankrupt in 1755, suggesting that his pottery coincided almost exactly with Lund's tenure of the lease. If Lund had indeed sublet part of these premises to Townsend then it would also help clarify Pococke's observation about two types of ware being produced at the factory. It may also help us understand why Lund's creditors did not find it easy in 1740 to identify his ownership of the lease when the most obvious form of activity on the site was that of potters at work rather than brass-making. Most importantly of all, this relocation of the site to Avon Street also helps explain the Bristol Weekly Intelligencer advertisements of November and December 1750 asking apprentice painters to report to him at St Philip's Plain where we are also told that it was possible to purchase a "six or four leaved Screen". The latter may well have been made of brass and suggests that Lund could have been continuing his old occupation alongside the new. It is also worth studying the way in which the advertisement appears to attempt to disguise Lund's association with the factory by only referring to his name in the advertisement about the screens which at first glance appears to be separate from that for the apprentice painters. This not only fits in with what we know about a man who was forever pursuing numerous speculative schemes and constantly trying to evade his creditors but also begins to explain the otherwise inexplicable mysteries which appear to enshroud the Limehouse-Bristol-Worcester connection.

WHO WAS THE "PRINCIPAL AT LIMEHOUSE?"

Our knowledge of the Limehouse factory has expanded rapidly in recent years thanks to new invaluable archaeological information and fresh documentary evidence. We can now be reasonably certain about the original site of the factory[25] and the identity of one of the chief operatives, Joseph Wilson. These developments in our knowledge have added immensely to the work of earlier ceramic historians who pursued the origins of the mysterious factory which, like Bristol and Worcester, enjoyed an advantageous riverside setting. However despite the almost unbelievable advances, of which Toppin et al would scarcely conceive in the 1930s and 1940s, it has not been possible to pin down the identity of the man who, according to Pococke, was not only a Limehouse partner but also established the Bristol factory. The only names we can draw from documentary evidence do not show any cross-over between the two factories. Lund and Miller are the only two names we have for Bristol whilst Joseph Wilson "& Co" is all we have for Limehouse. We only have therefore the following three options to consider.

Firstly, Pococke was in error and there was no Limehouse partner who was also involved in Bristol. Given that Pococke appears to be speaking about a direct conversation he himself had, rather than reporting hearsay evidence, it seems unlikely that he could be mistaken, especially when in all other respects his attention to detail would give one confidence in his testimony. He takes such great trouble in describing the different appearance, raw materials and prices of the Bristol products it is difficult to think he could be careless.[26] The fact that there is no further supporting documentary proof surely says more about the nature of the written evidence than it does about our best individual witness to events in Bristol in 1750.

It is just possible that his reference to one of the principals of the manufacturers might just refer to an actual workman or foreman like the artisan he later met in Staffordshire who "disagreed with his employers" but this does seem to stretch the likely ambiguity of language a shade too far. Frank Hurlbutt[27] made the suggestion in 1928 that Pococke may have confused Limehouse with Bow and that the partner concerned was Edward Heyleyn. Heyleyn had jointly applied with Thomas Frye for a patent to produce porcelain using unaker in 1744 but when Frye's second patent was taken out in 1748, Heyleyn is no longer mentioned. This would, of course, help explain why at just the time the Bristol factory was setting up, Heyleyn may have returned to his native Bristol armed with the expertise to assist Lund. There are also personal connections between the two men. Both Lund and Heyleyn were Quakers from Bristol and Heyleyn acted on behalf of Lund's creditors in the latter's bankruptcy in the hearing in 1741. Both men were described as brass and copper merchants. Hurlbutt was even able to explain the reference to the manufacture that "failed" by suggesting that the Bow factory run by Thomas Frye closed temporarily in 1749. The argument could also be promoted by another means thanks to the research at Limehouse which might suggest a different sort of connection with Bow, which does not depend upon supposing Pococke's confusion of the two factories. Ian Freestone's technical analysis of Limehouse ware has shown very significant similarities between the glass to clay ratio of Limehouse and the Bow patent of 1744.[28] Given this particular interpretation of the chronology it might be hypothesised that Heyleyn and Frye had a falling out and that Heyleyn then took the Bow recipe to Limehouse where, in order to conceal his espionage, he remained an *eminence gris* until the winding up of the latter factory. He then may have returned to Bristol to work with Lund.

However this version of events does not really seem to fit with what we now know of Bow and Limehouse. As Adams and Redstone show, there is no documented reason to believe that the absence of Heyleyn's name from the second patent indicated his departure from Bow and every reason to believe he was "a partner in the Bow concern from c 1744 right through to his bankruptcy in December 1757."[29] Moreover Hurlbutt's hypothesis was made before the existence of a separate factory at Limehouse was confirmed and when it was possible to believe that Limehouse was simply the term used to describe the wharf side facilities at Bow. Nor can we accept with confidence Hurlbutt's explanation about a "failure" of Bow rather than Limehouse. By the time that Pococke was writing, the Bow works had surely recommenced production as the dated New Canton inkwells now testify. We also need to point out that Freestone is careful to point out that there appear to be differences between the 1744 patent which specified a glass made from its own raw materials and the Limehouse body which seems to have included cullet. He also shows that the Bow glaze corresponds with that on early Limehouse earthen ware rather than on its porcelain.[30] In any case, the different commercial strategies of the two firms (see Chapter 4) do not support the notion of any Bow-Limehouse continuum. There is, in short, no documented reason to suppose that Heyleyn, either in the guise of a partner at Bow or Limehouse, ever left his business interests in London to take up with Lund and Miller.

A second explanation of Pococke's claim might be that both factories may have benefited from the influence of a partner who is not named in the documentation of either factory. In this category we might consider William Cookworthy, the inventor of English hard paste porcelain and creator of factories at Plymouth and Bristol. Yet, as F. Severne Mackenna pointed out,[31] there is not even any significant circumstantial evidence linking Cookworthy to Limehouse or Lund's Bristol other than two letters which require considerable imagination to have any weight in the argument. The famous letter to Edward Hingston of May 30 1745 claiming to have met "the person who has discovered the China Earth" - usually thought to refer to Andre Duché - only tells us that he had an interest in porcelain at this date and that since this is after the first Bow patent, this interest was more likely to be expressed in Limehouse or possibly Chelsea. We also have Sarah Champion's retrospective Journal of January 1764 which refers to him as "the inventor of the Bristol China" but his

No 87 (detail)

identification with the quest for hard paste porcelain would surely mean that she is referring to the later firm taken over by her brother. Mackenna postulated that Edward Cave may be a contender. This suggestion would appear to be based solely upon the observation that Cave was based in London and, as a partner of the later Worcester factory, presumably interested from the outset in porcelain production. There is, however, nothing that can positively link Cave to Limehouse or Bristol and the suggestion is also made less convincing by the knowledge that Cave does not appear to have played any active part in the affairs of the Worcester factory other than promoting it in his *"Gentleman's Magazine"*.

A third possibility is that one of the two factories may have had a "hidden" partner who is mentioned in the documentation as one of the known partners of the other factory. Even allowing for the fact that it is a common name, there would appear to be a strong *prima facie* case for discounting Joseph Wilson, the only named entrepreneur at Limehouse. The baptismal registers in Newcastle-under-Lyme record the birth of a son to Joseph Wilson, potter, on November 29th 1751, the same Joseph Wilson who was already a tenant of a property containing a pot-oven, warehouses and workhouses on the death of its owner John Bell who died in 1752. Since he was not listed as burgess he probably came from outside the district and this sort of timing would coincide with the closure of Limehouse, particularly if we can bring the date forward even further by referring again to Pococke's correspondence. Rather than identify Wilson as the former Limehouse man at Bristol, it would be far more logical to argue that this was the individual Pococke describes as having met at Newcastle in his letter dated July 14th 1750 "whom I saw at Limehouse, who promised to make the china ware, but who disagreed with his Employers". This also perhaps raises another interesting possibility. If it was indeed Joseph Wilson of whom Pococke speaks here, then it suggests that he was merely a front for his nameless "Employers" rather than the actual proprietor at Limehouse. This, in turn, might strengthen the case for the candidature of Benjamin Lund as the former "principal of the manufacturers at Limehouse". As we have already seen, given the frequent impecuniosity of Lund which was probably a key factor in the sell-out of the Bristol works to the Worcester partners, he may well have had a reason for preserving his anonymity in London; to avoid his creditors he may well have needed to conceal his investment in the Limehouse factory just as he had done in Bristol. We might speculate further that the apparent haste with which Lund sold up his stake in Bristol and moved up to Worcester might reflect that his creditors had indeed located him and his days on the run were numbered. Without possessing any documentary proof, the present authors would concur that of all the *known* candidates for Pococke's Limehouse principal the circumstantial evidence would probably point to Lund as being the strongest contender.

WAS THE WORCESTER PORCELAIN FACTORY CREATED TO TAKE OVER THE BRISTOL FACTORY?

Several factors could explain the inability of the Bristol factory to build upon its promising start, some of which have been alluded to in the previous chapter, in contrast to Worcester. With hindsight there were long term factors which meant Worcester was more likely to sustain the new industry. These do not, however, really explain why Bristol was such a short-lived enterprise. The latter seems to be almost entirely a question of a lack of sound financing. Lund, as we have seen, seems to have been a serial bankrupt whilst Miller's contribution is untraceable. There appears to be no documentary evidence of any other investors or partners. This, perhaps coupled with an understandable caution in the wake of the Limehouse failure, (if there were significant commercial connections between the two enterprises), led to a limited range of inferior ware dealt with in the next chapter. Even more intriguingly it has also been suggested that the factory was not intended to last and was in fact nothing more than an experimental project for the Worcester partners.

"It is clear from the Partnership Deed that the Company was formed for the purpose of taking over an already existing manufacture with which Dr Wall and William Davis had some earlier contact"[32]

The precise sequence of documented events by which the Worcester factory came into being is very well known but needs once more to be rehearsed in order to ascertain the precise nature of the relationship between the Worcester factory and Lund's concern in Bristol. On May 16th 1751 a Quaker glover Richard Holdship took up a twenty-six year lease on Warmstry House on the banks of the Severn from a fellow glover William Evett. Nineteen days later on June 4th 1751 the deeds of the partnership were drawn up, outlining the purpose of the enterprise and the financial commitments of the Worcester partners. The business was to be carried on at Warmstry House for the next twenty-one years. On February 6th 1752 Richard Holdship purchased from Lund his soaprock licence and a fortnight later on February 21st he also purchased the stock utensils and effects of the Bristol factory. Then on July 24th 1752 a notice was published in the *Bristol Intelligencer* that the Bristol factory "was now united with the Worcester Porcelain where for the future the whole business will be carried on". This was confirmed by Edward Cave's advertisement in *The Gentleman's Magazine* of the new factory in August 1752 and announcing that the sale of the new ware would begin at the Three Choirs Festival on September 20th.

Some earlier historians like Hobson and Pountney have speculated that the supposed merger of the two factories may have been part of a planned strategy with the Bristol works representing a small scale prototype whose wares served to convince Wall and Davis' partners that their scheme was viable. It was a view that seemed to hold general sway up to the 1970s.[33] Apart from the mere coincidence of timing, this reading of events is based upon the following observations.

Firstly, there is considerable circumstantial evidence to make such a prior connection between the two factories feasible. Wall's interest in stained glass or even his extensive medical rounds could easily have led him into contact with businesses in the Bristol area. We certainly know that the creation of the Worcester Infirmary in 1746, in which Wall gave every support to Bishop Maddox, its prime mover, involved the purchase of the rules of the recently opened Bristol Infirmary to serve as a model. There would have been Quaker links between Bristolians like Lund and Worcester families like the Holdships and nor should we forget the commercial ties between the two cities. Edward Jackson's trows plying the Severn would no doubt have been able to keep Worcester informed of riverside developments in Bristol. It has even been asserted by Hurlbutt[34] that the James Davis mentioned in the Lowdin's glasshouse lease of 1745 was the brother of William Davis although absolutely no evidence corroborating this is known to exist. Benjamin Lund, according to Pountney,[35] may well have been acting from the very beginning as an agent for the Worcester Company which did not declare its hand until it saw that the experiment at Bristol, and in particular the successful development of the soapstone body, made a full blown venture appear a viable commercial proposition. Hence the timing of the formation of the Worcester partnership in June 1751 and for the new conditions of secrecy surrounding the Bristol factory in July 1751 from which date all further sales were carried out at Castle Green and the factory itself was to be closed to all visitors. This may also have been due to the dismantling of the factory and its equipment in preparation for the move which would not be announced until June 24th 1752. The continued use of Castle Green as a retail outlet for Worcester stock long after the closure of the Bristol factory might suggest that its manager Robert Carpenter was acting as an agent for the Worcester Company right from the outset.

Secondly, one can interpret the surviving documentation and ware in such a way as to show a degree of continuity in the early production of the two factories. Hobson averred his belief that the reference in the preamble and second article in the partnership deeds of 1751 to Dr Wall having "invented" a "new Manufacture of Earthen Ware" can be taken to mean "brought in". The second article certainly suggests that the research was by no means completed and they were going to be taking up a product brought in from outside. Article 24 also makes it clear that a patent would only be taken out after experience had made "the success thereof certain" and this in fact never happened. The workmen referred to in Articles 19 and 20, and particular attention is drawn here to the names of Robert Podmore and John Lyes, who assisted Wall prior to the creation of the Worcester partnership, may well have been Bristolians and part of a dual process of simultaneous experimentation in both cities This might appear to be confirmed by the blurring of the shapes, decoration and even stock in the early output of the two factories traced in Chapter 4.

However there is a school of thought that would argue that the Worcester partnership was set up quite independently of the Bristol factory with no advance knowledge of the sudden demise of the Bristol factory. If it was created to take over anything it was the experimental team and research initiated by Wall and Davis. The evidence to support this view can be summarised in three main ways.

Firstly there appears every reason to suppose that Wall and Davis really had set up a separate experimental works in a small backyard kiln in Davis' house in Broad Street with presumably every intention of producing their own paste quite independently of Bristol. John Sandon[36] is of the opinion that it would have been perfectly possible to have conducted such trials on a small scale and this in turn would appear to obviate the need for a simultaneous dry run in Bristol. The two men had already experience of scientific experimentation together with Malvern water and there is clear evidence in the partnership deeds of materials and workmen being assembled before the takeover of Bristol. Reference is made to "workmen and boys now employed by the inventors be deemed to have entered into the service of the subscribers…from the 11th day of May last". This would appear to suggest that Wall and Davis (the inventors) had been conducting significant experiments from May 1750 onwards, twenty months before Holdship bought out the assets of the Bristol factory. If the Worcester partnership was indeed set up to take over an existing concern, it surely refers to that of Wall, Davis, Podmore and Lyes. More crucially still, as the Warmstry House lower levels excavations suggested, they may well have produced a paste not containing the soapstone which was Bristol's most significant contribution to eighteenth century porcelain production. Why would they have gone to such trouble if they knew they would be able to have access to the mysteries of the soapstone paste? Indeed, surely the reason why the Wall-Davis formula of June 1751 was never patented was the *unexpected* acquisition of the superior Bristol soaprock recipe.

Secondly, there are too many symptoms of the take-over being unplanned and the consequence of opportunism. The Bristol factory appears to have been set up without any provable documentary links between it and the Worcester factory prior to the knowledge that payments for Lund's soaprock can be backdated to December 25th 1751. In addition, as the first year of production at Bristol was not marked by any overt attempt at secrecy, hence Pococke's ability to tour the factory, it is difficult to see the enterprise as some sort of "experiment" by the Worcester partners away from prying eyes. We should also bear in mind that Lund's factory was using twenty tons of soaprock per annum which was the same quantity as the Worcester factory well after its establishment which seems surprising if Bristol was not intended to be a serious long term commercial proposition. One is also entitled to ask why, if the Worcester partners knew of the imminent collapse of Bristol beforehand, they would have gone to such trouble to advertise their intention to embark upon porcelain production in such a fulsome fashion in June 1751 and thus highlight a possible point of contact with Lund if secrecy was a key priority. Moreover, if the Worcester partners had been informed of this plan all along, why did they have to rely upon what was ultimately a fatal financial over-commitment by just one of its number, Richard Holdship, to make the funds available for the purchase of Lund's lease and his stock? This clearly lop-sided development threatened the apparent equilibrium of the newly created partnership; there would either be a dangerous overdependence upon one of its members or the need to dig even deeper into their pockets to raise funds seemingly unanticipated by the initial capital put up in February 1751.

Thirdly the evidence of the supposed commercial strategies and the products themselves do not point to any anticipation of a merger. The Holdship bankruptcy papers of 1760 would suggest that the original purpose of the Worcester factory had been to decorate in the Dresden style whilst that of Bristol was in the Oriental taste. Whilst this is difficult to reconcile with the actual output of the two factories, it would indicate that the two firms were *intended* to be separate concerns and it is difficult to see what advantage could be gained some ten years after the event in misleading a disinterested audience. Perhaps even more convincingly, one may pose the question why the Bristol factory would have developed its own raised "Bristoll" mark and why the Worcester factory felt so obliged to paint over the mark when it bought out Lund's remaining stock? This is surely proof that the Bristol proprietors were not acting as the agents for a senior Worcester partnership.

In conclusion, it should also be remembered that it was by no means unusual for businesses to fold in early eighteenth century Britain; not only were production methods unpredictable but so were the means of raising credit. It is perfectly reasonable to suggest that the closure of the Bristol enterprise was much more likely to have been the consequence of Lund's impecunity, Miller's withdrawal of funds or a combination of both than any plan by the Worcester partners to use it as a dry run. The most likely explanation for the union is coincidence and opportunism. Lund had a product but inadequate financial backing; Wall had financial backing but an inadequate product. A marriage of convenience would have seemed an obvious answer to their mutual problems. At some point in 1751 there was contact made between the two partnerships and, with Miller probably unwilling to continue with the project, a buy-out rather than a merger took place.

HOW DID THE WORCESTER FACTORY OPERATE?

We are particularly fortunate in possessing the partnership deeds of June 1751 which spell out in great detail the terms and conditions of business operations. The terms have already been published in full but it is worth examining some of the key features not already mentioned. I hope, too, by grouping the Articles in a more thematic way that some broader analytical conclusions might be drawn.

In Chapter 2 it was suggested that a fresh spirit of accountability was to be found in the running of the new business which was in accord with the experience of the partners gained from their involvement in "Patriot" politics, the supervision of the Poor and the establishment of the Infirmary. Here I suspect Brodribb's involvement in these earlier enterprises may well have been most instrumental in this important aspect of the partnership. All voting was weighted according to the value of their shareholding. Articles 7, 9, 10, 11, 12, 17, and 28 spell out the collective nature of the enterprise. A committee of not less than three of the subscribers would be elected, they would meet at 10 a.m. every Tuesday in order to oversee the drawing up of regulations, the construction of buildings, the employment of workers and the buying of materials, all of which would be recorded in a book. Proper accounts were to be kept by clerks. On the first Tuesday of the month the committee was obliged to give an account of their proceedings to the subscribers who, after voicing their opinions and passing resolutions on the basis of their shareholdings, would give the committee directions for the future. The subscribers were also empowered to inspect, audit and pass the accounts at intervals and a general state of accounts would be given every six months. They were also at their monthly meetings to appoint a new Treasurer and any other officers on their deaths or removal.

Another somewhat contradictory key element was secrecy which was understandable in a time when industrial espionage was rife and the partners clearly believed that they had a product to protect. As already suggested, given that there was no such secrecy at Bristol and that this document was drawn up before the acquisition of soaprock, this would tend to suggest that the partners were anticipating discoveries which were yet to be made, discoveries which imply that Wall and Davis had conducted research quite independently of Lund and which were not yet perfected. This would seem to be confirmed by the wording of Article 2 in which it is said that they would bind themselves to discover "the real, true and full art, mystery and secret by them hitherto invented and found out with such further improvements and secrets as shall from time to time hereafter be made …for the making, finishing or perfecting". Wall and Davis were to forfeit £4,000 apiece if they passed on their knowledge and could be called to make a voluntary oath at the monthly shareholder meetings as to the "truth and reality" of their discovery and future improvements. They were ordered to write out their recipe and processes and this was to be secured in a box with three locks and keys, with one key given to Wall and Davis and the other two in the possession of two subscribers elected by their fellows. Article 14 goes on to say that the secret would remain there until "a proper superintendant" was appointed who would be apprised of the secret in order to carry out production. The theme of secrecy is illustrated further in Articles 18, 20, 22 and 27. Wall and Davis were not only to be recompensed for the expenditure on goods and utensils but were also allowed to carry on making purchases of necessary equipment without producing detailed receipts for accounting purposes. Robert Podmore and John Lyes, the two workmen employed by Wall and Davis, were to be rewarded each year for their discretion by a gratuity, after profit-taking of 10% by the subscribers, of at least one half share of further profits. Should they disclose their secrets or leave the partnership they would be liable to pay back all such gratuities. They were also to be entrusted with an inner door key whilst a clerk of the works was to be appointed and issued with an outer door key, an arrangement which was designed to prevent strangers being admitted to the works and "they and the clerks may be checks upon each other". Even the subscribers were themselves pledged to forfeit £4,000 if they revealed any secrets they had acquired.

It is also worth considering the financial details of the deeds in order to understand the scale of the commitment and anticipated profits which can be inferred from the document especially Articles 3, 4, 5, 6, 8, 13, 16, and 25. The fifteen signatories all subscribed sums measured in forty units of £112.10s and varying between £112.10s and £675. The subscribers were obliged to pay an immediate deposit of 8% and the rest by means of absolute promissory notes paid at intervals to Thomas Moore a city hop merchant for the use of Richard Brodribb, the Treasurer and the funds drawn upon by the latter one month after the due date. Failure to pay subscription money in full would result in forfeiture of all monies already paid and any profits accruing. These appear quite stringent conditions when it is difficult to believe that Wall and Davis had convincing evidence of a viable product. The partners must have been totally confident in Wall, mesmerised by the hope of profit or as has been argued earlier, capable of embracing a broader view of their investment. Given that Wall and Davis were not entitled to receive a further one-off bonus of £100 until a 10% profit had been raised and the additional incentives due to Podmore and Lyes were only payable in the same circumstances, it could be suggested that the Worcester partners were cautious in their estimation of instant financial success.

The £4,500 thus raised by the fifteen subscribers was then divided into 45 shares valued at £100. The five additional shares thus created were allocated to Wall and Davis as reward for the discovery of the porcelain secret along with the additional five accompanying voting rights. The other forty shares were distributed according to the sums subscribed. Thus Baylies, Cave and the two Holdships between them exercised 20 votes with the other eleven partners (including the extra votes allocated to Wall and Davis) holding 25. It is also worth noting the arrangement by which John Brodribb, the brother of the treasurer Richard Brodribb, and John Berwick were "co-partners" for the sum of £225 worth two votes. Since they are both listed as woollen drapers one can only assume that their investment came from an existing business partnership and that they enjoyed one vote each. This balance of shareholdings would suggest it was intended to make it difficult for any one interest to become too dominant, an intention which may have been undermined by Richard Holdship's position as tenant of Warmstry House and later holder of the soaprock lease and owner of the stock and utensils of Lund's factory in 1751.

WHAT IS KNOWN OF THE ROLE OF THE PARTNERS IN THE COMPANY?

There are two other notable aspects of the partnership, its size and the wide range of practical skills it brought to the running of the new factory. No other early factory comes remotely close to matching its fifteen partners and one is struck by the number of partners who were actively involved in day to day affairs, in addition to their investment of money. Given that its survival was still by no means inevitable, it does make a remarkable contrast with the nominally two man operation of Lund and Miller and reinforces the point made earlier. This was an enterprise that reflected a new form of Hogarthian patriotism eschewing aristocratic patronage and opting instead for the active participation of a full range of partners drawn from trade and the professions. Wall and Davis are credited with the discovery of the porcelain paste - whether by direct or indirect means remains- as we have seen, a debatable point. At all events, Wall is usually identified as the charismatic talisman whose personality and contacts put together the partnership and whose artistic inclinations probably influenced at least some design decisions. Edward Jackson's experience in transporting salt down the Severn may well have been used to direct the bringing in of raw materials and the distribution of the precious finished product. Davis seems to have supervised the administration of routine affairs such as indenturing apprentices and issuing the tokens sometimes used for payment. His importance is perhaps reflected in the fact that the Giles Account book refers to the Worcester firm as "Davis and Company". The two Holdship brothers were responsible for the operation of the transfer printing department and the supervision of apprentices. The goldsmith Samuel Bradley was involved in the retailing of the finished products at his shop in the High Street and possibly also supervising enamelling work in his workshop. A letter from Wedgwood to Thomas Bentley on December 24th 1770 refers to Mr Bradley hiring Jefferyes Hamett O'Neale as a China painter.[37] He was described in the *London Evening Post* in 1781 as "chinaman, toyman, dealer and chapman" whose stock in trade were "jewels, plate, china, as well foreign as of Worcester".[38] His importance to the provincial retail operation is reflected in the notice appearing in *"The Public Advertiser"* of April 7th 1768 which declared that dealers could not only buy from the new London warehouse in Gough Square but also "as usual, by sending their Orders to Mr Samuel Bradley, in Worcester".[39] The Staffordshire potter John Baddeley even refers to the firm as "Messrs Bradley, Wall and Co".[40] He also certainly took in apprentices. Even a more peripheral figure such as London based partner and principal shareholder Edward Cave was able to promote the newly opened factory in his publication *"The Gentleman's Magazine"* whilst John Thorneloe, according to one tradition, ventured into Cornwall in the late 1750s in search of a new source of soapstone.[41] By 1760 Thorneloe acquired on behalf of the partnership a ten year lease from Viscount Falmouth who subsequently sold the mineral rights to John Hunt of Llanhydrock. There is a strong possibility that the draughtsman, land surveyor and cartographer John Doharty[42] planned the extension and development of Warmstry House. There is some ground for believing, as already indicated, that the role of Richard Brodribb as Treasurer for the company may have been of greater importance than hitherto believed given his previous experience acting as Treasurer of both the Infirmary and the influential Constitution Club, supervising Thomas Vernon's election expenses and his representation of the Guardians of the Poor in their dispute with the Corporation. If this is the case then it would not be unnatural to assume that his younger brother John may also have helped in this capacity and perhaps adds to the significance of the splendid mask head jug dedicated to him and his new wife on their wedding and now housed in the Museum of Worcester Porcelain.

HOW DID THE FACTORY DEVELOP 1753-57?

The development of the factory in the five years after the merger with Bristol does appear to proceed with less ambiguity. Firstly the evidence of newspaper advertisements located by Geoffrey Wills and Nancy Valpy allows us to trace the rapid way in which Worcester sought to capture the crucial London market. Whilst the importance of the local market, as mentioned in Chapter 2, should not be overlooked, it was the concentration of fashionable taste, wealth and population in the capital that would determine Worcester's future. This is explored more fully in Chapter 6. The whole point of the strategy of avoiding a duplication of the wares produced at Bow and Chelsea was surely based upon the premise that Worcester would find its niche in the malls of the West End as shopping developed as a new leisure activity. Moreover, it was by placing one's goods in the capital, that one gained most effective access to the distribution network radiating from the capital. From the outset it was Worcester's practice to sell to dealers rather than private customers and to encourage provincial dealers to either attend auctions in London or place orders by post rather than trade directly with the factory. *The Daily Advertiser* of 29th May 1753 gave details of six London dealers who had been appointed as London agents[43] and on March 1st 1754 we find the first mention of the factory selling its wares by auction to dealers in London with a notice in *The Public Advertiser* when 40,000 pieces were to be shown and sold at London House in Aldersgate Street on Friday 14th of that month. *The General Evening Post* for 9-12 August 1755[44] gave early advance warning to "Country Traders" of a three day auction of goods at the Royal Exchange Coffee House between 17th and 19th September.[45] This was because the company "do not send Riders to vend their Ware by Pattern or Description, making London their only Mart of Sale". By March 20th 1756 the firm were now selling not just by auction but also direct to trade at the same Aldersgate Street premises which they had now taken over for their own exclusive use. Significantly there is also mention of selling not just to home but also to "foreign trade". Worcester's pointed attempt to penetrate the market in this way was, as Hilary Young[46] has argued, in contrast to Bow which tried to deal directly with personal customers as well as trade and provincial dealers in addition to those based in the capital. Worcester's strategy, however, was to become that followed by most companies in the next two decades.

The strategy made sense for a number of reasons. Firstly, transport costs to a point of sale were obviously reduced if all goods could be sent in bulk to one place and the expanding canal network certainly allowed safer and quicker transport. Secondly, and this seems confirmed by a survey of Chinamen who advertised in the Norwich press in the second half of the eighteenth century,[47] for exactly the same reason most provincial dealers seem to have travelled up to London to make all their purchases because it allowed them to buy in and send back in one consignment a whole range of products from different factories, including the East India Company. Thirdly, payment by dealers was significantly prompter than was the custom with personal customers, within three to six months rather than the two years or more credit which Duesbury the Younger allowed at Derby. With luxury goods in particular this was a vital consideration for a firm wishing to remain solvent. Wealthy aristocratic clients, as Sir Everard Knatchbull told Thomas Chippendale, would often only pay their bills at the end of the financial year when they had collected their rents.[48] It was probably about 1756 that the important but undated price list of wares was produced which not only gives discounted wholesale prices of the various wares but also offers a further discount of 15% for prompt payment on top of the discount given to trade. Finally, a further consideration was that by shifting large quantities of stock to dealers at a warehouse, Worcester did not have to fit out lavish premises to attract personal clients and accommodate expensive stock. Defoe commented that London shopkeepers now had to invest two thirds of their wealth on displaying their wares.[49] In this way, Worcester was able to overcome the disadvantages of being a provincial company and compete alongside Bow and Chelsea in their own backyard.

No 97 (reverse)

Another vital development during these years was the perfection of the process of overglaze transfer printing. Although there is only one token - albeit extremely rare - printed piece in the A. J. Smith Collection (see Chapter 12), the new process was to have a major impact upon the success of Worcester. Despite the efforts of other firms as they began to exploit the new medium about this time, none matched the quality of the Worcester prints the making of which, as Lady Shelburne's visit in 1770 revealed,[50] was still kept a secret. The precise origins are still difficult to trace and may even have their roots in a visit by Captain Delamain in 1753, an Irishman who claimed to the Irish Parliament that he had "purchased the art of transfer printing". In all probability, the success of Worcester was based on collaboration between the two Holdship brothers and the engraver Robert Hancock who seems to have arrived in the city shortly after 1754. It would have been at some point between 1755 and 1756 that the process of the Holdships and Robert Hancock would allow Worcester to enter the highly lucrative commemoratives market of the late 1750s and 1760s.

The rise of patriotism and Hanoverian loyalism that was outlined in Chapter 2 was something that sought an outlet in art and consumer goods and this was something which the Worcester partners, with their particular political outlook, were able to understand and exploit better than most. Depictions of George II and his family, the achievements of his politicians and generals, the successes of his ally Frederick of Prussia and the philanthropic schemes such as the Marine Society all reflected the earlier "Patriot" political activity of men like Wall and Brodribb. Even more significantly this development, particularly when it was later extended to under glaze blue printing, allowed more rapid decoration of basic items by less accomplished craftsmen and artists, thus speeding up production and keeping costs down. Constant innovation and simultaneous cost-cutting was a difficult but necessary survival strategy in the volatile world of eighteenth century ceramics production and Worcester's success in the 1750s was built upon it.

One of the key figures in introducing Worcester to the London market, Edward Cave, died on June 18th 1754 and although his main task was, in a sense, already accomplished, his death did lead to a reorganisation of the company which reasserted the spirit of 1751. The bringing in of another nine small shareholders to replace him - making a total of twenty three - both broadened and stabilised the financial base by bringing in an additional £2,960. The new shareholders also appear to have had interests closely interwoven with the existing shareholders. They were the Reverend Benjamin and Mr Robert Blayney, Mr David Henry and his wife Mary, the Reverend Richard Pritchett, the surgeon William Russell, Thomas Salway, John Stillingfleet and the Reverend Thomas Vernon. The last named is of particular interest because he was the rector of Hanbury and the cousin of Sir Thomas Vernon MP.[51] This would lend further confirmation of the speculation that there was a political connection between the factory and the local Whig interest, although of the new shareholders only the Reverend Benjamin Blayney can be traced in the 1747 poll books who, like the 1751 partners, voted for Vernon and Tracy. This association might well be extended to Robert Blayney since we find in the Vernon election papers that a Mr Blayney - probably either Robert or Benjamin's father Thomas - was acting as one of Vernon's agents in 1754 with instructions on how much to pay constituents for the allocation of their votes. The Stillingfleets were certainly amongst the early subscribers to the Infirmary whilst William Russell was one of Wall's colleagues in the said institution. The Reverend Pritchett was in all probability a relative of Samuel, another of the original 1751 partners.

It certainly reinforces the view that the Worcester partnership, despite thrusting itself into the London market, was determined to remain in the hands of local men and women. As if to emphasise this concern we also have the first documented information of apprentices being taken on with the indenturing of John Williams, son of Richard Williams of St Nicholas, weaver to Richard Holdship "to learn the art of a potter" on June 25th 1755. The number of apprentices recorded in the Worcester enrolment book only increased dramatically a decade later - thirty-five were apprenticed to Bradley and Davis between 1763-67 - but analysis of this list shows that two-thirds came from within the city.[52] This would appear to bear out the suggestion that the partners did have a paternalist interest to provide local employment and the first indenture seems in retrospect a highly significant metaphor as the increasingly defunct woollen business outlined in Chapter 2 was replaced by a new industry with which the city's name was to become synonymous.

Yet, even at this early stage, there were some signs of the danger that commercial pressures could put upon the close knit relationship. In June 1755 the workman Robert Podmore defected to the Liverpool concern of Chaffers and Christian. The articles of agreement for employment which survive[53] show that he was to receive a guinea a week as factory manager and one twelfth of the profits in return for teaching "the art and mystery" of making soaprock porcelain and not to "communicate or make known the said Art to any other Person or Persons". The cause of his defection was presumably dissatisfaction with the remuneration he received at Worcester which may well tell us that profits in the first few years did not exceed 10% and thus allow Podmore his payment of a half share.

Another potential source of discord lay in the role of the Holdships, and in particular, Richard Holdship, within the partnership. Mention has already been made of his dangerously dominant role within the partnership; by 1757 he and his brother controlled 20% of the shares, were joint landlords and sole suppliers of the vital soaprock. More worryingly, Richard had overstretched himself financially, selling off his wife's inherited property worth £1,500 in Somerset in order to buy out Lund and Miller. Despite agreeing to set up a trust into which he was to pay £100 for twenty years to recompense his wife, his mounting difficulties prevented him from doing this. Furthermore, there appear to have been some other character flaws which contributed to his eventual downfall. By 1757 it was evident that there were tensions in the printing department between the Holdships and Robert Hancock over who should gain the credit for the King of Prussia mugs which appeared that year. This was well-documented in the local and national press and also reflected in the appearance of both the Holdship anchor rebus and the name or initials of Hancock on transfer printed ware. A contributor to Berrow's Worcester Journal, calling himself "Philomath", challenged in similar style some lines in verse by "Cynthio" which had appeared in the *Gentleman's Magazine* in December 20th 1757 praising Josiah Holdship for inventing transfer printing; "Philomath" attributes the invention to Hancock and consoled the latter with the couplet

"Hancock, my friend, don't grieve, tho Holdship has the praise,
'Tis yours to execute, 'tis his to wear the bays"

The fact that some of the later prints contained his hidden signatures suggested that Hancock had been forbidden by the Holdships to share the credit but was nevertheless determined to fight his cause. Brian Smith[54] has also suggested that John Doharty may also have been increasingly alienated by the Holdships and that it was he who, as Philomath, castigated the Holdships' ambition.

That there was an element of truth in this seems to be borne out by two further acts of financial recklessness which would lead to Richard's bankruptcy. During 1756 he bought three small houses next to the factory and built a "large commodious dwelling place for himself" which was shown in Hancock's splendid engraving the following year and then, in 1759, bought jointly with Josiah the freehold of Warmstry House for £600. Doharty may have been hired as designer or architect for the project but Holdship's impending financial catastrophe may well have left him out of pocket. Doharty, who had also lapsed into a depression following his father's death and the evident disappointment of his financial expectations, made a marginal and inaccurate sketch of the new site which he intriguingly entitled "The Naughty China Works at Worcester". He seems to have had more reason than most to view the elder Holdship's defection from the factory in 1759 in order to trade its secrets of soaprock production and transfer printing elsewhere[55] as an act of treachery. Even brother Josiah by this time seems to have regarded his elder sibling's behaviour as beyond the pale and it was he who was to petition against him on behalf of Richard's wife Betty to secure her the compensation now threatened by the impending bankruptcy proceedings. Thus the building of his splendid residence was the last financial miscalculation Holdship was to make and it caused great internal conflict in the partnership; yet although his confidence in his future personal prosperity was to prove misplaced, it was, nevertheless, a gesture which was to mark the fact that the Worcester Porcelain Company had arrived and was here to stay.

NOTES

Chapter 3   **The foundation of the Bristol and Worcester porcelain factories**

1   John Sandon "A Dictionary of Worcester Porcelain 1751-1851" (Antique Collectors Club 1993 &1996).

2   Although he could infer from the Warmstry House leases and the soaprock licence that the Holdships, Samuel Bradley, Samuel Pritchett, William Oliver, William Davis and Benjamin Blayney were likely to be business associates.

3   Later published as H Eccles and B Rackham "Analysed Specimens of English Porcelain" (London 1922).

4   R. L. Hobson "Worcester Porcelain" (Bernard Quaritch 1910 p.12).

5   W. J. Pountney "Old Bristol Potteries" (E P Publishing 1920 reprint 1972).

6   C. W. Dyson Perrins "John Wall and the Worcester Porcelain Company" (EEC Transactions vol 2 no 8 1942 p.128)

7   e.g. Dr H Bellamy Gardener "The Earliest Reference to Chelsea Porcelain " (English Porcelain Circle Transactions Vol 1 No 1 1928 pp16-22) W E Elliott "Soft Paste Porcelain and the Intimate Relationship of the factory at Lowdin's Glass House with Limehouse and Worcester" (EPC Transactions No 1, 1929) and Mr A J Toppin "A Note on the Limehouse China Factory" (EPC Transactions No 3 1931 pp70-73).

8   This was deduced from a letter dated 28th December 1745 written by a Mr James Middleton of Shelton to William Tams of "the Pot Works in Fore Street nigh Duke shore in Limehouse, London" , the references to four Limehouse Ware sauceboats at 15s in the personal and household accounts of John Campbell, Lord Glenorchy dated November 25th 1747 and a series of advertisements in the London press discovered by A J B Kiddell which concludes on June 3rd 1748 with notice of a meeting of the creditors of the factory. Ref B Watney in D Drakard (ed)"Limehouse Ware Revealed" (English Ceramic Circle 1993 p.1).

9   It is also possible that Limehouse introduced the use of the soapstone paste used by Bristol and then Worcester although there is no documentary proof of this and there is some ambiguity relating to the composition of surviving Limehouse pieces. Lund's licence - which was the first soaprock licence - was dated June 1748 whereas the Limehouse factory had failed by March.

10   PRO Bankruptcy Order Book No 40 pp19 seq :ref F A Barrett "Worcester Porcelain and Lund's Bristol" Faber and Faber 2nd edition 1966 p.3).

11   Rodney Dowling informs me that "grocer" in 18th century Bristol can mean "merchant" as the latter phrase was used to distinguish members of the Bristol Merchant Adventurers. He also tells me that a William Miller he has traced had shares in a Bristol glasshouse.

12   A. J. Toppin "The Proprietors of the early Bristol China Factory: Identified as William Miller and Benjamin Lund" (ECC Transactions vol 3 part 3 p130 Jan 1954 pp.129-40).

13   PRO Ref C54 5922/7 ref B. Watney "English Blue and White Porcelain" (Faber and Faber 1963 reprint 1979 p.31)

14   Toppin (ibid).

15   E. Morton Nance "Soaprock Licences" (EEC Transactions vol 1 no 3 1935 p.76 and p.82).

16   Pountney (ibid p.187).

17   Pountney (ibid p.185).

18   Pountney (ibid p.205).

19   Research file available at Bristol Record Office and archive of Museum of Worcester Porcelain.

20   R. and P. Jackson & R Price "Bristol Potters and Potteries 1600-1800" (Journal of Ceramic History no12, Stoke-on-Trent City Museums 1982).

21   Toppin (ibid p.130).

22   Research article deposited with Bristol Record Office.

23   Pountney (ibid p.192).

24   Toppin (ibid p.140).

25   In 1983 Mrs Nancy Valpy discovered an advertisement in the Daily Advertiser between 4th and 8th October 1746 advising "Pot, Fan or Box Painters" to apply to Mr Wilson's manufactory near Duke Shore, Limehouse which corroborated Bernard Watney's earlier research into local Land Tax returns which had located a Joseph Wilson at 20 Fore Street. The subsequent archaeological dig between March and April 1990 revealed the long lost site of the Limehouse kilns. Watney (ibid) pp.2-3.

26   One would also like to hope that the fact that he later became the bishop of Ossory and then of Meath would strengthen his claims to be a reliable source!

27   F. Hurlbutt "Bristol Porcelain" (London and Boston The Medici Society 1928 p.33).

28   I. Freestone in D Drakard (ibid) chapter 7. Freestone suggests that the patent might have been taken out to obstruct experimentation at Limehouse but the known dating would suggest that they were perhaps already too late.

29   Elizabeth Adams and David Redstone "Bow Porcelain" (Faber and Faber 1981 p.32) It is shown that he and Alderman Arnold purchased jointly the first premises and buildings in Stepney in 1744; he is mentioned in the Sun Assurance policies of July 7th 1749 and November 22nd 1750; and the firm is referred to as Edward Heyleyn and Co between 1752 and 1754. They also point out that he was a clothier rather than a copper merchant, which was the occupation of his brother Henry. The apparent confusion in contemporary references may be the source of a misapprehension or perhaps Edward had a financial stake in his brother's business.

30   Freestone (ibid p.73) Freestone's technical analysis shows that there was no evidence of soapstone present in the Limehouse samples but that this does not rule out the possibility altogether. The sample taken was small and some attributed Limehouse pieces have been shown by X ray diffraction to contain soapstone. The reference to "improved" ware and continued experimentation at Limehouse may yet explain this apparent ambiguity

31   F. S. Mackenna "Worcester Porcelain: The Wall Period and its Antecedents" (F Lewis 1950 pp.8-10).

32   Franklin A Barrett "Worcester Porcelain and Lund's Bristol" (Faber and Faber 1966 p.1).

33   Barrett, with a suitable note of caution, appeared to endorse this interpretation even though he did develop thoroughly a line of argument which favoured the view that the two factories had quite separate origins.

34   Hurlbutt (ibid p.33).

35   Pountney (ibid p.192).

36   J. Sandon "A Dictionary of Worcester Porcelain 1751-1851" (Antique Collectors club 1996) p.11.

37   Major W H Tapp "Jefferyes Hamett O'Neale" (University of London Press 1938 p.7).

38   Nancy Valpy "Extracts from 18th century newspapers" (ECC Transactions, XII, Pt 1 1984, pp.58-89).

39   Gerald Coke "In Search Of James Giles" (Micawber Publications 1983) p.108.

40   J. V. G. Mallett "John Baddeley of Shelton: an Early Staffordshire Maker of Pottery and Porcelain" (Parts I-II ECC Transactions VI 2-3 1966-67 p.192 and 225).

41   B. K. Hobbs "New Perspectives on Soapstone" (ECC Transactions XV pt 3 1995 pp.368-92).

42   B. S. Smith "Two Early Sketches of the Worcester Porcelain Works" (Transactions of the Worcestershire Archaeological Society vol 16 1998 pp.221-225).

43   Nancy Valpy "Extracts from 18th century newspapers " (ECC Transactions XI, Pt 3, 1983 pp.187-211) The six dealers were Farrer & Co, Cotterrell, Lamden & Woods, Vere, Bridge and Taylor.

44   Geoffrey Wills "Some notes on the Worcester Porcelain Factory" (Apollo Jan 1954 pp.7-9).

45   In the event the sale had to be postponed until October 8-11th "on account of the large Quantity of Goods which could not be got ready so soon".

46   Hilary Young "English Porcelain 1745-95: Its Making, Design, Marketing and Consumption" (V&A Publications 1999 chapter 8) I have plundered quite shamelessly from this magnificent book throughout this section. It also has by far the best bibliography for any student of the period.

47   S. Smith "Norwich China Dealers of the Mid-Eighteenth Century" (ECC Transactions, IX, Pt 2, 1974).

48   Young (ibid p.167).

49   "The Compleat English Tradesman" 1726.

50   J. V. G. Mallett "Lady Shelburne's Visit to Worcester in 1770" (ECC Transactions XI, Part 2 1982 pp.109-11).

51   The reverend was the son of Captain Thomas Vernon (d 1734) who was the younger brother of Bowater Vernon the father of the MP Sir Thomas Vernon (1724-71).

52   I am grateful to David Everett for this information.

53   Boney Knowles "Liverpool Porcelain of the Eighteenth Century and its Makers" (Portman Press 1989 Appendix 1 pp.193-195).

54   B. S. Smith "Two Early Sketches of the Worcester Porcelain Works" (Transactions of the Worcestershire Archaeological Society vol 16 1998 pp.221-225) The phrasing and its appearance in the local newspaper does suggest some inside knowledge and land surveyors like Doharty often called themselves "philomaths". Doharty had also made a previous anonymous contribution to the Worcester Journal in 1755.

55   He had certainly entered into an agreement with Duesbury and John Heath at Derby by 1764 but might have been here earlier or possibly at Bow. John Sandon (ibid p.198).

CHAPTER 4   LUND'S BRISTOL

The factory established by Benjamin Lund in Bristol in 1749 was the first English porcelain factory to be located outside London. Despite a long standing tradition for tin-glazed earthenware in the area, this venture was a leap into the unknown. The porcelain industry in 1750 was dominated by the two existing factories, Chelsea and Bow, and by the mass importation of Chinese wares from the East India Company. Chelsea concentrated exclusively on a narrow but affluent market, providing for the fashionable London tastes for wares in the oriental and Meissen style. Bow, a far larger and more overtly commercial enterprise, sought to compete directly with Chinese importations, whilst also catering for the Meissen taste, especially in their figure models. It was therefore necessary for Lund to identify a window of opportunity in this financially hazardous and highly competitive market.

Bristol was described in 1753, by R R Angerstein, a Swedish traveller, diarist and industrial observer, as " . . . a large and powerful commercial city, competing with London both in business and wealth. They trade with every place on earth . . .".[1] Although only one tenth the size of London, Bristol was the largest and longest-established of the ports facing west towards the Atlantic, and Britain's burgeoning overseas empire. It was an excellent location for a porcelain factory, a major port situated on the River Severn, the busiest and most important tidal artery aside from the Thames. A still more fundamental asset was Lund's access to a soaprock formula. This licence, dated 7th March 1748/9, had been granted to him for a term of twenty-one years. In terms of his projected market, Lund was faced by two options: he could compete directly with the porcelain made at Bow and with the Chinese importations, or he could offer the public something new and not available elsewhere. He shrewdly chose the latter course, using as his model, the defunct Limehouse factory. Dr. Richard Pococke, a traveller and writer, had visited the Bristol factory in November 1750, describing it as " . . . a manufacture lately established here by one of the principle manufacturers at Limehouse which failed". It is likely that the man referred to was Benjamin Lund himself.

The Limehouse factory, situated in East London, on the Thames, was in operation between 1746 and 1748. Production was almost entirely confined to blue and white wares, with an emphasis on pickle leaves, shell-shaped pickle dishes, sauceboats, creamboats, teapots and tankards, with a significant absence of teawares, bowls, plates and dishes. In three particular respects, this production stood apart from both the contemporary Bow and the Chinese importations: an innovative use of moulded ornamentation, especially on sauceboats and creamboats, a series of models associated with silver forms and almost certainly, the first use of soaprock on a commercial scale, probably introduced only during the final stages of the factory's brief existence. Judging from surviving pieces, Lund determined to mirror both the Limehouse concentration on blue and white wares and the output itself. Indeed, several Bristol shapes echoed specific Limehouse models, nos. 1 and 11. The perceived importance of high quality moulded decoration is reflected in an advertisement in November 1750, for young apprentices to learn the skills of pottery as practised in Staffordshire, which was the centre of the saltglazed stoneware industry. The apprentices were also exhorted to learn how to paint porcelain "in the India or Roman taste", meaning the oriental style.[2] The enterprise was retrospectively described several years later as " a porcelain manufactory in imitation of East India China ware". A later advertisement in July 1751, referring to wares made in imitation of foreign china is more puzzling and suggests a proposed decorative idiom which was never developed, possibly involving overglaze painting in polychrome. At any event it seems almost certain that no polychrome decoration was undertaken at Bristol, although a small proportion of wares left "in the white" were subsequently painted in enamel colours at Worcester.

The output of Lund's factory, seemingly idiosyncratic, was defined by its small size, limited resources, the benefits afforded by its soapstone formula, the closely observed precedent of Limehouse and by an awareness of what was already available on the market in terms of blue and white wares. The imported Chinese porcelain could hardly be matched in terms of either its thinness and excellence of potting for teabowls, saucers and bowls, or their supreme ability to mass produce sturdily potted plates, dishes and dinner services. On the other hand, many smaller products, alien to the Chinese culture, such as pickle leaves, small shell-shaped dishes, creamboats, patty pans and coffee cans, though robustly potted and functional, were plain in shape and repetitive in their decoration. Sauceboats too, were serviceable, yet designed with an emphasis on utility rather than visual sophistication. Furthermore, the glaze on the more thickly potted oriental vessels had a distressing tendency to shear off, leaving an uneven surface to the rims of coffee cups, sauceboats and tankards. These deficiencies might have seemed comparatively trivial to a consumer earlier in the century, exhilarated at the availability of this fashionable new material, tougher and more durable than delftware and imbued with the magical quality of translucency. Yet with the development of an indigenous English porcelain industry in the 1740s, the consumer was offered a choice. At Bow, embarking on a large scale expansion, the challenge of the Chinese importations was met directly, competing for the same market, deploying a series of comparable shapes and decorated in much the same idiom. Where possible, Bow sought to undersell the Chinese, though this endeavour was seldom achieved. Relatively little attempt was made to offer the public blue and white wares which were inherently different to the Chinese.

Bristol, a much smaller enterprise, sought like Limehouse what might be termed today a 'niche' market. Resources were concentrated into shapes at which the Chinese did *not* excel. Pickle leaves and small shell-shaped dishes were more finely potted and more imaginatively decorated than their imported counterparts. Sauceboats and creamboats, embellished with high quality moulded rococo ornamentation, were far superior to the more humdrum Chinese models. These moulding skills, exemplified in the Limehouse output and learned from the Staffordshire saltglaze industry, had luxury associations with silver, a correlation emphasised by the shapes of some sauceboats. Neither the Chinese nor Bow offered the public such allusive novelties. Yet the Bristol production was narrower and more restricted than that of Limehouse and in several respects, less accomplished. In retrospect, it has very much the appearance of the first tentative stage of a factory's genesis, prior to the main phase of development. The next phase may have been signalled by the advertisement of July 1751, referring to wares made in imitation of foreign china, an intended expansion which was overtaken by events.[3] In this sense, it is possible to view the short-lived Bristol production as the initial phase in the evolution of soapstone porcelain, continued at Worcester in 1752, after the two factories had been "united".

It might be instructive to look more closely at the Bristol production as gauged from surviving examples. What was *not* produced at the factory is almost as significant as the production itself. In terms of the size of its output, it might be compared to the blue and white wares of Samuel Gilbody's Liverpool factory, in operation during the later 1750s, offering a far more conventional range of shapes. As is evident from the following notes, almost all the surviving models made at Bristol are extremely scarce today, and in many instances, only one or two examples are recorded.

The known or recorded models are described here in ascending order of rarity.

Pickle leaf dishes of three-pointed outline, moulded with veins on the undersides, resemble the slightly later Worcester version, no. 58. Whilst at Limehouse, pickle leaves were issued in several differing shapes and sizes and in a range of patterns, the Bristol examples were confined to one model and one size, most often decorated in a Chinese figure pattern,[4] in the manner of the creamboat, no. 2, and the small shell dish, no. 11. The model remained in production at Worcester until about 1756-57. This is perhaps the least scarce today of all Bristol shapes.

Small shell-shaped dishes, no. 11, moulded on the undersides, were almost certainly inspired by Limehouse precursors. Yet unlike the London factory, they were issued in only two sizes and in a far more limited range of patterns, generally incorporating a Chinese figure.

Sauceboats were issued in four basic press-moulded models, all later employed at Worcester. A low shallow "panneled" form was made in three sizes, nos. 3, 4 and 5. The two moulded versions, nos. 3 and 4, occasionally bear the embossed *Bristol* mark but this is not recorded on the unmoulded model, no. 5. A pedestal sauceboat, no. 6, was issued in two sizes and was the forerunner of the classic Worcester shape, no. 88. A panel-moulded sauceboat of tapering shape, with an angular handle and pronounced thumbrest, similar to no. 95, was made in one size, but only three examples of Lund's are known, all at present in North American private collections.[5] The fourth and most ambitious sauceboat model is the Bristol version of no. 43. This corresponds to those described by the traveller Dr. Richard Pococke, who visited the factory in November 1750, writing to his mother of ". . . beautiful white china sauce boats, adorned with reliefs of festoons which sell for sixteen shillings a pair". Issued in two sizes, these elaborately designed and extremely expensive sauceboats, resembling contemporary Bow counterparts, were redolent of silver models. One single blue and white example is recorded, together with some left "in the white" and a number which were subsequently decorated in enamel colours, most often at Worcester, but in at least one instance, in London.[6] The polychrome examples are sometimes embossed with the *Bristol* mark placed inside the footrim and almost invariably overpainted in green enamel so as to conceal the letters.[7]

Five models of creamboats are recorded, all moulded in the rococo taste. A hexagonal form with a moulded leaf under the lip, closely replicates a Limehouse original[8] and was itself copied at Worcester, no. 109. A slightly larger hexagonal shape, no. 1, is an even rarer variation on this rococo theme, with more generously proportioned panels. Related to both is the more rounded form, sharing the same angular handle and curved thumbrest, no. 2. A smaller lobed model on four pad feet also occurs "in the white" and with slightly later polychrome decoration.[9] All four of these models are recorded with the embossed *Bristol* mark and it would appear that the small fluted examples on pad feet are almost invariably marked in this way. A fifth slightly larger creamboat, fluted and on a low oval base, has recently been recorded.[10] In addition to these five basic models are several undecorated creamboats[11] and small sauceboats,[12] conforming to known models in their shape, but with detailed *chinoiserie* moulding in high relief.

Mugs and tankards were issued in two models. A cylindrical example with a widely flared base, no. 8, forerunner of the Worcester shape, no. 18, was made in two sizes. Of these, two are recorded in the larger size[13] and three in the smaller. A less conventional mug, probably based upon a German stoneware model, has a bulbous body and horizontally ribbed cylindrical neck. Only two of these are recorded.[14]

Coffee cans were of plain cylindrical shape, not dissimilar from Chinese or Bow models, but with angular handles and cursive thumbrests, resembling those on hexagonal creamboats, and a fine ridge around the base.[15] Sturdily potted and of practical design, it seems curious that only some seven examples are known to have survived.

More unconventional in shape are cream pails on pad feet, applied with highly vulnerable loop handles in the manner of George II silver models, nos. 9 and 10. These have no precise counterparts in other factories' productions. Only six examples are recorded.

Four Lund's Bristol teapots have so far come to light, two of plain globular shape, no. 7, one lobed in the manner of the Worcester example, no. 82, and the fourth of hexagonal form.[16] This poor survival rate of a staple porcelain model echoes that of Limehouse teapots, advertised as a speciality in September 1748,[17] issued in several differing shapes, yet extremely scarce today.

Deep shell-shaped dishes, adapted from earlier silver models on three feet, were issued in two sizes. Three are recorded in the larger size, no. 12, together with one single smaller example. The model was later replicated at Worcester.

Only three coffee pots[18] and three coffee cups[19] are known and only two cider jugs.[20] Two large and imposing baluster vases, formerly in the Jenkins Collection, are the only ones of their kind recorded and no other small flared vase, no. 13, is known to exist.

The small size and apparent vagaries of the Bristol production is further emphasised by the following tabulation of contemporary porcelain shapes, available also in Chinese and Bow porcelain.

One single Bristol example known	No Bristol examples recorded
Creamjug[21]	Bowl, hand thrown
Patty pan[22]	*Bottle-shaped vase
Pierced strainer dish[23]	Cutlery
Small pot and cover[24]	*Miniature teawares
Spirally fluted bowl, no. 14	Plate or *dish
Sugar box and cover[25]	*Potting pot
	*Saucer
	*Teabowl
	*Tureen
	*Leaf-shaped dishes, large

*Indicates a shape made at Limehouse

From this tabulation it may be deduced that there was a very low survival rate of Bristol porcelain, but almost certainly not lower than that of blue and white Bow or Limehouse. Indeed, Bristol was probably a tougher, more durable and heat resistant material. Yet it seems clear that this was not only a short-lived enterprise, but also a small-scale one. Its marketing priorities are thrown into vivid relief by the concentration on sauceboats, pickle leaves and shell-shaped dishes to the partial exclusion of other shapes. The absence of teawares, particularly teabowls and saucers, is explained by a natural reluctance to compete with the superbly potted and comparatively cheap Chinese importations, a disinclination shared by all other English factories prior to about 1754, with the single exception of Bow. Much of the surviving output mirrors that of Limehouse, especially the recurring emphasis on sauceboats, pickle leaves and shell-shaped dishes, by far the most frequently encountered Limehouse shapes today. Yet a whole range of models made at Limehouse seem not to have been attempted at Bristol. Hand thrown, as opposed to press-moulded wares are notably deficient in both productions. Yet the absence of large leaf-shaped dishes and bottle-shaped vases and the far more restricted range of sauceboat models and pickle leaves, is indicative of more limited commercial aspirations. Perhaps it was the recent experience of the failure of Limehouse, two years earlier, which created this spirit of caution.

Far more enterprising was Benjamin Lund's attempt to promote the factory through a series of slip-cast figures representing the Chinese Immortal *Lu Tung-Pin*. At least nine of these models are known, imitating Chinese *blanc de chine* porcelain and directly moulded from *Fujian* porcelain, seven of which are undecorated and two streaked in underglaze manganese. This experimental underglaze colour, never satisfactorily employed on English porcelain, is also recorded on one single shell-shaped pickle dish. Seven of the models of *Lu Tung-Pin* are embossed from the mould, at the back of the figure on the base, with the name *Bristoll* and the date *1750*.[26] These figures were probably intended to promote the newly established factory in a manner akin to the Bow inkpots inscribed *New Canton*. They must have effectively conveyed the required sense of beguiling exoticism associated with the mysterious orient. Yet if the models of *Lu Tung-Pin* embodied the artistic spirit of the Bristol production, they hardly represented the output itself, firmly rooted in tablewares. But these too occasionally bore the embossed *Bristol* mark, sometimes spelt *Bristoll,* nos. 1 and 2. The mark, employed only on sauceboats and creamboats, appears on both blue and white and undecorated pieces. Most of the latter were subsequently painted in colour at Worcester, the embossed mark being deliberately concealed by a wash of green enamel. This is confirmed by the high-handled Bristol pedestal sauceboats which are decorated in a manner corresponding exactly to Worcester versions, no. 43. A small number of Bristol pieces were evidently decorated elsewhere, including a high-handled sauceboat painted in one of the London ateliers.[27] Significantly, the embossed mark has *not* been obscured. In all, at least twenty-five examples of Lund's Bristol bear this embossed mark, together with seven of the recorded models of *Lu Tung-Pin*.[28]

If the Bristol production was narrower and less innovative than that of Limehouse, it did succeed in developing one facet of the London factory's production. This was the juxtaposition between essentially European shapes, with Chinese decorative themes. The range of Bristol shapes displays unmistakable silver influences, especially evident in sauceboats, creamboats, tankards, cream pails and deep shell-shaped dishes. Yet regardless of form, these were invariably decorated with oriental landscapes. This correlation of European shapes and oriental decorative themes, initiated at Limehouse on a small scale and amplified at Bristol, was to become a defining feature of the Worcester production, both in polychrome and underglaze blue, during the factory's initial phase. So too was the use of Chinese landscapes enclosed within rococo moulded reserved panels, a delightful and inventive decorative conceit common to Limehouse, Bristol and Worcester, but more sparingly employed elsewhere. The landscapes themselves display a limited variety in their scope and it is possible to speculate as to the same hand working on different pieces. At so relatively small a factory concentrating on one single decorative idiom, it is reasonable to assume that only a tiny handful of painters were employed. For example, the teapot, no. 7, featuring the Chinese junk in full sail and a rudimentary two-tier structure incorporating the three dot motif, may have been decorated by the same hand as the moulded sauceboat, no. 3, the smaller sauceboat, no. 4, and perhaps even the pair of unmoulded sauceboats, no. 5. A connecting thread also links the tankard, no. 8, the smaller cream pail, no. 9, and the shell-shaped dish, no. 11. All are painted with a sinuous Chinese figure, sketchily drawn in an identical pose and wearing a distinctive Micky Mouse-like coiffure sometimes resembling a flying helmet. This unusual hairstyle is also conspicuous on the reclining lady on the small vase, no. 13. The two cream pails, nos. 9 and 10, may also have been painted by the same hand, judging by a comparison between the treatment of their vegetation and even the formation of the flights of birds. Recurrent motifs such as studded hilltops, no. 4, Chinese junks with billowing sails, no. 8, and the ubiquitous triangular formations of three dots, no. 6, may have constituted an established factory style, but the interconnected chain of similarly painted motifs indicate that there may possibly have been as few as two or three painters at Bristol. Several of these decorative motifs, including the studded hilltops and the junk with billowing sails, also occur on early Worcester.[29]

The tone of underglaze blue varied from a characteristic rich deep colour, with a touch of indigo, to a paler more misty tone. The blue itself was generally less pale than that of Worcester and less well-defined than either Limehouse or Worcester. It tended to blur in the glaze, creating an unfocused effect, as if viewing the scene depicted through a wet window, no. 2. This serious fault remained uncorrected until Worcester employed a "hardening on" firing process which obviated the blurring. The Bristol glaze, far thicker than either that of Limehouse or Worcester, militated against clarity of decoration. It also served to dilute the impact of the fine cursive rococo moulding in high relief, which was such a feature of sauceboats and creamboats, with their elegantly formed handles and curved thumbrests.

In a letter to his mother in November 1750, Dr. Richard Pococke described what he had seen during his visit to the Bristol factory. He divided the ceramics which he saw into two main categories, "One called stone-china - which has a yellow caste, both in the ware and the glazing, that I suppose is made of pipe clay and calcin'd flint". This was probably a stoneware or pottery rather than porcelain and has never been satisfactorily identified. Pococke's observations on the second category are far more pertinent:

"That called "old china that is whiter" and I suppose this is made of calcin'd flint and the soapy rock at Lizard Point, which 'tis known they use - this is painted blue and somewhat like old white china of a yellowish cast, another kind is white with a bluish cast and both called fine ornamental white china".[30]

These somewhat ambiguous comments suggest that Pococke saw both blue and white porcelain and "white", or undecorated ornamental wares. Yet it seems clear that he was drawing a distinction between two types of porcelain, apparently being produced simultaneously. The explanation for this apparent anomaly probably lies in the colour of the glaze. Three models of *Lu Tung-Pin* in the Victoria and Albert Museum, all marked *Bristoll* and dated *1750*, vary in their glaze tone from white, to cream, to a bluish colour. Similarly, in this Collection, some pieces have a very bluish glaze, nos. 5 and 6, whilst in other instances, the glaze is colourless, no. 11. There may have been an intention that the main underglaze blue production had a slightly bluish glaze, possibly in imitation of oriental porcelain, whereas undecorated pieces should appear as white as possible. Yet even if Richard Pococke was mistaken in his assumption of "two sorts of ware", it does seem likely that the factory did at some point alter their porcelain recipe. The pair of sauceboats, no. 5, differ from their counterparts, nos. 3 and 4, in being unmoulded, far more clearly painted and having a thinner, smoother and better controlled glaze, distinctly grey in tone. The superb spirally fluted bowl, no. 14, shares these characteristics. Both are more thinly potted than other Bristol wares and share a friable, brittle quality, as if more underfired than the mainstream production. One might speculate that this was an attempt to make more delicately potted wares, less heavily glazed, with a consequent improvement in the clarity and definition of the decoration. This "improvement" is palpable in a comparison between the single sauceboat, no. 3, and the unmoulded pair of the same shape, no. 5. The plain sauceboats are more cleanly modelled, both in their contours and in their curved handles and their decoration is entirely free of blurring. They are also less heavily glazed and lighter in weight. Indeed, this tiny group of wares, represented in the Collection by nos. 5 and 14, are conspicuously superior in both their potting and their painted decoration, to the earliest phase of underglaze blue decoration at Worcester in 1752-53. Thus it would seem that in the months prior to the "unification" with the nascent Worcester enterprise, there were significant improvements in the production at Bristol.

The translucency by artificial light of Lund's Bristol varies from a pale bluish green, sometimes with tiny specks of greater luminosity, to a greenish yellow or even straw colour. Even the most heavily potted hand-thrown pieces, such as large tankards, are fairly translucent, but moulded wares, far less so. Intriguingly, the unmoulded sauceboats, no. 5, are opaque to artificial light.

The porcelain body is compact and finely grained and the glaze has a tendency to pool in places, whilst in others, small areas are left almost free of glaze. Fire cracks occur occasionally, especially around handle terminals and mould lines. Glaze bubbling and areas of tiny black speckling are frequent and there is sometimes pitting in the glaze. However, Bristol was generally a very tough sturdy material, far more so than Limehouse. This attribute, allied to its generally thickly potted character, has lent it a literally enduring quality, familiar to collectors of this rare class of porcelain. An unusually high proportion of the small number of surviving pieces have remained in perfect condition, surely a testament of sorts, to the expertise of the Bristol potters.

A. J. Smith displayed a particular interest in Lund's Bristol, and endeavoured to purchase as many as possible of the pieces which he encountered. Yet from the little shell-shaped dish, no. 11, bought in Dawlish in 1962, until the tankard, no. 8, his final purchase in 1981, he was only able to acquire fourteen examples. Admittedly he excluded several duplicates during this twenty year span, but this affords an illuminating insight into the rarity of this small class of porcelain on the open market during the 1960s and 1970s. In this time, he nevertheless assembled what is currently the most extensive public collection of Lund's Bristol, representative of most aspects of the factory's production, including two *Bristol* marked pieces. It demonstrates the unified and coherent nature of the decorative idioms, the surprising variations in glaze tones and the range of shapes and decorative motifs which both echo the preceding Limehouse venture and foreshadow that of Worcester. Yet perhaps most of all, this short-lived production, abruptly curtailed by the unification with Worcester in 1752, should be perceived less as an entity in itself, than as an initial pioneering phase in the distinguished evolution of soapstone porcelain.

1. "BRISTOL" MARKED CREAMBOAT circa 1750

MARK: Embossed *Bristol*

LENGTH: 4¼ ins

A hexagonal form derived from a Limehouse model[31] which was issued in two sizes. The Lund's version occurs in two slight variations. Although the painting is far less blurred than on other examples in this collection, the thickly applied glaze has somewhat obscured the detail and definition of the moulded ornamentation. The central painted motif of a Chinese figure, holding a flower or fan, recurs frequently on Lund's porcelain and a little later, on both blue and white and polychrome Worcester.

Despite the thick glaze evident on the underside of the base, the embossed *Bristol* mark stands out clearly in relief. Not only is it more distinct, but the lettering is different to that on no. 2, indicating that it emanated from a different mould. A close examination of the glaze above the embossed mark shows the sanding in the glaze which is so characteristic of Lund's porcelain. So too are the indications of staining on the hexagonal footrim. Both imperfections occur infrequently on early Worcester. Unlike the initial decade at Worcester, when the majority of underglaze blue is accompanied by a painter's symbol, no. 19, no painter's marks were used at Bristol.

Illustrated: W J Pountney, *Old Bristol Potteries*, plate 18a
　　　　　　 Frank Hurlbutt, *Bristol Porcelain*, plate 10a

cf. Geoffrey Godden, *Eighteenth-Century English Porcelain*, colour plate VI, for a variation on this Lund's model.

PROVENANCE: *The F C Dykes Collection*
　　　　　　　 The C H B Caldwell Collection

71

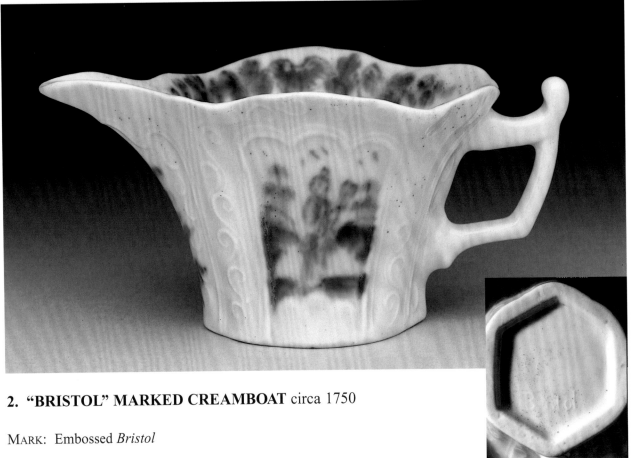

2. "BRISTOL" MARKED CREAMBOAT circa 1750

MARK: Embossed *Bristol*

LENGTH: 4½ ins

Judging from the pieces which have survived, it seems that after the small shell-shaped dishes, no.11, pickle leaves and sauceboats, creamboats were the next most common element in the output of Benjamin Lund's factory. They were issued in five basic shapes, four of which are recorded with the embossed *Bristol* mark, placed within the footrim, facing the handle. In addition to the two creamboats in this Collection, there is a fluted model on pad feet, recorded also in polychrome and "in the white", which seems invariably to bear the *Bristol* mark. A further model embossed with a moulded leaf under the lip, closely follows the shape, contours and handle form of a Limehouse original. A fifth shape has recently been recorded, also fluted and a little larger than the other four basic models.

This *Bristol* marked creamboat illustrates both the strengths and the deficiencies of the Lund's production during the brief lifetime of the factory. The shape is well-designed and practical and the moulded ornamentation in low relief is subtly suggestive of some distant silver precursor. Yet the underglaze blue has run in the glaze causing a lack of definition, and the heavy glaze has lessened the impact of the moulding. A comparison with the low moulded Worcester sauceboat, no. 32, demonstrates the crucial technical improvements achieved within a four year span. Yet this problem of loss of definition in the decoration varied considerably from piece to piece. The creamboat, no. 1, the small vase, no. 13, and especially the pair of unmoulded sauceboats, no. 5, display far less blurring.

Illustrated: R J Charleston, (ed) *English Porcelain 1745-1850*, plate 28A
Bernard Watney, *English Blue and White Porcelain of the 18th Century*, plate 21a

cf. Simon Spero, *Exhibition 2001,* cat. no. 44, for the fifth of the Lund's Bristol creamboat types.

PROVENANCE: *The H E Marshall Collection*

3. LUND'S BRISTOL SAUCEBOAT circa 1750

MARK: None
LENGTH: 8 ins

The larger of the two sizes of shallow moulded Bristol sauceboats, seven of which bear the embossed *Bristol* mark inside the footrim. It shares, with several other Lund's pieces in this Collection, such characteristic deficiencies of manufacture as the slightly unfocused landscape scene and the severe running of the underglaze blue border painting. Looking at this decoration, it is no wonder that moulded ornamentation was employed to lend definition by acting as a framework for the blurred vistas within. The moulding also served to disguise the mould lines under the lip of the sauceboat. Somewhat haphazardly, the moulding on the two sides of these sauceboats did not always correspond.

An interesting, if not entirely illuminating comparison, is with the pair of Lund's sauceboats, no.5. These lack the moulded cartouches, replacing them with a painted double line frame, enclosing decoration of remarkable clarity. This possibly underlines the supposition that moulded reserved panels and decoration in high relief was a deliberate device to compensate for the hazy and blurred nature of so much of the Bristol painting. Once these firing difficulties were brought under better control, the need for moulded panels as a *divertissement,* became less necessary. From this, it might logically follow that the unmoulded sauceboats are very slightly later in date than this moulded example. It is tempting to pursue this train of thought still further and speculate whether the greyer-toned glaze on the pair of sauceboats, no. 5, the spirally flared bowl, no. 14, and even the small pedestal sauceboat, no. 6, denote a slightly later class of Bristol wares.

cf. Geoffrey Godden, *Eighteenth-Century English Porcelain*, plates 43-46 for a similar sauceboat bearing the embossed *Bristol* mark within the footrim.

PROVENANCE: *The H E Marshall Collection*

4. LUND'S BRISTOL SAUCEBOAT circa 1750

MARK: None
LENGTH: 6 ins

A low moulded model issued at Bristol in two sizes. The shape was introduced at Worcester in colour, in about 1752-53 and two years or so later, in underglaze blue. Comparisons with the Worcester version, no. 32, are instructive. The Worcester moulding is sharper in outline, although not superior in detail or intricacy. The Worcester handle has the added ornamentation of bosses echoing those on silver, but the Lund's handle is more generous and has a more gracefully curved thumbrest. The Lund's decoration, displaying typical motifs such as the studded hilltops, Chinese junks and the recurrent formation of three dots, lacks the clarity, the definition and the thematic organisation of the Worcester decoration. The same hand may have also painted the teapot, no. 7, and the pedestal sauceboat, no. 6. The tendency to stain around cracks and unglazed areas is a characteristic of some Lund's and very early Worcester, no. 65, which by about 1753-54 had been almost entirely eradicated.

At least one Lund's sauceboat of this size and form bears the embossed mark *Bristol* within the footrim, close to the base of the handle. A small sherd from a sauceboat of this shape, also with the embossed Bristol mark, was recovered during excavations at the lowest level of the Worcester factory site.[32] It seems probable that this fragment was brought to Worcester after the purchase of the Bristol factory in February 1752.

One single Lund's Bristol sauceboat of this model and size with very similar moulding, in a private collection in London, is decorated in enamel colours. Whether this remarkable piece, formerly in the H E Marshall Collection, was decorated outside the factory or constitutes an instance of polychrome painting on Bristol, remains problematical.

cf. no. 32 for the corresponding model in Worcester, of three or four years later in period.

5. PAIR OF LUND'S BRISTOL SAUCEBOATS circa 1750-51

MARK: None

LENGTH: 7 ins

Although basically the same shape as the archetypal Lund's Bristol sauceboat, no. 3, a close examination of these sauceboats reveals more variations than similarities. The moulded cartouches have been replaced by a double line border and the ornamentation around the lip is also absent. The painted landscapes, whilst typical of the factory's idiomatic style, are more clearly defined and display little of the characteristic blurring or misty sense of focus. By comparison with the *Bristol* marked creamboats, nos. 1 and 2, and the two moulded sauceboats, nos. 3 and 4, they are more thinly potted and have a brittle quality, shared by the spirally flared bowl, no. 14. They also lack such characteristic Lund's firing blemishes as the bubbling of the glaze. Indeed, their glaze is remarkably smooth and less thickly applied. Yet above all, they are distinguished by a greyish caste to their glaze. Coincidentally, none of the pieces which share these atypical Lund's features bear the embossed *Bristol* mark.

Yet despite these intriguing disparities, all the characteristic Lund's Bristol decorative motifs are present, including the studded mountain peaks, the billowing junk and the triangles of dots, and there are clear similarities with the painting on the teapot, no. 7. Perhaps significantly, one unmoulded sauceboat of this greyish glaze class bears on its handle thumbrest, an incised letter B.

This short-lived Bristol production must surely have been to some degree experimental, insofar that a process of improvement was necessary to obviate glazing deficiencies and prevent the persistent blurring of the underglaze blue. The presence of two distinctly different classes of Lund's porcelain is echoed in a letter from Dr Richard Pococke to his mother, dated 2nd November 1750, giving an account of his visit to the factory.[33]

cf. the spirally flared bowl, no. 14 in this catalogue, which shares several potting and glazing features with these sauceboats.

PROVENANCE: *The H E Marshall Collection*

6. LUND'S BRISTOL PEDESTAL SAUCEBOAT circa 1750

MARK: None
LENGTH: 6½ ins

The smaller of the two sizes of "high footed" sauceboat made at Bristol. The shape was copied at Worcester, no. 88, in both colour and underglaze blue and issued in three sizes, approximately 6½ inches, 7½ inches and 9 inches. In this sauceboat are embodied both the strengths and the weaknesses of Lund's porcelain. The high footed shape suggested by, but not copying, a silver model, was a design which endured for nearly a decade. The detailed moulding is perhaps used in a more sophisticated manner than on its Limehouse precursors and the scroll handle is both decorative and highly practical. Yet on the other hand the underglaze blue, possibly too heavily applied, is blurred and the decoration seems consequently slightly out of focus. The blue has also 'run' in the firing, especially the decoration on the interior border which is indecipherable in parts. The rich bright cobalt blue differs appreciably from the grey-blue of Worcester, no. 27, and the potting is somewhat thicker. Recurrent motifs on Lund's porcelain include the studded mountain tops, tiny sailing boats and the ubiquitous triangular formations of dots. The Chinese emblems inside the lip foreshadow the idiom used with such success on early polychrome Worcester, no. 52. Unlike their Worcester counterparts, Lund's Bristol pedestal sauceboats never bear painter's marks.

cf. Simon Spero and John Sandon, *Worcester Porcelain, 1751-1790: The Zorensky Collection,* nos. 525 and 527 for two middle size Worcester sauceboats of this shape.

7. LUND'S BRISTOL TEAPOT circa 1750

MARK: None

HEIGHT: 3 ins

A plain globular teapot, much simpler in shape than either the Limehouse models which preceded it, or the subsequent Worcester examples. Of the four recorded surviving Lund's Bristol teapots, two are a plain globular form, one is a lobed shape resembling no. 35, and the fourth is a small octagonal model. The overall effect here is far more akin to contemporary Bow teapots which offered a straightforward and uncomplicated alternative to the Chinese export version.

Characteristic features of the decoration include the fern-like motifs on the spout and the Chinese junk in full sail. This idiom, seen also on the Lund's sauceboat, no. 4, became familiar on the series of interconnected Worcester patterns of the 1752-53 period. On coffee cans, coffee cups and mugs, it tended to be a secondary motif rather than an element of the principal pattern. On this teapot, the arrangement of the three dots which recur almost obsessively in Lund's decoration, have been realigned and incorporated into the pair of two-tier structures which flank the central Chinese junk. In this fresh guise, they represent rudimentary windows, doors and even chimneys. This almost child-like composition, literal yet naive in execution, contrasts with the more fluid, artful and sometimes abstract technique, expressed by a different hand on such pieces as the small vase, no.13, and more especially, the larger of the two cream pails, no. 10. The apparently artless method employed on this teapot may well be indicative of the work of a painter accustomed to working on tin-glazed earthenware, attempting to make the transition to, and adapt his technique for, the less porous surface of porcelain.

cf. no. 3, for a moulded sauceboat probably painted by the same hand.

ccf. Geoffrey Godden, *English Blue and White Porcelain,* plate 4, for the only other recorded Lund's Bristol plain globular teapot.

8. LUND'S BRISTOL TANKARD circa 1750

MARK: None
HEIGHT: 4½ ins

Lund's Bristol tankards, cylindrical in shape but with widely spreading bases, were issued in two sizes, measuring 4½ inches and 6⅖ inches. The massive larger size has an elaborate scroll handle applied with a thumbrest.[34] Five of these tankards are recorded, two in the larger size. Two are in private collections in London and two are in North America. All five are decorated in ambitious and complex landscapes, featuring mountain tops and extensive rocky outcrops. They share a confused sense of perspective which is somewhat subordinate to the individual details of the design. A sense prevails of a vividly realised landscape containing motifs which have been copied without being fully understood. Perspective has taken flight. For instance, the curving line of small boulder-like objects below the Chinese figure, represent stylised cliffs, derived from the river landscapes depicted on large oriental vases. The "comma" marks around the handle terminals are decorative features copied from Chinese porcelain which at other English factories were used to disguise firing flaws. At least two of these tankards seem to be direct copies of Chinese mugs inspired by English silver models and made for the export market. All share an accentuated spreading base derived from metalwork.

These five tankards are amongst the largest and most impressive surviving examples of Lund's Bristol, aside from the celebrated vases formerly in the Anthony Lyttleton (Lord Chandos) Collection.[35] In each instance, the painter has endeavoured to compensate for the characteristic blurring and lack of definition by emphasising areas shaded in a lighter tone of blue. This technique however conspicuously fails to lift the veil of impenetrability which pervades much of the decoration on these fine tankards.

Two further Lund's Bristol mugs are recorded, originally from the J W Jenkins Collection, their shapes derived from seventeenth century German stoneware. These too, are decorated with highly detailed, yet somewhat indecipherable Chinese landscape scenes.

cf. John Sandon, *The Dictionary of Worcester Porcelain Volume 1 1751 – 1851,* colour plates 15 and 16.

9 & 10. TWO LUND'S BRISTOL CREAM PAILS circa 1750

MARKS: No mark (left) and incised and P marks (right)
HEIGHTS: 2⅞ ins and 3¼ ins

An extremely rare shape in porcelain, freely adapted from a George II silver model of the 1740s. The silver originals were more flared in outline, often horizontally ribbed and had swing handles. They generally lacked the porcelain embellishment of pad feet. The shape is more commonly encountered in Georgian glass of the second half of the eighteenth century.

Although only six Lund's models are recorded, they display considerable variations in size, varying from 2¾ ins to 3⅗ ins in height. The moulding on the handles and the decorative motif surmounting the handles, also shows variations. Whilst all six examples share several decorative motifs, none are painted with exactly the same pattern. These discrepancies in both proportions and patterns suggest that whilst few of these cream pails have survived, they may originally have been produced in substantial numbers. The fragile handle would have been very vulnerable, and once broken, there would have been little reason to preserve it. At any event, six surviving examples are in perfect condition. However, only two, one of which is in the Fitzwilliam Museum in Cambridge, have retained its fragile ladle, an undecorated acorn shaped cup with twig handle.

This is one of a small number of Lund's models which was not subsequently adapted for use at Worcester. Others include a flared moulded bowl, no. 14, a small pot and cover, an unmoulded sugar box and cover, a pierced circular strainer and the large pair of baluster vases, formerly in the Anthony Lyttleton Collection. However, two other factories did produce cream pails in the 1750s, Chaffers' Liverpool and the "sprig'd" examples made at Bow. The latter are much plainer in form, lacking the associations with metalwork.

cf. Bernard Watney, *English Blue and White Porcelain of the 18th Century,* Plate 55A, for a Chaffers' Liverpool cream pail.

PROVENANCE: *The H E Marshall Collection* (left hand example)

11. LUND'S BRISTOL SHELL- SHAPED DISH circa 1750

MARK: None

HEIGHT: 3⅝ ins

Small shell-shaped pickle dishes, often moulded from scallop shells were among the earliest objects made in English porcelain. Press moulded, and relatively easy to make, replacing the real scallop shells previously used, they were staple products in the output of Limehouse, Lund's Bristol and Worcester. It seems likely that some rather poor quality examples, underfired and very crazed, were made experimentally at Worcester, prior to the purchase of Benjamin Lund's factory in February 1752. The Limehouse, Lund's and early Worcester examples were more thinly potted and more imaginatively decorated than the ". . . blue and white scallopt shells" imported from China in the 1740s, valued at one shilling each.

The diaper design on the borders of this example corresponds to moulded ornamentation on silver, but as with nearly all English blue and white porcelain of the 1750s, the painting is in the oriental taste. Here, the Long Eliza figure has a cartoon-like quality, as if swiftly sketched. A delftware painter, used to working on a more porous surface, might draw in this manner. This *Lange Lijzen* style, originating in China, was adapted by the Dutch for decoration on their delftware. In England, it was used in underglaze blue at Limehouse, Bristol and Worcester and became a component in the polychrome Worcester *indianische Blumen* style which evolved during the early 1750s. The rapidly drawn somewhat rudimentary and impressionistic representation on this little shell and on the Lund's tankard, no. 8, gradually mutated into the far more sophisticated and elongated figure seen on the Worcester bottle, no. 19, and the *Willow Root mug,* no. 17.

cf. Simon Spero, *Exhibition 2001,* cat. no. 45, for an experimental Worcester shell of exactly the same pattern.

12. LUND'S BRISTOL DEEP SHELL-SHAPED DISH circa 1750

MARK: None
HEIGHT: 5 ins
WIDTH: 4¾ ins

A rare shape, probably loosely adapted from a silver model of the middle 1740s, supported upon three dolphin feet. It is one of only three examples known, together with one smaller specimen. Two are in private collections in London. The model did not appear at Worcester until the early 1760s, in underglaze blue, in *The Bluebell Spray,* and several years later in *The Marrow* transfer-print. Polychrome decorated versions of this form were issued also in two sizes during the 1753-58 period. The shape was later copied at John Pennington's Liverpool factory.

The underglaze blue painting exhibits several characteristic features of Lund's Bristol, including the sinuous Long Eliza figure and the blurred, somewhat unfocused decoration beneath the thick glaze. The formations of three dots which recur frequently in Lund's porcelain were copied directly from motifs on imported Chinese wares. They represented groups of boulders, depicted in a progressively more stylised manner, so that the English imitators had no idea what they were copying.

The precise purpose of this deep shell-shaped dish is uncertain. It is sometimes suggested to be a receptacle for salt. Yet two features suggest otherwise. The relatively scarce polychrome examples almost invariably show signs of severe wear, indicating that the acids in pickles may have eroded areas of the overglaze decoration. Inspired by the fashion of Indian Chutney, pickling had become a convenient method for preserving the summer harvest during the winter months. Alongside pickled herring, oysters and even salmon, were a variety of vegetables, including marrow, mushrooms and walnuts, all of which were incorporated into a Worcester underglaze blue print, specifically designed for this shape of shell-dish.

cf. Simon Spero and John Sandon, *Worcester Porcelain, 1751-1790: The Zorensky Collection,* cat no. 637 for an example printed in underglaze blue with *The Marrow.*

ccf. Simon Spero, *Worcester Porcelain The Klepser collection,* no. 57 for a polychrome model.

13. LUND'S BRISTOL SMALL VASE circa 1750

MARK: None

HEIGHT: 3¼ ins

This small vase, the only recorded example of its type, is the precursor of the more elongated Worcester model introduced in about 1754.[36] The decorative idiom too, was slightly modified, yet utterly transformed in spirit, by its conversion into a series of polychrome designs, exemplified by the creamjug, no.106, and the lobed teapot, no. 82. Here may be the genesis of the *chinoiserie* style developed at Worcester in the early 1750s, far more subtle and far more effective in colour than in underglaze blue. As with so many designs on Lund's Bristol, it does not constitute a set pattern, although one cannot resist the impression of an emerging idiom. The design resembles that on the rather blurred deep shell-shaped dish, no. 12, yet the treatment of the lady, and especially her Micky Mouse-like coiffure, is strikingly similar to that on the Lund's tankard, no. 8.

The decoration here is far more well-defined than on the deep shell dish, no. 12, or the smaller cream pail, no. 9, and the reverse design of mountain tops and small boats is also clearly executed. Yet a characteristic firing blemish is evident in the glaze bubbling just above and below the tall willow tree behind the Chinese figure. Further indications of potting imperfections can be seen in the somewhat uneven base. Yet for all its naivety and technical frailties, this little vase anticipates a genre which defined both the innovative decorative idiom, which so distinguished Worcester during the early 1750s, and its consequent commercial prosperity.

The Lund's Bristol output, to a larger extent than any contemporary English factory, was confined to purely utilitarian wares. This small vase therefore represents an unusual excursion into decorative forms, foreshadowing a significant aspect of the Worcester production during the 1750s.

cf. The creamjug, no. 106 in this Collection, decorated with a seated lady, legs akimbo, her companion holding a parasol.

PROVENANCE: *The Dr and Mrs Statham Collection*

14. LUND'S BRISTOL SPIRALLY FLUTED BOWL circa 1750-51

MARK: None

HEIGHT: 2½ ins

DIAMETER: 6 ins

A remarkable press-moulded flared bowl which is perhaps the most sophisticated of all recorded Lund's Bristol shapes. The rhythmic spirally fluted contours, swirling upwards from its acanthus moulded base are clearly inspired by, and loosely adapted from, a silver model of the 1730s. One single polychrome example is known, from the Rissik Marshall Collection, now in the Ashmolean Museum in Oxford. This is almost certainly a Worcester piece rather than Lund's Bristol. No others have so far come to light.

It belongs to the small class of Lund's characterised by a greyish cast to the glaze, relatively thin potting and a slightly brittle appearance, more vulnerable to cracking. As with the pair of sauceboats, no.5, the underglaze blue is a darker, more purplish tone than on the mainstream wares. These discrepancies can be clearly discerned as improvements, especially in terms of the thinner potting, the eradication of the blurred decoration and the tendency for the blue to 'run' in the glaze. Here, the interior border is far more satisfactory than on the pedestal sauceboat, no. 6, or the low moulded sauceboat, no.3. This enhanced facility for controlling the underglaze blue resulted in a far more careful and deliberate appearance to the decoration, largely free of the blurred and misty effects which bedevilled so much of the output. Wares exhibiting this distinctly grey-toned glaze and the evident advances in potting and glazing techniques, constitute a small proportion of the surviving Lund's Bristol output, probably as little as ten percent.

cf. H Rissik Marshall, *Coloured Worcester Porcelain of the First Period*, colour plate 4, for a polychrome bowl of this model.

PROVENANCE: *The Dr and Mrs Statham Collection*

NOTES

Chapter 4   Lund's Bristol

1. Angerstein, (2001).
2. Watney, (1973), p.32.
3. Godden, (2004), pp.119-120.
4. Spero, *Exhibition Catalogue* (2003), no.45.
5. Godden, (2004), Colour plate 30.
6. Barrett, (1966), plate 3B.
7. Spero, *Exhibition Catalogue* (1997), no.16.
8. Godden (2004), Colour plate 28 (left).
9. Spero, *Exhibition Catalogue* (1984), Colour plate 8 (no.20).
10. Spero, *Exhibition Catalogue* (2001), no.44.
11. Spero, *Exhibition Catalogue* (1995), no.17.
12. Spero, *Exhibition Catalogue* (1989), no.24.
13. Watney (1973), plate 22A.
14. Spero, *Exhibition Catalogue* (1995), no. 156, pp.149-150.
15. Watney, (1973), plate 22B.
16. Bonham's Auction Catalogue, (2003), Lot 89.
17. English Ceramic Circle, (1993), p.74.
18. Branyan, *et al.,* (1989), p.40.
19. Godden, (2004), Colour plate 28 and plates 130 and 131.
20. Sandon, J (1993), Colour plate 83.
21. Sandon, J (1993), Colour plate 11.
22. Watney, (1973), plate 21C.
23. "Miscellany of Pieces", *ECC Transactions*, Vol. 15, part 3, 1995, p.394.
24. Phillips' Auction Catalogue (11 September 1991), Lot 528.
25. Sotheby's Auction Catalogue (27 April 1976), Lot 144.
26. Spero *Exhibition Catalogue* (1989), no.23.
27. Barrett, (1966), plate 3B.
28. Spero *Exhibition Catalogue* (1989), p.180.
29. Branyan, *et al*, (1989), p.43.
30. Watney, (1973), p.32.
31. Godden, (2004), plate 86, for a comparable Limehouse model.
32. Sandon, J (1993), p.83.
33. Godden, (2004), p.113.
34. Watney, (1973), plate 22A.
35. English Ceramic Circle, (1993), plate 93, illustrated as Limehouse.
36. Spero and Sandon, J (1996), no.486.

BLUE AND WHITE WORCESTER

From the outset, the Worcester Tonquin Manufacture was a venture with aspirations far beyond those of Benjamin Lund at Bristol. The factory came into existence on the 4th of June 1751, when an agreement was drawn up bearing the names of the fifteen original partners comprising prominent local figures, businessmen and merchants. Together they subscribed a total of £4,500 in order to finance the new enterprise, a substantial sum at that time. Three weeks or so prior to this Deed of Partnership, on the 16th May 1751, a 21 year lease on the Warmstry House premises had been granted to Richard Holdship and this was to be the location for the new factory. It is clear from these positive developments that a substantial enterprise was being envisaged and that Dr. John Wall and William Davis, the principal instigators, had gained the full confidence of the other investors.

The "Articles for carrying on the Worcester Tonquin Manufacture", as drawn up on 4th of June 1751, commenced by stating that:

"Whereas a new Manufacture of Earthen Ware has been Invented by JOHN WALL of the City of Worcester Doctor of Physic and WILLIAM DAVIS of the same Apothecary under the denomination of Worcester Porcellain : - "

This wording suggests that not only had John Wall and William Davis succeeded in making porcelain of some kind, but in all probability they had used these experimental wares as evidence in convincing their potential backers what might be achieved in the future.

Within the limitations of their experience and the materials and technology available, it is likely that these 'trial' pieces, dating from 1751, were low-fired, almost certainly blue and white and probably closely imitating porcelain shapes readily at hand. A small surviving class of wares conforms to this proposed criteria, comprising some small shell-shaped dishes,[1] moulded and amongst the simplest of all ceramic forms to create. These, together with some shallow unmoulded sauceboats,[2] constitute the recorded shapes of this tiny class. Both directly mirror contemporary Lund's Bristol models, nos. 5 and 11, not only in shape, but also in their decorative idiom. Yet by comparison with their Bristol counterparts, they display understandable technical deficiencies. They are less vitrified, suggesting that they were fired at a temperature too low for the body and glaze to mature together. This has created a network of light crazing throughout the entire glaze, an uncharacteristic feature on either Bristol or early Worcester pieces. Low firing is common to both experimental wares and those in the earliest phase of production, such as Lowestoft for example. Yet to an untrained eye, such as those of the potential investors, these experimental pieces may have appeared in no way inferior to comparable Bristol. Furthermore, the decoration, especially on the small outline sketched shell-shaped dishes, is almost uncannily similar to that on Bristol. According to their earliest biographer, Wall and Davis created the first Worcester porcelain in the fireplace of Davis' apothecary shop in Broad Street, using an iron pot around which fire was heaped.[3] These few surviving low-fired wares may be the fruits of the Broad Street experiments. This remains conjecture. Yet one must surely accept that the claim that Wall and Davis had invented "a new Manufacture of Earthen Ware . . .",[4] had sufficient substance to impress the other thirteen potential investors. However, it seems a little doubtful whether these friable-looking imitations of Bristol would in themselves have provided the necessary grounds to convince the interested parties that porcelain could be made at Worcester on a significant enough commercial scale to justify their investment and indeed, the ambitious plans for Warmstry House.

This begs the question as to what incentive Wall and Davis could offer their backers, aside from this narrow range of experimental pieces. They were certainly aware of Benjamin Lund's activities in

Bristol, the nature and details of his production and most crucially, his possession of a soapstone formula. This might be the key to the success of their enterprise. It is conceivable that at the time of the partnership agreement in June 1751, negotiations had already begun with Lund for the purchase of his factory and the transfer of the entire stock and utensils from Bristol to Worcester. If this was so, the fifteen partners in the new company not only had the promise of the soapstone formula itself, but also the possibility of the presence of Benjamin Lund and several of his workmen. Whether or not there was a foreknowledge of the impending "unification" with Lund's factory, it seems likely that further attempts to produce porcelain were made during the eight month period between the partnership agreement in June 1751 and the eventual purchase of the Bristol factory in February 1752.

Sherds excavated in 1979, from the very lowest levels of occupation on the Warmestry House site, revealed about thirty fragments of plates and dishes, somewhat underfired and decorated in underglaze blue.[5] Some were probably from a failed firing but there was evidence to suggest that others of this type may have been successfully produced and offered for sale. As might have been anticipated from this period, these sherds did not contain soaprock.[6] The only recorded piece*` which may correspond to the sherds and to this short-lived experimental production, prior to the unification with Bristol and the possession of the soapstone formula, is an extraordinary plate, now in a North American Collection.[7] It is painted in underglaze blue with such naivety as to suggest an inexperienced hand unused to painting on porcelain. The painting is tentative, with streaky washes and blobs of blue and the various elements of the decoration are unrelated, as if on a 'trial' plate. The improvised decorative idiom includes such motifs as the junks with billowing sails, studded mountaintops and embryonic clusters of three dots, all motifs familiar from contemporary Lund's Bristol but painted with far less skill.

A globular teapot, no. 15, in this Collection has since its purchase in 1974, presented an intriguing conundrum as to its attribution and precise date. The rudimentary pattern is painted in a distinctively purplish tone of underglaze blue and exactly repeated on the reverse. The porcelain appears *not* to be a soapstone body and the glaze is well-controlled and free of crazing, although it does exhibit firing blemishes. The pattern itself appears on both Bow[8] and Worcester[9] of the early 1750s. The teapot has been variously ascribed to Limehouse and Lund's Bristol, though without much conviction. The decoration is far inferior to that of either factory and certainly displays no similarities to that of Limehouse. A comparison with the Bristol teapot, no. 7, shows a less well-designed shape, a thicker and more lumpy handle and far less well-defined decoration. The decoration is darker in tone, painted with less confidence and with a less accomplished technique. There is an experimental, tentative appearance to the decoration, as if the painter was only beginning to learn his craft. As on the 'trial' plate, he may have had a background in the delftware industry and not yet adapted his technique from that of the more porous pottery surface to that of porcelain. This tantalising piece which has so successfully eluded attribution shares many similarities with the 'trial' plate, with its primitive rendering of a sailing junk, wispy fern-like trees near the handle, its triangular formation of blobs and the artless treatment of a cliff, blocking in areas with a solid wash of underglaze blue, devoid of detail.* A recently discovered glazed shard from the factory site, probably from a bowl or tankard of about 1751-52, displays the wispy fronds which exactly match those on the teapot, adjacent to its handle. Yet for all its lack of accomplishment, this teapot betrays an awareness of decorative motifs on Bristol, whilst conveying something of the challenge confronting a delftware painter modifying his technique to the differing demands of porcelain decoration. This distinction might be compared to that between blotting paper and ordinary writing paper.

*See page 122

No 20 (detail)

Brushstrokes on delftware were required to be firm, confident and unhesitating as the paint was swiftly absorbed into the porous surface. On porcelain, a more impermeable surface, a deliberate and calculated method was preferable. The inept and naive treatment of the sailing junk, the child-like depiction of the tree and the vestigial house surmounting the cliff, all testify to the painter's inexperience at working on porcelain. Yet these motifs were all to be developed and incorporated into the early landscape scenes. The almost unrecognisable sailing junk derived from Bristol, no. 8, evolved into the more sea-worthy vessel on the sauceboat, no. 32, whilst the artless depiction of a tree developed through that on the bell-shaped mug, no. 16, to the more sophisticated representation on the large vase, no. 20. The rudimentary hut above the cliff underwent a series of developments from its tentative extension on the mug, no. 16, to an eventual architectural elegance on the octagonal teapot, no. 29. This lidless teapot thus represents the starting point in the evolution of underglaze blue landscape decoration, which had its roots in the long tin-glazed earthenware tradition stretching back into the seventeenth century, but which was by now in decline. The porcelain industry, which had not existed in England until the middle 1740s, was the chief beneficiary of this shift in consumer taste brought about by the mass importation of Chinese porcelain. Within ten years, a workforce of many hundreds of painters was employed in the emerging porcelain industry, many of whom had learned their craft as delftware painters.

Once the purchase of Benjamin Lund's factory had been accomplished, in July 1752, and with it the possession of the soapstone formula, production commenced immediately. Indeed, *The Gentleman's Magazine* for August 1752 stated that "the sale of this manufacture will begin at the Worcester Music Meeting on 20 September 1752". We can be reasonably sure of the accuracy of this statement as Edward Cave, the proprietor of the magazine was one of the original subscribers to the new company and consequently eager to promote its activities and progress.

The purpose of the venture, retrospectively disclosed several years later, was as "a porcelain manufactory in imitation of Dresden ware". This implies an emphasis on polychrome wares and as is explained in Chapters 6 and 7, alluded to a highly innovative approach to both shapes and decoration. The Bristol factory which had been concerned predominantly with underglaze blue decoration, was described in the same document as a "porcelain manufactory in imitation of Indian China Ware", meaning Chinese porcelain. The apparent objective in uniting the two factories was to produce both kinds of ware. Yet whereas it is evident that the polychrome output was assiduously devised so as to create the maximum impact as a novelty production, entirely fresh to the public, no such inventive procedure seems to have been envisaged specifically for the blue and white wares. However, it is possible that the range of new shapes devised for the polychrome wares was originally intended to include the underglaze blue production too. A handful of surviving blue and white pieces testify to this, corresponding in form to the twelve-sided teabowl, no. 64,[10] the plain creamjug, no. 66,[11] the quatrefoil lobed cup, no. 89,[12] and the octagonal coffee cup, no. 56.[13] In each instance, only one or two such examples are known, all far inferior to their polychrome counterparts. This was partly because underglaze blue decoration was less suited to these elegant shapes and partly because the decorative idioms would have appeared humdrum and repetitive in monochrome, alongside the vibrant palette and allusive themes in polychrome. Furthermore, the standard of underglaze blue painting was far less technically accomplished than that in polychrome, executed over the glaze. Blurring remained a problem, as did the definition of outlines. Even the more successful pieces, such as the bell-shaped mug, no. 16, compares unfavourably when matched with its sparkling polychrome counterpart, no. 72. Understandably in these circumstances, this underglaze blue production was swiftly abandoned, to be replaced by a restricted series of hand-thrown shapes, chiefly comprising coffee cups, coffee cans and mugs, most of which still exhibited technical deficiencies in their decoration. These hand-thrown shapes were generally not representative of those made at Bristol and it was not until two years or so later that the output of blue and white

No 27 (detail)

Worcester began to echo that of the earlier factory. Thus, it seems likely that for much of 1753, Worcester concentrated chiefly on their more innovative and artistically sophisticated polychrome wares, whilst endeavouring to eradicate the technical faults in their underglaze blue production.[14] This was achieved largely through a "hardening-on" process, whereby after painting, the porcelain was fired again at a lower temperature, fusing the cobalt into the biscuit body.

The improvement in painting and firing techniques led to a rapid expansion in production, so that by about 1753-54, standards of potting and decoration were comparable to those of Chinese porcelain, a pivotal benchmark. The first group of wares to display the benefits from these technical and artistic advances were hand-thrown and turned pieces such as bowls, beakers, mugs and coffee cans, decorated with motifs such as tall "Long Eliza" figures, triangular fences, rockwork, mountain tops and sailing junks. These elements were often assembled almost at random, coalescing for the first time into a conventional pattern in *The Willow Root*, nos. 17 and 18. This versatile composition, mirroring a contemporary polychrome style, no. 82, was the forerunner of a long series of evocative Worcester hand painted oriental landscape designs, stretching into the late 1760s. These first loosely organised rhythmical compositions, wreathing freely around circular forms such as teapots, mugs and bowls, were readily adapted to the flatter surfaces of saucers, plates and dishes, nos. 21-23. Gradually, these supple oriental compositions became condensed into more orderly systematic patterns, often executed with great care and subtlety, nos. 27 and 28. The idiom was also scaled down for use in the reserved panels of moulded sauceboats, creamboats and tewares, nos. 29-33. These moulded shapes, some echoing Bristol models, had been in production since 1752-53, (Chapters 6 - 9), but it was not until two years or so later that they were considered suited to underglaze blue decoration. Thus, such archetypal early Worcester models as hexagonal teapots, no. 29, hexagonal creamboats, two-handled sauceboats, no. 33, and low shallow sauceboats, no. 32, are invariably two years or so later in period than their corresponding polychrome counterparts, nos. 70, 93 and 109. As the tone of underglaze blue was altered from a rich intense tone, no. 18, to a greyer shade, no. 27, and painting techniques allowed for greater detail and definition, a decorative idiom was developed which could be successfully marketed alongside the comparable polychrome production. Ironically, this new range of underglaze blue patterns on moulded shapes endured for longer than the corresponding polychrome style.

Whilst the potting of tankards, plates, large jugs and potting pots was robust, often loosly echoing the contours of earlier silver models, bowls, teawares and moulded creamboats were thinly potted, without losing any of their characteristic durability, no. 26. No factory mark was used at Worcester until about 1760. Instead, a series of painter's or workman's symbols appear on blue and white wares, most often placed either within the footrim or else under a handle, no. 19. The significance and purpose of these marks is unknown, but they may have been "tally" marks devised to identify a team or bench of painters working together, with variations of related clusters of symbols referring to each group. For a brief period in about 1754-56, many hand-thrown and turned pieces were marked with a single cross or stroke, incised into the porcelain body prior to firing, no. 103. This mark occurs principally within the footrim, most often placed under a handle. It is associated with a range of pieces with a greyish-toned glaze, usually painted in the Chinese style, and appears on tankards, potting pots, beer jugs, coffee cans, teawares and many other shapes of the period, though not on press-moulded items. As with the painted symbols, its significance remains obscure.[15]

From about 1754, the production of blue and white widened both in scope and volume. Most crucially among the fresh range of shapes introduced, were tea services. These had been previously available only in Chinese porcelain and in Bow and comprised a highly profitable aspect of the market - and it was an aspect at which Worcester excelled. Their tea services were far more expertly potted than those of Bow, more durable and more imaginatively and skilfully painted. Perhaps more surprisingly, teapots, creamjugs, coffee pots and spoontrays were also far superior to the Chinese importations in the thinness of their potting and the sophistication and variety of their decorative idioms. The soapstone recipe was of particular benefit in the production of teawares. In this respect, the ability of the porcelain body to withstand the thermal impact of hot liquids was a decisive factor. Teabowls and saucers, elegantly potted and highly translucent, surpassed all their English competitors of the middle and later 1750s and astonishingly, bore comparison with their Chinese counterparts.

London was still the focus of the porcelain market and was to remain so throughout the century. As the port of entry for Chinese importations and the location for three major factories, Chelsea, Bow and Vauxhall, it was the most important centre for distribution in the retail trade. It was also both the social and economic hub of England, at the forefront of all appreciation of changing fashions and tastes. Prices for luxury commodities such as porcelain, were higher than in the provinces, and the Worcester partners considered a commercial presence in London to be essential. In March 1754, the factory opened a shop termed "The Worcester Porcelain Warehouse" and in the same month announced a sale to include "ABOUT 40,000 Pieces of China Ware. . .".[16] A wholesale price list from about 1755-56, concerned chiefly with blue and white wares,[17] conveys a detailed picture of what porcelain was produced at this period. It also offers an illuminating insight into the low survival rate of such purely functional forms as "Wash hand Basons", only one of which is known, and the somewhat enigmatic "Decanters", which may correspond to no. 19, a great rarity of which only a handful are recorded. Less surprisingly not a single "Chamber pot" from this early period has survived the ravages of time. Yet perhaps more significant, are the striking omissions from this detailed price card. There is no mention of either plates or dishes, both of which had been issued two years or so earlier, nos. 21-23, nor were the optional components of a tea service listed: sugar boxes, spoontrays or saucer dishes. Production of plates and dishes was probably abandoned in the face of superior Chinese examples, less expensive and more consistently well potted. Bow also made a speciality of flatware and these two mass market enterprises dominated this key sphere to the effective exclusion of all competition. The price list also confirms that it was not until a little later in the decade that the "full" tea service was available, a commodity which became a feature of the Worcester production, contributing significantly to the factory's prosperity, especially during the 1760s and 1770s.

As the production widened during the later 1750s with an expanding output, so the workforce of painters increased. Patterns became more simplified and for the first time the monopoly of oriental idioms was challenged. The emerging European style, derived from Meissen, had more impact on the polychrome style than on the oriental themes which remained predominant in underglaze blue throughout the 1760s. The new idiom was almost entirely confined to European shapes, especially those associated with Meissen: dessert wares, leaf shaped dishes, openwork baskets, no. 40, and moulded cider jugs, all models which had exact counterparts in colour. The rare beaker vase, no. 41, also has a polychrome counterpart in both shape and pattern and is strongly related in style to the baluster vase, no. 145, a component of a corresponding garniture set.

In the four years or so since the Deed of Partnership in 1751, the Worcester factory had become widely recognised alongside Bow, as one of the two principle porcelain factories in competition with Chinese importations. Underglaze blue decoration had developed an imaginative and innovative style, unmatched by either Chinese wares or any English competitor. Standards of both hand throwing and press moulding were superior to all other factories and Worcester had gained a pre-eminence in the crucial market for porcelain for the tea table. Elegant shapes, often suggestive of metalwork, such as teapots, creamjugs, tankards, large jugs, sauceboats, creamboats and even coffee cups, had a refinement of design, a finesse and an attention to detail which readily justified prices at a higher level than those of either Chinese importations or other English factories. The path to commercial prosperity was formulated.

15. TEAPOT circa 1750-52

MARK: None

LENGTH: 4½ ins

A plain globular teapot with a slightly curved spout and thickly potted handle, painted in a rudimentary oriental landscape, in a distinctive purplish tone of underglaze blue. The potting, the tone of blue, the firing blemishes around the footrim and especially the highly primitive nature of the decoration suggest that this is a very early example from its factory, almost experimental in its decorative technique.

The tentative painting technique, creating an almost indecipherable pattern indicates a very inexperienced hand, perhaps more accustomed to decorating the more porous surface of tin-glazed earthenware. This speculative technique is reminiscent of that on wasters excavated on the lowest levels of the factory site at Warmstry House. There are also similarities with the painting on a unique "trial" plate, now in a private collection in California. This plate, corresponding to early factory wasters, is decorated with a series of randomly placed motifs, including sailing junks, small islands, wispy pine trees and triangular formations of large dots. All are painted in an awkward, unpractised manner which reveal several similarities with this teapot.*

Both pieces offer an insight into the initial difficulties experienced by the Worcester painters, struggling to master the unaccustomed technique of painting on porcelain in underglaze blue. Perhaps the primitive tree evolved into that on the bell-shaped mug, no. 16, and the embryonic hut perched on the cliff, into the house on the island. The triangle of blob-like dots adjoining the spout echo the familiar motifs on Lund's Bristol, nos. 4 and 8, and the unseaworthy junk below them eventually developed into a delightful fishing boat no. 28.

cf. John Sandon, *The Dictionary of Worcester Porcelain Volume I 1751-1851*, colour plate 1 and plate 1.

*See page 122

16. BELL SHAPED MUG circa 1752-53

MARK: Painter's in the form of a cross

HEIGHT: 3¾ ins

The only recorded example of a pattern which has been designated *The Primitive Bridge*. Although it contains elements which recur on other early Worcester landscapes, the decoration has a confused, somewhat random appearance, suggesting that it may not be a set pattern. This feature is characteristic of the earliest phase of underglaze blue decoration at Worcester. The treatment of the tufted tree to the right of the distant house resembles the idiosyncratic depictions of those on the Lund's mug, no. 8, whilst the comma marks around the handle have parallels in Chinese porcelain. The potting accords to the high standard of throwing and turning but the painting is poorly defined. A comparison with the superb mug from the Lady Corah Collection, no.72, is instructive. It affords a revealing insight into the remarkable disparity in accomplishment at this early stage of production, between the delicacy and refinement attained in overglaze decoration, and the evident difficulties in underglaze blue experienced in two mugs, identical in shape and period. This dichotomy accounts for the frequency with which potting shapes were issued in polychrome, a year or so prior to their appearance in underglaze blue. From this it follows, that for at least a year, in about 1752-53, the majority of Worcester decoration was overglaze. Once the technical problems of controlling the blue under the glaze had been overcome and the china painters had become more experienced, this proportion was reversed.

This early baluster shape was adapted from a silver model of the 1740s and issued in two sizes. It remained in production for only two years or so. The silver influence is evident in the thumbrest, the pronounced scroll at the base of the handle and the folded foot.

Illustrated: Branyan, French and John Sandon, *Worcester Blue and White Porcelain 1751-1790,* ID.1A

cf. no. 72 in this Collection for a mug of identical date and shape, painted in polychrome.

17. BELL- SHAPED MUG circa 1753

MARK: Painter's and incised line

HEIGHT: 3¾ ins

The Willow Root was probably the earliest of the established Worcester landscape patterns in underglaze blue. Elements such as the Long Eliza figure, the twin peaks divided by a ragged flagstaff and the highly stylised cliffs below the triangular fence, echo motifs on Lund's Bristol. A most unusual feature is that the arrangement of hollow rocks, the gnarled willow tree and the fretwork fence, are all loosely replicated in colour on a coffee cup in this collection, no. 112. The painting of this pattern, invariably vivid and somewhat liquid in its appearance, displays considerable variations according to the proportions of the shapes upon which it occurs. For instance, on cylindrical coffee cans, due to limitations of height and space, the Long Eliza figure is sometimes replaced by a tiny figure in a sampan.[18] The pattern was issued on a range of thrown and turned shapes including cylindrical and bell-shaped mugs, in two sizes, coffee cans, bowls in several sizes and tall flared conical beakers with handles.[19] No tea wares in this pattern are recorded, except one single teabowl.

Although closely resembling *The Primitive Bridge* mug, no. 16, in its contours, folded foot and overall shape, this mug varies in the treatment of its handle. It has no thumbrest, a less accentuated lower handle terminal and its inner surface is deliberately flattened.

A retail invoice dated May 1753, listed "3 Pint Worcester muggs at 0 7s 6d". This was expensive by comparison with contemporary Chinese and Bow porcelain, especially for a product which compared unfavourably with its polychrome counterpart, no. 72. A temporary concentration on the artistically and technically more accomplished overglaze decoration at this time, was a commercially logical response. Hence, the brief period in 1752-53 when the bulk of the production was in polychrome.

cf. Simon Spero and John Sandon, *Worcester Porcelain, 1751-1790: The Zorensky Collection*, no. 517, for a conical flared beaker and a coffee can in this pattern.

PROVENANCE: *The Dr and Mrs Statham Collection*

18. CYLINDRICAL MUG circa 1753

MARK: Incised cross and painter's

HEIGHT: 3¾ ins

By comparison with the bell-shaped *Willow Root* mug, no.17, the treatment of the landscape is far clearer and more organised as if the painter had become a little more experienced. The arrangement of the willow tree growing from the hollow rocks has become simplified and is far more effective in its use of space. The shape, with its flared base and generous strap handle, was adapted from a silver model which first emerged in the 1680s. The flared base had disappeared by the 1760s as this classic Worcester shape developed through three decades.

There are clear parallels with the Lund's Bristol tankard of about three years earlier, no. 8. Elements in common include the Long Eliza figure, the twin peaks, the stylised cliffs and the tree emerging from hollow rocks. Yet the underglaze blue is far better controlled and the landscape has a sense of clarity and spaciousness, enabling the painter to convey greater detail. The contrast between the heavy blue of the hollow rocks and the airy cross hatching of the stylised willow tree is especially effective. Thus, these three mugs in the Collection, nos. 8, 16, and 18, illustrate a progression and an evolution in the early stages of underglaze blue landscape decoration. Alongside this gradual mastery of underglaze blue painting were improvements in throwing, turning, glazing and design. The awkward looking handle on the Lund's Bristol tankard, no. 8, evolved into a graceful strap form, elegantly grooved to facilitate the task in hand. According to the price card of the factory's London Warehouse, Worcester mugs of this size cost 2 guineas per dozen which seems excellent value by comparison with the contemporary "Nankeen mugs at £1, 4 shillings for 3". However, the London Warehouse price card was for wholesale prices. A retail invoice for May 1753 noted "3 Pint Worcester muggs 0 7s 6d".

Parallels between polychrome and underglaze blue painting on early Worcester are relatively scarce. Yet the tall figure on this mug may be gainfully compared with that on the polychrome pedestal sauceboat, no. 88. So too, might the treatment of the stylised triangular bushes, resembling distant men o' war.

cf. Branyan, French and John Sandon, *Worcester Blue and White Porcelain 1751-1790,* IA3.

No 19 (reverse)

Detail of underside of base

19. BOTTLE circa 1753-54

MARK: Painter's
HEIGHT: 10 ins

This graceful form often onomatopoeically termed a "guglet", possibly corresponds to the factory price list of about 1755-56, describing "Decanters pint. Quart and 3 pint…21/- 30/-. 42/-", although only two sizes are recorded from this period. A more likely purpose is that of a bottle to match with the "Wash Hand Bason" referred to in the same price list. Seven bottles of this type are recorded, together with a single basin. This pattern, designated as *The Lange Lijzen,* is closely related to both *The Writhing Rock*, no. 21, and *The Willow Root*, no. 17. The detailed elements of this complex pattern, specifically devised for this shape, display considerable variations, yet the standard of painting is invariably most accomplished. The shape was issued in three further main patterns: *The Crescent Moon, The Willow Bridge Fisherman* and *The Pine Cone.* Over a production period of about eighteen years, the shape altered in outline considerably, the rim becoming progressively less flared and by the middle 1760s, evolving into a simple trumpet shape. At the same time, the graceful contours evident in this bottle gradually lost much of their linear subtlety. As with so many utilitarian Worcester potting shapes, the majority of bottles are in underglaze blue.

From 1753 until about 1760, the majority of blue and white Worcester bears a painter's or workman's mark. These take the form of pseudo Chinese symbols and occur in great variety. Their purpose may either have been as tally marks in order to identify the work of a single painter or a group of painters, or else as some form of factory code.

Illustrated: Bernard Watney, *English Blue and White Porcelain of the 18th Century,* fig. 27c

cf. Franklin A Barrett, *Worcester Porcelain,* fig. 27A for a polychrome bottle and basin.

ccf. p. 96 for the reverse.

PROVENANCE: *The C W Jenkins Collection*

No 20 (alternative view)

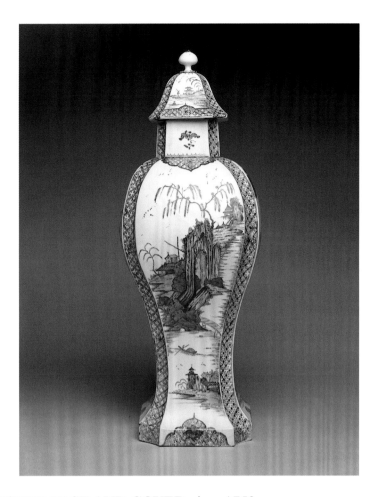

20. LARGE BALUSTER VASE AND COVER circa 1753

MARK: Cross in underglaze blue

HEIGHT: 22½ ins

An apparently unique Worcester vase of massive proportions. The shape was issued in colour at this same early date, though in smaller sizes. It was presumably conceived as part of a mantelpiece garniture with matching flared beaker-shaped vases, though none of the latter have so far been recorded. The shapes are unique to Worcester in English porcelain. The enormous difficulties which the factory experienced in firing so large a piece are manifest in the extensive areas remaining free of glaze due to firing deficiencies. Yet the vase represents an extraordinary achievement insofar that it is relatively free from potting distortions and displays its detailed riverscape with admirably clear definition. Neither the designs, nor their treatment, except in the broadest sense, have parallels in other Worcester decoration, but the free, expansive style allowed by the breadth of canvas, evokes the landscapes on large delftware vases. Indeed, at this early period, it is likely that the more proficient underglaze blue painters had a background in the delftware industry, which by the 1750s, was beginning a process of decline. The Brislington and Lime-kiln potteries had closed in the 1740s, releasing a skilled workforce onto the market and coinciding with a rapid expansion of the porcelain industry, from the late 1740s onwards.

The shape itself accurately mirrors a Chinese model, apart from modifications to the cover and knop. These would have been issued in garniture sets of either five or seven.

cf. J L Dixon, *English Porcelain of the 18th century,* fig 69, for a polychrome vase of this form and period.

PROVENANCE: *The H Rissik Marshall Collection*
The Hon Anthony Lyttleton Collection

21. PLATE circa 1753

MARKS: Pseudo Chinese characters within a double circle

DIAMETER: 9 ins

The Writhing Rock is one of four patterns recorded on early Worcester plates of this type, all of which occur on this shape only. It is closely related to *The Lange Lijzen*, a more expansive design associated with early guglets or bottles, no. 19. Fragments of plates were recovered from the very lowest levels of excavations on the factory site and two finished plates of differing shapes are recorded from this experimental period of manufacture (circa 1751). Both display serious firing blemishes. The small number of blue and white Worcester plates from the 1750s (with two exceptions) all conform to the basic shape of this example, usually with wide flanges and double lines around the well. Their shape and diaper border design links them to the Bristol delft plates from earlier in the century, produced in huge quantities. A polychrome counterpart from the same period is no. 75 in this Collection. The underglaze blue plates of this type usually bear the three Chinese characters, *Cheng Hua* marks within a double circle. Somewhat surprisingly, these are copied accurately, although they relate to different periods.

In 1755, *The Prince George* sailed from Canton with a cargo which included 80,000 pieces of Chinese porcelain, most of which was blue and white. This consignment included 10,236 single plates. This vessel was one of seven East India Company ships to sail from Canton in 1755, all carrying porcelain amongst their cargo. Faced by competition of these proportions, it is no wonder that the Worcester wholesale price list for about 1755-56 shows no evidence of the production of plates.

cf. Branyan, French and John Sandon, *Blue and White Worcester Porcelain 1751-1790,* pp. 45, 65, 149 and 150, for the four recorded patterns on plates of this type.

PROVENANCE: *The J W Jenkins Collection*

22. PLATE circa 1753

MARKS: Pseudo Chinese characters within a double line border
DIAMETER: 9 ins

The Zig Zag Fence Bird shares many elements of the more familiar *Zig Zag Fence* pattern and seems to be an exact copy of a Chinese *Kangxi* original. The idiom depicting fences meandering at angles to one another, recurs frequently on Chinese porcelain. Fences were invariably painted in this manner as evil spirits were thought to travel only in straight lines.

Whilst it is true that Worcester had some difficulties in firing plates and dishes during the 1750s, an examination of the well-potted and aesthetically pleasing examples in this Collection, nos. 21 and 22, suggests that the problems had been largely overcome by about 1753-54. Yet judging from the few surviving examples and from the absence of plates mentioned in the wholesale price list of about 1755-56, this staple product for a porcelain factory, was largely avoided. The reasons for this omission were almost certainly commercial rather than practical. The still-active delftware industry and the Bow factory both made a speciality of plates, inferior to the best Worcester examples but also less expensive. Delft plates generally cost about 6d each at this period, depending upon quality. Yet more significantly, it was the mass market production of imported Chinese plates that constrained the Worcester output. The Chinese plates were well potted, durable, attractively decorated and cost 9d or 10d each, a price which Worcester found impossible to match. A further factor was that plates take up more space in a kiln than might have been cost effective for a relatively small factory, adept at the manufacture of small scale material.

cf. John Sandon, *The Dictionary of Worcester Porcelain Volume I 1751-1851,* plate 1 for a trial plate apparently corresponding to wasters from the earliest levels excavated at the Worcester factory site.

23. RECTANGULAR DISH, circa 1754

MARK: Painter's mark
WIDTH: 10⅞ ins

The Two-level Fence and Rock pattern was confined to large punch pots[20] and rectangular dishes. The design incorporates components which are related to other Worcester patterns of the middle 1750s, including *The Prunus Fence* and *The Zig-Zag Fence*. The large scale of this press moulded dish has enabled the painter to express himself in a loose relaxed style, reminiscent of delftware. The slightly primitive treatment of the three large peonies and the rambling outer border decoration are a reminder of the early period of this rare dish. The octagonal shape itself, as with so much of the production of the middle 1750s, was issued in three sizes, of which this is the middle size. It occurs only in this pattern. A similar shape was made in Chinese export porcelain and in tin-glazed earthenware.

Unlike the Bow factory which made a speciality of plates and dishes in direct competition with Chinese importations, Worcester did not develop a large-scale production of flatware until the late 1760s. Prior to that time, firing difficulties were experienced and plates and dishes tended to warp and become distorted. Furthermore, larger pieces naturally took up more space in the kiln than the coffee cans, pickle trays, mugs, creamboats and teawares which characterised the output of the early and middle 1750s, which were smaller and therefore more cost effective. No polychrome counterpart is recorded.

cf. Anton Gabszewicz, *Made at New Canton,* no. 8 for comparable decoration on an early Bow plate.

24. COFFEE CAN circa 1753-54

MARK: Incised cross mark

HEIGHT: 2¼ ins

An intriguing pattern, *The Floral Swag, Ribbon and Scroll,* is recorded only on "scratch cross" coffee cups and coffee cans, suggesting that they may not be components of an orthodox tea service. Examples are known with two entirely different lower border designs, while others have none.[21] The treatment of the pattern itself varies widely. Whilst this decoration is somewhat blurred, in other instances the blue is pale and subtly defined. A technique is evident here, known as "trekking", designed to assist the more inexperienced hand. A darker tone of cobalt blue outline is employed in order to prevent the underglaze blue from running. This occurs only on early pieces, prior to the introduction of the hardening-on firing process.

The lower border design is painted in a primitive almost childlike manner, giving rise to speculation that it might be by a delftware painter, unaccustomed to working on a less porous porcelain surface. The pattern itself, comprising ribbons and garlands, lies outside the conventional idiom for blue and white Worcester of the 1750s. Idiosyncratically, it faintly echoes the moulded garlands and ribbons on Lund's Bristol and early Worcester pedestal sauceboats, nos. 43 and 44.

Coffee cans with flared bases were issued without saucers and may have been intended either for children or as small-sized mugs, possibly for beer. They are among the earliest Worcester shapes in underglaze blue, uncharacteristically pre-dating the rarer polychrome versions of the shape.

cf. Simon Spero and John Sandon, *Worcester Porcelain 1751—1790 The Zorensky Collection,* no. 524, for a coffee cup painted in a pale tone of underglaze blue, with a variation of this distinctive pattern.

25. WINE FUNNEL circa 1754-56

MARK: None
HEIGHT: 4 ins
DIAMETER: 3⅝ ins

One of the rarest of all utilitarian forms in early English porcelain, made only at Worcester. Their function rendered them very susceptible to damage and only about twenty or so examples are known to have survived. Of the six underglaze blue wine funnels, four are transfer-printed with floral sprays and date from the late 1760s. A further specimen is painted with a bird design and the present example, with a meandering spray of flowers and leaves. Both in its tone of underglaze blue and in the loose treatment of the floral spray, the painting is reminiscent of that on contemporary "scratch cross" tankards. Modelled after a George I silver funnel, this shape is hand thrown and consequently displays wide variations in diameter, the later versions being distinctly larger. This rare form was in production from about 1754 to 1756 and then briefly reintroduced in the late 1760s, coinciding with an expansion of the Worcester output of domestic wares. No other example of this pattern is recorded.

On the Continent, wine was almost invariably diluted with water. French wine was heavily taxed and its high cost and unpatriotic associations led to an increase in the consumption of port, rather than claret.

cf. Simon Spero and John Sandon, *Worcester Porcelain, 1751-1790: The Zorensky Collection,* no. 34 for a polychrome wine funnel and no. 651 for a later blue and white example.

ccf. no. 110 in this Collection.

26. TEABOWL AND SAUCER circa 1755

MARKS: Painter's and incised marks

DIAMETER OF SAUCER: 4½ ins

The Cormorant is one of the earliest set teaware patterns to come into production at Worcester. It was also used on tankards of various sizes and shapes, coffee cans, potting pans and finger bowls and stands. The pattern was subject to numerous variations depending upon the scale and shape of the object. Almost invariably, pieces are marked with incised lines or crosses, together with a painter's mark. Most examples date from about 1754-56. Curiously, finger bowls and stands are always of slightly later date, about 1756-58, evident from the style of their decoration and the absence of incised marks. Glost wasters of this pattern were found on the factory site during excavations.

Worcester teabowls and saucers of this period and type were unique in early English porcelain, in being as thinly and elegantly potted as the finest Chinese importations. Being also painted with more individuality and flair than their somewhat repetitive oriental counterparts, they were an excellent commercial commodity even at their higher retail price. In January 1757, Robert Carpenter, the factory's Bristol agent, was advertising for sale in his shop in Temple Street; "Good Blue and White Tea Cups and Saucers at 3s 6d per Sett", a wholesale price.[22] The slightly flared rim to this teabowl, echoed on the edge of the saucer, is a typical feature of the superb standards of turning and throwing at the factory during the middle 1750s.

cf. Branyan, French and John Sandon, *Worcester Blue & White Porcelain 1751-1790,* I.B.28 for slightly differing treatment of the pattern on two finger bowl stands.

ccf. Anton Gabszewicz, *Made at New Canton,* no. 9 for a Bow teabowl and a saucer of approximately the same period.

27. LARGE PATTY PAN circa 1754-55

MARK: Painter's and incised marks
DIAMETER: 8¾ ins

The four known examples of this large-scale early Worcester patty pan display the *chinoiserie* river landscape genre to superb effect. A fifth patty pan is decorated in a previously unrecorded Chinese figure landscape. Most often confined within the reserved panels of sauceboats, creamboats and tearwares, the idiom has been liberated onto an expansive canvas and presented in a pale, well-defined tone of underglaze blue. By comparison with the smaller version of *The Patty Pan Angler*, no. 28, there is little specific additional detail except for the outer panelled diaper border. Yet the painter has seized the opportunity to depict a more fluid and serene landscape, expanding such elements as the branches of the willow tree and the two fishing boats, to delightful effect. Made in two slightly differing shapes, this corresponds to the larger size of "Tart Pan", itemised in the factory's wholesale price list of about 1755-56, selling at 8/- (40p) per dozen.

Patty pans were a significant element in the underglaze blue production of most early English porcelain factories, including Bow, Lowestoft, Caughley, Isleworth, Christian's Liverpool, Champions Bristol and in delftware, though intriguingly, not Longton Hall or Derby. The Worcester examples of the 1750s tended to be more ambitiously decorated than their contemporary English and imported Chinese counterparts.

Tarts, both savoury and sweet, were popular during the eighteenth century, sweet spinach tart being a particular delicacy. They were served during the second course at dinner. Some patty pans show signs that they have been used in an oven, suggesting that they may sometimes have served the same purpose as a potted meat dish. Indeed, Hannah Glasse, the celebrated contemporary cookery writer, recommended filling china tart pans or saucers with preserved fruit or meat, covered with a thin puff-pastry and cooked in a warm oven.

28. PATTY PAN circa 1754-55

MARK: Painter's mark
DIAMETER: 5½ ins

A delightful *chinoiserie* landscape, *The Patty Pan Angler,* is invariably painted with the greatest delicacy in a fairly pale tone of underglaze blue. It occurs only on the earliest forms of Worcester patty pan which correspond to the wholesale price list of about 1755-56, referring to "Tart pans 1st, 2nd, 3rd [at] 4/-, 6/-, 8/- per dozen". This type continued in production for only two years or so, judging from the few which have survived. It was replaced, first by a more thickly potted example painted in the equally scarce pattern *The Club Rock Patty Pan,*[23] and later by the standard shape decorated in *The Bare Tree and Speared Bird* pattern. By the early 1760s patty pans were becoming more plentiful, painted in such designs as *The Prunus Root* and *The Mansfield* patterns. The shape continued in production into the early 1770s. As at most other factories, no polychrome examples are recorded. At this period Chinese patty pans were being imported in their thousands. Sturdy and functional, yet far plainer than the early Worcester models, they cost just under one shilling each, by comparison to the Worcester wholesale price of approximately half.

Tarts were popular components of the second course at dinner, served as side dishes. The smallest size of "Tart pan" was probably an individual portion. Professional cooks vied with one another to produce intricate designs for the crust of puff-pastry which covered the tarts. These were purely for decoration and not eaten.

cf. Branyan, French and John Sandon, *Worcester Blue and White Porcelain 1751-1790,* I.B.37 and I.B.38 for two further patty pans with landscapes.

29. OCTAGONAL TEAPOT AND COVER circa 1754-55

MARK: TF monogram on base

HEIGHT: 5 ins

Octagonal Worcester teapots in underglaze blue, issued in two slightly differing moulded shapes, are both rarer and slightly later in date than their polychrome counterparts. *The Captive Bird* pattern occurs also on press-moulded teapots and hexagonal creamboats and was specifically suited to fit within reserved panels. Both the straight spout and the generous loop handle are echoed on other contemporary Worcester teapots, no. 35 but the origins of the overall shape are more problematical. Although octagonal teapots were made in silver during the 1720s and in Chinese porcelain during approximately the same period, this Worcester shape is somewhat more reminiscent of Staffordshire saltglaze and redwares. Octagonal lead-glazed red earthenware slip cast teapots, made by Samuel Bell at Newcastle Under Lyme in Staffordshire, in about 1740-44, have large reserved panels containing moulded ornamentation of motifs such as birds and Chinese figures. As with so many Worcester shapes and patterns of the early and middle 1750s, it is an amalgam of several disparate influences, coalescing into one innovative form.

In terms of early English porcelain, this octagonal shape follows the Limehouse tradition of the middle 1740s,[24] though with the crucial embellishment of moulded ornamentation. The Worcester octagonal version was exactly twice the wholesale price of a plain globular teapot, yet no more expensive than the exactly contemporary Bow "sprig'd upright tea-pot"[25] mentioned in Bowcock's Notebook of 1756.[26] Four years later, in 1760, the retail price for a Chinese blue and white teapot, at 2 shillings, was slightly less.

cf. Henry Sandon, *Coffeepots* and *Teapots,* plate 11 for a Chinese precursor and plate 15 for an octagonal panelled Staffordshire saltglaze teapot.

PROVENANCE: *The Rev Sharp Collection*
The C W Jenkins Collection

30. MOULDED CREAMBOAT circa 1754

MARK: Painter's mark in interior

LENGTH: 5 ins

A creamboat associated with the name *Wigornia*, the latin word for the City of Worcester. One polychrome example, painted in a palette reminiscent of saltglaze, bears the embossed word *Wigornia* on its base, within the footrim.[27] This celebrated creamboat, now in the Museum of Worcester Porcelain, has given its name to a range of models, all with the same distinctive scroll handle, but varying in their moulded ornamentation. At least nine separate *chinoiserie* landscapes moulded in low relief have been identified by Dr Paul Riley. He has categorised this design as Moulding G and notes that it is the only such example so far recorded.[28] In all instances, it seems that each creamboat is moulded with a separate design on each side. Underglaze blue examples are most often left free of decoration, as here, with an interior floral border painted in blue. More rarely, the landscape is outlined in blue, no.31. The inspiration for a moulded landscape scene is likely to have come from either Staffordshire redware or saltglaze stoneware. It serves to underline the influence, experience and expertise of the Staffordshire potters who contributed so much to the individuality of the Worcester style in the early and middle 1750s, especially through the medium of moulded decoration.

cf. Henry Sandon, *Worcester Porcelain,* fig. 5 for the same moulding, together with a similar unglazed waster from the factory site, illustrating the depth and detail of the design.

31. MOULDED CREAMBOAT circa 1754

MARK: Painter's mark
LENGTH: 4½ ins

Whereas creamboats of this type are sometimes decorated with the *chinoiserie* landscape fully embellished in vivid "saltglaze" colours, this extremely rare version outlines details of the moulded scene, creating an utterly different and far more subtle effect. Even so, the detail and delicacy of the moulded landscape and the sense of depth evident in no. 30, is hardly accentuated by the addition of painted decoration. Yet unlike Chelsea and Bow in their early years, Worcester were reluctant to leave their domestic forms 'in the white', possibly because no sculptural tradition existed as at most other contemporary factories. This class of creamboat, with its exuberant scroll handle, spanned a brief period from about 1753 to 1755, although at least one Lund's Bristol example is recorded.[29]

Research into the moulded patterns of this class of creamboat has been carried out by Dr Paul Riley. He has identified nine different moulded designs of which this specimen is catagorised as Moulding B.[30] Only two examples of this mould are known, one in colour and this present creamboat. One other blue and white example is recorded with moulded ornamentation outlined in underglaze blue.[31] All "Wigornia" type moulded designs are illustrated and described by Dr Paul Riley, *English Ceramic Circle Transactions* Volume 13 Part 3, 1989, page 166.

cf. Simon Spero, *Worcester Porcelain The Klepser Collection,* no. 21, colour plate 8, for a polychrome version of this model.

ccf. Simon Spero, *Exhibition* 1995, no. 17, for a Lund's Bristol model, "in the white".

PROVENANCE: *The Dr Maurice Harper Collection, Bath*

32. MOULDED SAUCEBOAT circa 1755-56

MARK: Painter's mark
LENGTH: 6 ins

A low moulded form of sauceboat dating from the middle 1750s and echoing an archetypal Lund's Bristol model. It probably corresponds to the "Pannel'd Boats 1st and 2nd at 9/- and 10/- per dozen" in the London warehouse price list of about 1755-56. However, unlike the Lund's Bristol examples, nos. 3 and 4, the Worcester version is only known in one size. By comparison with its Lund's Bristol counterpart, no. 4, the moulding is far more detailed and sharper and the tone of underglaze blue is greyer and more clearly defined. The handle is less generous in size, although more thickly formed and has a far less pronounced thumbrest. Unlike the contemporary two-handled sauceboats, no.33, both the moulded ornamentation and the Chinese landscapes within the panels display great variations. The Worcester version of this model is invariably painted with an interior landscape of great detail, whereas the interior decoration on the Lund's Bristol sauceboats is perfunctory. This particularly finely moulded example illustrates a version of *The Boatman* pattern, the eponymous crew of which is active on a whole range of related river landscapes including *The Patty Pan Angler*, no. 27 and *The Captive Bird*, no. 29.

In terms of the detail, definition and complexity of their moulded ornamentation, Worcester sauceboats were not only far superior to their Chinese, Bow or delftware counterparts, but also to their smaller contemporary competitors, such as Longton Hall, Lowestoft and the Liverpool factories. Only at Vauxhall were sauceboats sometimes produced which were stylistically and technically as accomplished as corresponding Worcester examples.

cf. no. 4 for an earlier Lund's Bristol model of this size.

33. TWO-HANDLED SAUCEBOAT circa 1755-56

MARK: Painter's mark

LENGTH: 7½ ins

Issued in three sizes, of which this is the middle, two-handled sauceboats span a brief period from about 1754-58 and were also produced in colour, no. 147, and with overglaze transfer-prints.[32] Corresponding to the "Two Handle Boats 1st 2nd 3rd . . . 24/-, 30/-, 40/-", they were among the most expensive items on the factory's London Warehouse wholesale price list of 1755-56. Yet although at 2/6 each (12.5 pence) they were significantly more expensive than their contemporary Chinese export counterparts, they were infinitely superior in their potting, painted decoration and moulding.[33] Indeed, their overall appearance had a sophistication of design which must have made the Chinese sauceboats seem very plain, even humdrum by comparison. The superb clarity, detail and definition of the moulding, was far in advance of anything which was produced in Chinese export wares or indeed at Bow.

The interior decoration on these sauceboats displays very little variation, almost all examples being painted in the same *chinoiserie* landscape, now designated *The Two-Handled Sauceboat Landscape.* By contrast, the decoration within the exterior panels displays substantial variation.

cf. Anton Gabszewicz, *Bow Porcelain,* no. 68, for a pair of Bow sauceboats far closer in design to their Chinese counterparts.

34. CONICAL TEAPOT circa 1755-57

MARKS: Incised and Painters. Incised numeral 2 under cover.
DIAMETER: 7¾ ins

The only recorded example of this curious model, resembling a watering can and conceivably derived from Chinese porcelain. Perhaps more plausibly it is either an amplification of a Staffordshire saltglaze model, somewhat exaggerated in its contours or else an adaptation of a late red anchor period Chelsea model. The rustic triple twig finial and the straight spout emphasise the oriental influence. It is painted in *The Prunus Fence*, the pattern being repeated on the reverse.

   The diversity and variety of Worcester teapot shapes available to the public during the initial five years of production was matched by no other factory, nor by imported Chinese wares. More than a dozen separate shapes were made during this brief period, including: three types of octagonal, two panelled, lobed, ribbed, faceted, fluted, plain globular, and even a fluid rococo form on four scroll feet (Zorensky Collection no. 7). This determination to offer the public as wide a choice of shapes as possible was mirrored by both the variety of patterns and decorative themes available and the innovative manner in which entirely fresh idioms were created, often for use on specific shapes. No other contemporary factory based its commercial strategy so explicitly upon variety and novelty, and these two commercial imperatives defined Worcester's success in competing with the mass importation of Chinese porcelain during the 1750s.

Illustrated: *Bernard Watney, English Blue and White Porcelain of the Eighteenth Century,* plate 28c

PROVENANCE: *The H E Marshall Collection*

35. LOBED TEAPOT AND COVER circa 1755-56

MARK: Painter's mark
HEIGHT: 5½ ins

This lobed form, loosely adapted from a silver model, was introduced at Worcester in polychrome, no. 82, in 1752-53. The underglaze blue version was not issued until about 1754, occurring in *The Prunus Root* and in a more complex embossed design with wide floral panels containing *chinoiserie* landscapes, including *The Indian Fisherman* pattern. The model is characterised by a generous loop handle, a rather straight spout and a turned mushroom finial with a flattened top. Whereas the earlier polychrome version was issued in two sizes, the underglaze blue teapots seem only to occur in one size. The models span a brief period from about 1752-53 until about 1755-56, being replaced by a faceted shape. One single Lund's Bristol example of this shape is recorded in an American Collection.

As with octagonal and moulded teapots, these Worcester models offered the public a novel shape, often evocative of silver, which was seldom if ever, available in either Bow or Chinese porcelain. Unlike their contemporary Chelsea, Bow, Derby and Longton Hall counterparts, Worcester teapots had the crucial advantage of being resistant to the thermal impact of hot liquid and therefore did not suffer damage during the process of making tea.

cf nos. 82 and 83 for polychrome versions of this model.

ccf. Anton Gabszewicz *Made at New Canton* no. 14 for a Bow teaport of approximately similar period.

36. CYLINDRICAL MUG circa 1755-56

MARKS: Incised and Painter's marks
HEIGHT: 3ins

A delightful form probably derived from English silver and in production for no more than two years or so. The unusual grooved and ridged base occurs in two versions and the handle too, is grooved. The ridged base probably derives from the early Fulham saltglazed models, although it also occurs on late seventeenth century Chinese importations. A further unusual feature is the underside of the base, which is unglazed, a most uncharacteristic trait on Worcester. This model is recorded in four underglaze blue patterns, *The Warbler, The High Island, The Cormorant* and *The Prunus Root*. Two polychrome examples are known, one formerly in the Bernard Watney Collection, both decorated in a version of *The Banded Hedge* pattern.

The Prunus Root, perhaps the most versatile of all early Worcester designs, varies considerably in its interpretation. Here the roots, beset by tiny dots, are far more tangled and the painting more rudimentary than on other examples of the pattern, nos. 35 and 37.

cf. Simon Spero and John Sandon, *Worcester Porcelain, 1751-1790: The Zorensky Collection, n*o. 555 for the same model decorated in *The Warbler* pattern.

37. HEXAGONAL TEAPOT STAND circa 1756-58

MARK: Painter's mark
DIAMETER: 5¾ ins

A classic Worcester form originating in Chinese export porcelain[34] and introduced at the factory in about 1755-56. During the 1750s the shape was sparingly used in underglaze blue, being limited to a handful of patterns which included *The Prunus Root, The Warbler* and *The Landslip*. It was not until the early 1770s that teapot stands became more common in underglaze blue. The later examples are deeper and have more steeply angled sides.[35] All examples have unglazed bases. Teapot stands were components of "full" tea services, alongside spoontrays, sugar pots, tea canisters, milkjugs and covers, and saucerdishes. Production of these "full" tea services was restricted until the early 1760s, unaccountably coinciding with the abrupt expansion of overglaze transfer printing on Worcester tewares.[36]

cf. Simon Spero and John Sandon, *Worcester Porcelain, 1751-1790: The Zorensky Collection,* no.50, for a polychrome example of the model.

38. OCTAGONAL TEABOWL AND SAUCER circa 1756-58

MARK: Painter's marks
DIAMETER OF SAUCER: 4½ ins

The Prunus Root was the most common Worcester underglaze blue pattern of the 1750s and occurs on the most extensive range of shapes. In production from about 1755 until the early 1770s, the basic design remained unchanged, yet its chameleon quality tended to alter its appearance, depending upon the tone of underglaze blue and the manner in which the pattern was entwined around the contours of the object. Teawares in this popular pattern were issued in octagonal, fluted, indented and plain forms and one rare version was deployed in an overglaze iron red monochrome.[37]

Octagonal teabowls and saucers in underglaze blue were issued in four patterns: *The Prunus Root, The Romantic Rocks, The Mansfield* and *The Plantation Print*, in almost all instances dating from the 1750s. However, unlike their contemporary polychrome counterparts, no teapots or coffee cups were made to match with the teabowls and saucers in underglaze blue. In all instances, the blue and white examples post-date polychrome octagonal teawares.

cf. no. 115.

39. CONICAL BOWL circa 1756-58

MARK: Painter's mark
DIAMETER: 4¼ ins

The precise function of this distinctive shape is unknown and it does not appear in the factory's London warehouse wholesale price list from about 1755-56. Unlike the majority of underglaze blue forms from this period, it is Chinese in origin. Dating from about 1756-58, these conical bowls vary only marginally in shape and are invariably decorated in *The Prunus Root* pattern. This is one of only two Worcester designs which extend into the interior of such shapes as bowls and coffee cans and spread onto the underside of saucers, the other being *The Dragon* pattern. This loose, abstract structure lends the design a versatility and enables it to flow naturally around any shape, adapting itself to the contours as necessary. This sense of fluidity undoubtedly contributed to the pattern's enduring popularity. Introduced at Worcester in about 1755, it remained in production into the early 1770s and was also issued at Bow, Longton Hall, Lowestoft and William Reid's Liverpool factory. It is likely that the pattern was used at Isleworth but as yet, no sherds have come to light.

cf. Simon Spero, *Exhibition Catalogue 2005,* cat no.36, for an exactly contemporary interpretation of this pattern on a Longton Hall creamjug.

40. CIRCULAR BASKET circa 1758-60

MARK: Arrow and annulet mark
DIAMETER: 4⅝ ins

A small openwork basket slightly earlier in date and smaller in size than the conventional Worcester baskets of this class. It has a painter's mark rather than a crescent and although the floral decoration is very much in the style of the two other patterns associated with these baskets (see: Branyan, French and J Sandon, IE24 and IE24A), it displays distinct variations and lacks the decoration around the openwork sides. These baskets range in date from about 1758 to 1765 and seem to have been issued in three sizes. The design is invariably of an anemone spray painted with particular care and attention to detail. Openwork baskets, circular and oval, were a speciality of the Worcester factory, both in colour and underglaze blue. Yet unlike Chelsea, Bow and Derby, widespread production did not get underway until the late 1750s. This apparent anomaly was due to the factory's preoccupation with oriental themes. Openwork baskets, essentially European in origin, were most often decorated either with flowers or birds, or else in the case of Derby, with stylised Chinese scenes in the manner of Meissen.

cf. Branyan, French and John Sandon, *Worcester Blue and White Porcelain 1751-1790,* pp.250 and 251 for the principal two floral designs associated with Worcester baskets of this type.

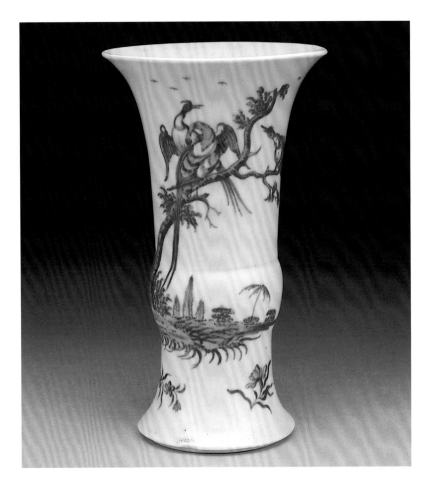

41. BEAKER VASE circa 1756-58

MARK: Painter's I.H. monogram

HEIGHT: 5⅜ ins

Underglaze blue designs painted in the European taste incorporating birds are generally confined to the late 1750s and occur on shapes associated with Meissen. These include tureens, mugs, teapots and especially vases. *The Mobbing Birds* was specifically devised for use on garniture sets of five vases, comprising two of baluster shape with covers, two of flared beaker shape, and a single, more substantial, wide baluster model with a high domed cover. The larger central vase was painted with an augmented arrangement which included a long-eared owl. Both variations were issued in colour on vases of the same shapes, no. 145, and the decoration is sometimes associated with the painter James Rogers. No firm evidence exists for this attribution. The patterns were derived from drawings by C Fenn, some of which were published as prints in the drawing book, *The Ladies Amusement.*

Although this flared beaker shape imitates a Meissen model, it originated in the ancient Chinese bronze *tsun*, recurring in transitional Ming porcelain of the late seventeenth century. However its antecedent harks back to the *Han* dynasty of about 200 BC, made in both bronze and pottery. The shape remained in production at Worcester into the early 1770s, becoming progressively more flared in its contours.

Illustrated: Bernard Watney, *English Blue and White Porcelain of the 18th Century*, plate 31B

cf. Branyan, French and John Sandon, *Worcester Blue and White Porcelain 1751-1790,* IC26 and IC27 for the other vase shapes comprising the garniture set.

PROVENANCE: *The J W Jenkins Collection*

42. LARGE BALUSTER VASE AND COVER circa 1758-60

MARKS: Painter's and Crescent marks
HEIGHT: 21½ ins

Together with the earlier vase of this shape, no. 20, this is almost certainly the largest model issued at Worcester during the first three decades of production. Unusually, it bears both a painter's and a crescent mark, each repeated on the cover. This massive and very ambitious form was in production during about 1752-53, most examples being decorated in colour and having slightly less imposing proportions. The shape was briefly reissued in the late 1750s, alongside the introduction of the celebrated octagonal and hexagonal press-moulded vases. Yet unlike the classic Worcester shape - echoing Meissen and originating in Japanese *kakiemon* porcelain - which endured for some twelve years, this larger and more ambitious baluster form continued to pose problems in manufacture and examples are consequently exceedingly rare. They may have also been intended for garnitures with their hexagonal counterparts. Both the two recorded surviving examples are decorated with *The Fancybird in a Tree,* the standard underglaze blue design on hexagonal vases.

cf. Simon Spero and John Sandon, *Worcester Porcelain, 1751-1790: The Zorensky Collection,* no. 567, for a pair of hexagonal vases in the same pattern, together with another large baluster vase.

NOTES

Chapter 5   Blue and white Worcester

1.   Spero, *Exhibition Catalogue* (2001), no.45.
2.   Spero, *Exhibition Catalogue* (1996), no.36.
3.   Sandon, J (1993), p.11.
4.   Sandon, J (1993), p.11.
5.   Sandon, J (1993), p.13.
6.   Sandon, J (1993), p.13.
7.   Sandon, J (1993), plate 1.
8.   Adams and Redstone, (1981), plate 24.
9.   Spero, *Exhibition Catalogue* (1991), no.37.
10.   Phillips Auction Catalogue, (22 September 1999), Lot 143.
11.   Spero, *Exhibition Catalogue* (1998), no.34.
12.   Watney, (1973), plate 23A.
13.   Spero, *Exhibition Catalogue* (1999), no.32.
14.   Branyan *et al.*, (1989), p.92 for a coffee cup inscribed *TB 1753*.
15.   Cole, (1995).
16.   Sandon, J (1993), p.18.
17.   Sandon, J (1993), p.223.
18.   Spero, *Exhibition Catalogue* (2004), no.32.
19.   Spero and Sandon, J (1996), no.517.
20.   Branyan *et al.*, (1989), p.206.
21.   Branyan *et al.*, (1989), p.285.
22.   Rod Dowling, private communication.
23.   Branyan *et al.*, (1989), p.136.
24.   Godden (2004), Colour plate 15.
25.   Adams and Redstone, (1981), plate 39.
26.   Adams and Redstone, (1981), p.210.
27.   J. Sandon (1993), p.364.
28.   Riley, (1989), plate 137.
29.   Spero, *Exhibition Catalogue* (1995), no.17.
30.   Riley, (1989), plate 131.
31.   Riley, (1989), plate 140.
32.   Handley, (1991), pp.20,46 and 47.
33.   Poole, (2002), p.160, *May 14th 1753 "4 Bow China Sauce Boats 0-10-"*.
34.   Godden, (2004), plate 3.
35.   Spero and Sandon, J (1996), no.639.
36.   Spero and Sandon, J (1996), no.371.
37.   Spero and Sandon, J (1996), no.129.

*A further plate with a sharply cursive rim, corresponds in outline to an undecorated sherd excavated at the lowest level of the factory site. This plate, not previously recorded, is strongly reminiscent in both shape and decoration, to a delftware precursor. The decoration is of small figures apparently engaged in the martial arts, within a broad diaper border design. These sherds are illustrated by John Sandon in *The Dictionary of Worcester Porcelain*, colour plate 1. A slightly later version of this rare pattern is illustrated on a plain circular plate from the *Godden Reference Collection*, by Branyan, French and John Sandon, *Worcester Blue and White Porcelain 1751-1790*, I.A.19, a pattern designated *The Children at Play.*

CHAPTER 6   THE *INDIANISCHE BLUMEN* DECORATION

The decorative idiom devised at Worcester in 1752, at the outset of their production of polychrome wares, was unlike anything seen on English ceramics up until that time. Certainly, it was very different from decoration on any contemporary English porcelain.

At this period the porcelain industry, in existence for only eight or so years, was almost entirely concentrated in London, at Chelsea, Bow and at the by now defunct Limehouse factory. Furthermore, London was also the exclusive port of entry for the Chinese porcelain imported by the East India Company, some of which was decorated in the City. London was ten times larger than the next biggest English city, Norwich, and thus represented a commercial and cultural pre-eminence far greater than today. It was the social and economic hub of England; a distribution point for produce from all over the country in what was essentially a market economy. From a ceramic standpoint, it was most crucially, a nursing ground for small new industries, especially those concerned with luxury trades.[1] Porcelain was in 1752, still perceived as a luxury and London was the magnet for many of those with the taste and resources to purchase such commodities. In these circumstances, the establishment of a porcelain factory outside London presented a leap into the unknown. Where would the market lie? What should be the focus of the production? And most importantly, what manner of decoration would appeal to an essentially provincial consumer, unacquainted with the prevailing tastes and fashions of distant London society?

The porcelain factories which were founded in England during the 1740s and 1750s lacked the royal and aristocratic patronage which defined their French, German, Austrian and Italian counterparts. As a consequence, the necessity for commercial survival led to their products being directed at a broad span of consumers rather than exclusively to a more narrow and discerning elite. Thus the character and individuality of early English porcelain was defined by its lack of patronage and the freedom which this allowed to the porcelain entrepreneurs. Up to a dozen of these ceramic enterprises foundered during the 1740s and 1750s buffeted aside by the economic hazards and uncertainties of the new industry. Aristocratic patronage would probably have ensured the survival of a favoured handful but any purely commercial competition would have been squeezed aside. Thus, two or three factories would have prospered, their output directed towards the wealthy classes, but the range and diversity of early English porcelain would have been sacrificed to this end. The choice and variety available to a broad range of consumers would surely have been deferred until the late eighteenth century or beyond. So too would the versatility of the early factories, adapting their styles, decorative idioms and potting forms to the constantly changing demands and tastes of a fickle public. The requirements of the middle class consumer had no place in the porcelain productions of mid-eighteenth century continental Europe, yet the newly established English factories, although commercial enterprises, were fully aware of the nature of the evolution of the porcelain industry abroad. This perception led to the creation in most of the early enterprises of a two tier production, directed in part towards the luxury nature of the porcelain industry, exemplified by decoration and shapes in the fashionable Meissen and Chinese tastes, and in part to competition with the more commercial Chinese importations. The rise of a broad middle class of consumers, hardly existing in this proportion elsewhere in Europe, facilitated this ambitious endeavour.

The Chelsea factory concentrated on specific patterns derived from Japanese and sometimes Chinese porcelain, almost invariably viewed through the prism of Meissen, and upon landscape and floral themes, also drawn from an essentially Meissen idiom. Almost nothing in terms of polychrome decoration was truly original, with the exception of the earliest animal decoration which foreshadowed the fable painting of Jefferyes Hamett O'Neale.[2] The mainstream fable subjects, together with the innovative botanical themes, lay two years or so ahead. Likewise, the restricted utilitarian production of Charles Gouyn's St. James' factory was decorated exclusively in a floral style derived from Meissen.

Bow was by far the largest English factory in 1752 and had the widest range of decorative idioms. Most were adaptations of Chinese *famille verte* and *famille rose* or Japanese *kakiemon* patterns, the latter often owing their direct inspiration to Meissen. Chinese and Japanese *Imari* themes were also replicated, as were white "sprigged" wares in the manner of Chinese *Fujian* porcelain. Perhaps significantly, one of the few areas of decorative innovation lay in a small class of Bow dating from the early 1750s, comprising mainly leaf-shaped dishes and small pickle leaves, which combined Chinese and Japanese motifs, often around a central banded hedge, enriched with a sparing use of gilding.[3] Whether these relatively few pieces, directed at a more prosperous market, preceded the nascent Worcester idiom and whether the Worcester designers were aware of this idiom, is pure conjecture.

Ironically, the Limehouse factory which had "failed" in 1748, had a far greater impact on Worcester than either Chelsea or Bow, but this influence was principally in terms of potting shapes and moulded ornamentation, derived through the agency of Lund's Bristol. The tiny amount of polychrome Limehouse produced was decorated outside the factory and bore little similarity to any other English porcelain.[4]

Outside London, the Derby and Longton Hall factories, making their first tentative steps towards a commercial production, were concentrating on figures and vases. In both instances, their minimal domestic output echoed Meissen in both form and decoration.

Nearer to home and closely observed by the interested parties in Worcester, was Benjamin Lund's factory in Bristol Here, the production was very different from anything being attempted either in London or in the Midlands. The output was almost entirely confined to underglaze blue decoration, but in a style very unlike that of Bow. The inspiration was clearly that of the Limehouse concern which had "failed" several years earlier. Yet Lund's factory seems not to have attempted polychrome decoration and the majority of such candidates were almost certainly painted outside the factory, either in London or a year or two later, at Worcester.

Thus, the Worcester factory's objective in producing polychrome domestic wares alongside their blue and white, would be in direct competition principally with Bow and also with the well-organised and large-scale importations of Chinese porcelain.

In several respects, the Worcester factory was advantageously placed to take up the challenges and hazards implicit in this new industry. Most crucially, the soapstone recipe developed by Benjamin Lund at Bristol would enable the factory to produce thinly potted teawares superior to those of Bow and equal in thinness to the Chinese importations. The potting shapes favoured at Bristol suggested the basis for the future Worcester production, especially high-footed sauceboats, no. 6, low sauceboats, no. 4, panelled octagonal creamboats, no. 1, flared base tankards, no. 8, small shell dishes, no. 11, and pickle leaf dishes, no. 58. An output such as this was a novelty in the industry, utilising domestic shapes inspired by silver models rather than by oriental and Meissen originals. As can be seen from this Collection, the range and crispness of the moulded ornamentation inspired by silver, was highly sophisticated. This too presented the public with something entirely new, for high quality moulding played little part in the production at Chelsea or Bow and was almost unknown on imported Chinese wares. The workforce of modellers and mould-makers probably came from Staffordshire where many would have gained experience in the manufacture of saltglaze stoneware, an industry in which high quality moulded ornamentation was a crucial ingredient.[5] The soapstone formula facilitating the making of a malleable clay which could be thinly pressed into moulds, was ideal for this new range of moulded utilitarian shapes. With the expertise and experience of workers engaged from Bristol and the practical knowledge of Benjamin Lund himself, the Worcester partners were close to having a production strategy in place: an entirely innovative range of shapes, the novelty of intricate moulded ornamentation, an experienced workforce, and a versatile soapstone formula unavailable to any commercial competitor. The final piece of this puzzle was the question of what idiom should be adopted for their polychrome decoration.

On 24 July 1752, the Bristol factory was "now united with the Worcester Porcelain Company where for the future the whole business will be carried on".[6] Several years later, the bankruptcy papers of Richard Holdship retrospectively distinguished between Bristol, a "porcelain manufactory in imitation of Indian China ware" and Worcester, a "porcelain manufactory in imitation of Dresden ware".[7] The purpose of this distinction was presumably to distinguish the Bristol production concerned almost exclusively with blue and white porcelain decorated with Chinese or "Indian" themes, from the new decorative idiom in overglaze decoration in the manner of Meissen. Yet this decoration "in imitation of Dresden ware" embodied in the small coffee pot, no. 50, was very far from the directly copied patterns and styles used at Chelsea, Bow and Derby. Instead, it presented the public with a sophisticated idiom, sufficiently versatile and flexible to be ideally suited to moulded panels, which was oriental in feeling yet entirely different to any porcelain with which the consumer might be familiar.

From this retrospective wording, it seems that the immediate inspiration for this new style was the *indianische Blumen*, a decorative idiom devised at Meissen in the early 1720s by J G Höroldt, using a sketch book of drawings of *chinoiserie* themes, the so-called *Schulz-Codex*. These sketches and the patterns which were created from them, generally incorporated Chinese figures, but the subsidiary motifs, of trees, birds, foliage, rockwork and fanciful flowers derived from peonies and chrysanthemums were depicted in a brilliant palette which combined both Chinese and Japanese colours. To English eyes, no distinction was made between the Chinese *famille verte* and *famille rose* on the one hand, and the Japanese *kakiemon* palette, on the other. Yet the Worcester interpretation of this distinctive style was far more informal and relaxed, seasoned with quite separate influences, from painters with backgrounds in the Staffordshire saltglaze industry and possibly the South Staffordshire tradition of decorating opaque white glass.[8] In this way, a style was created for the earliest Worcester polychrome production which interwove decorative idioms from China, Japan, Meissen and Staffordshire, with a series of models inspired by silver and embellished with complex rococo moulding. Despite the Meissen (or "Dresden") influence, explicit in the wording of Richard Holdship's bankruptcy papers, few if any pieces of Worcester of this period actually resemble Meissen in either shape or decoration. In the same way, although much of the production was imbued with a generalised silver influence, no shapes were precise imitations of metalwork models. Thus in a sense, these disparate layers of influence were instrumental in creating an entirely original style. And so it would have appeared at its introduction to the public in 1752.

The *indianische Blumen* oriental style as interpreted at Worcester is embodied to delightful effect in the lotus-moulded bowl, no. 49, the decoration arching rhythmically around the moulded contours. The composition is more informal than the highly structured Meissen designs and if there are similarities in the palette, the effect is altered by an absence of the characteristic symmetry. The juxtaposition of *famille verte* colours with those derived from the conventional *kakiemon* palette is used to great effect on many of the smaller objects produced at this period, such as the creamboat, no. 51, the octagonal cup, no. 56, the pickle leaf, no. 58, and the small shell-shaped dish, no. 59. For the most part, the *indianische Blumen* influence was so artlessly absorbed into this spontaneous Worcester idiom as to be almost undetectable and the decoration on the small coffee pot, no. 50, with its large chrysanthemums and peonies is a rare instance where a pattern might be associated with a corresponding Meissen idiom.

This adaptation of elements of the *indianische Blumen*, creating related motifs rather than a series of patterns, was ideally suited to the interior rims of sauceboats, no. 43, creamboats, no. 51, and the edges of pickle leaves, no. 58, all integral components of the early Worcester output. These motifs were also ingeniously incorporated into the moulded ornamentation on sauceboats, nos. 43 and 44, and creamboats, no. 52, thereby adding a further sense of novelty to shapes inspired by silver and enhanced by the skill of the mould-maker. The versatility of this relaxed and informal idiom, with its loose structure, was also well-suited to the decoration of the rhythmically moulded jugs and vases, their linear complexity softened by the meandering decorative style, nos. 45-47. Evocative and sophisticated vessels such as these, together with the beaker on three feet, no. 48, the lotus-moulded bowl, no. 49, the pair of decagonal bowls, no. 54, and the small hexagonal bottle-vase, no. 55, are indicative of the luxury market to which this earliest Worcester production aspired. The equivalent connoisseur-collector pieces in Chinese *famille verte* were no longer being imported and it is entirely possible that a proportion of the Worcester production from the earliest period was designed to supply this erudite market. If so, this might account for the sophistication of so many shapes and the richly allusive nature of their decoration.

Perceptions of novelty were an accepted marketing strategy at this embryonic stage of the English porcelain industry. Nicholas Sprimont at Chelsea, an inveterate newspaper advertiser, introduced his new range of shapes and patterns to the public in 1750, as "A Taste Entirely New",[9] whilst the Derby factory was termed "The Second Dresden".[10] Yet neither offered the public the multi-layered novelty of the initial Worcester production. Shapes such as the lobed jug on feet, no. 45, the helmet jug, no. 46, and the pair of vases, no. 47, were exciting models derived from unfamiliar European sources. Their decoration too, was new . . . oriental in spirit, yet somehow quite different to the Chinese importations available in England. And to this sense of novelty was added, a gradually evolving range of sturdy practical shapes, teawares, mugs, bowls and sauceboats, as durable as their oriental counterparts and far more imaginative and sophisticated in their decoration.

43. PAIR OF PEDESTAL SAUCEBOATS circa 1752

MARKS: None

LENGTH: 7½ ins

Sauceboats of this form with scroll handles in two sections and moulded festoons, correspond to those mentioned by the traveller and diarist, Dr. Richard Pococke, Bishop of Meath, who visited the Bristol factory in November 1750. Writing to his mother, he noted two sorts of ware made there, describing ". . . beautiful white china sauce boats adorned with reliefs of festoons which sell for sixteen shillings a pair".[11] Lund's Bristol models are recorded in colour, bearing the embossed *Bristol* or *Bristoll* mark,[12] and in the white,[13] together with one example painted in underglaze blue and another with additional polychrome decoration presumably embellished later at Worcester. Yet from their slightly creamy paste, this pair seem to date from the very earliest period at Worcester. However, the palette and the style of decoration are identical to that on several of the *Bristol* marked examples, reinforcing the likelihood that the Bristol sauceboats were decorated at Worcester. This of course would account for the green wash which almost invariably obscures the *Bristol* embossed mark.[14] The same tone of green recurs on this earliest class of Worcester pedestal sauceboat, idiosyncratically decorating the upper portion of handles.

At this early period, it was the Worcester procedure to adapt and modify silver models for their range of sauceboats, rather than to imitate directly, as at Bow and Vauxhall. Yet in this instance, the high handled sauceboats are somewhat closer to their silver progenitor. Silver was proportionally more expensive than it is today. The unpublished Accounts Day Book of Colonel William Sotheby reveal that he was paying nearly seven shillings an ounce for his silver. On May 13th 1761 "Silver bread basket of Le Sage, 9 gns," and on November 25th 1762. "Two Sauceboats £8 10s 6d". At this period, Worcester sauceboats would have cost approximately six shillings a pair. This disparity may explain the demand for porcelain sauceboats of silver form.

cf. Franklin A Barrett, *Worcester Porcelain*, plates 3A and 3B for two differing high handled Lund's Bristol sauceboats, both bearing the embossed *Bristoll* mark.

ccf. Anton Gabszewicz, *Bow Porcelain*, no. 35, for a corresponding Bow model of approximately the same date.

PROVENANCE: *The H E Marshall Collection*

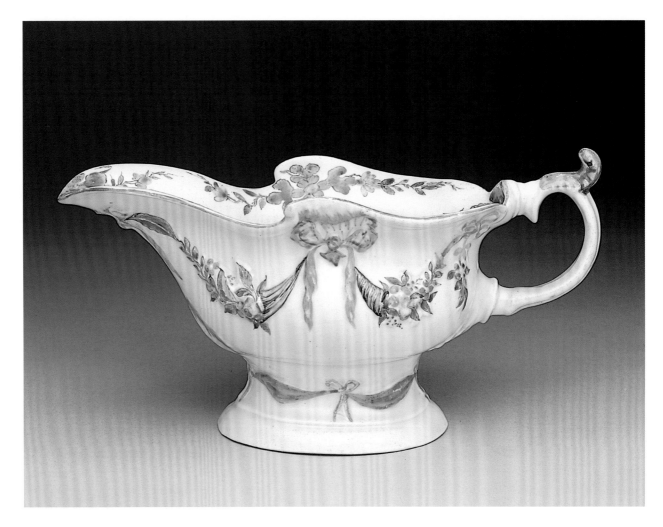

44. PEDESTAL SAUCEBOAT circa 1752-53

MARK: None

Length: 8¾ ins

This simplified shape was adapted from the model with a handle in two sections no. 43, first issued at Bristol. The modified handle, whilst more practical and less vulnerable, disturbs the sense of balance found in the original, and lends this adapted shape a slightly ungainly appearance. The palette is identical to both the high handled models and their Bristol precursors and they all share the distinctive feature of the upper section of the handle and thumbrest painted green. This does not occur on the mainstream production of early Worcester sauceboats.

Characteristically, the majority of Worcester sauceboats of the early and middle 1750s, whether polychrome or blue and white, combine oriental-style decoration with moulded ornamentation and an overall shape suggested by silver. Yet in this instance, the painted decoration generally emphasises the moulding. Only in the interior decoration and on the rim of the sauceboat, do motifs appear in an oriental idiom. Early Bow, Lund's Bristol and the earliest Worcester pedestal sauceboats all retain this emphasis on relief decoration, mirroring that of silver. But from the early 1750s onwards, no other factory was as adept and inventive as Worcester at adapting a *chinoiserie* idiom to the fluid contours of metalwork. Models applied with this simplified handle form do not bear the embossed *Bristol* mark.

cf. no. 43 in this catalogue, for a similar sauceboat with a two-piece "high" handle.

45. LOBED JUG ON THREE FEET circa 1752-53

MARK: None

HEIGHT: 7¼ ins

The small class of early polychrome Worcester models supported on three scroll feet comprise teapots,[15] lobed beakers and tall lobed jugs. The jugs are essentially similar in shape although their handles vary in complexity. Examples are recorded in at least three patterns. In this case, the decoration is particularly free, resembling in its palette, the beaker cup in this Collection, no. 48, and a slender lobed vase in the Klepser Collection in Seattle.[16]

The overall shape, especially the scroll handle, the splayed feet and the moulded leaf below the lip, is strongly suggestive of metalwork. German silver jugs and mugs on ball and claw feet were made at Nuremburg in the 1670s and comparable engraved designs were circulating in Europe during the 1730s and 1740s. However, on balance a derivation from English rococo silver seems more likely. The upper section of the handle, with its moulded ornamentation above the terminal, mirrors that on English silver wine jugs of about 1750.[17]

All of the Worcester models on splayed feet, teapots, beakers and jugs, share firing blemishes in the form of sanding on the underside of the base, and it is perhaps no wonder that these ambitious models, almost without parallel in English porcelain, had so fleeting a period of production. In the case of this allusive model, the placing of the pair of large overlapping green leaves has been determined by the need to camouflage a firing fault. The effect has been to add a further measure of individuality and rococo spirit to this remarkable jug. If any parallel exists, however distant, it might be drawn with the Chelsea strawberry leaf coffee pots of the triangle period, sharing both metalwork associations and splayed feet.[18]

cf. Franklin Barrett, *Worcester Porcelain and Lund's Bristol*, plate 13, for a similar jug painted with landscapes.

ccf. Henry Sandon, *Coffee Pots and Tea Pots,* 1973. plate 16, for a silver coffee pot of rococo form on three scroll feet made in 1738 by Paul de Lamerie.

46. HELMET SHAPED JUG circa 1752-53

MARK: None

HEIGHT: 4⅞ ins

A remarkable baroque shape utterly unrepresentative of the early Worcester production. Only two other comparable examples are known, one in the Museum of Worcester Porcelain and the other in the Klepser Collection in The Seattle Art Museum. They vary in height from 4⅞ inches to 7 inches and the Klepser example, much the largest of the three, has an entirely different style of moulded ornamentation. In their painted decoration too, they have little in common. Whereas the Museum of Worcester jug is painted in a relatively conventional Worcester *famille rose-verte* style, the Klepser jug depends primarily on its moulded swag and ribbon motifs for its decorative impact, echoing contemporary Worcester pedestal sauceboats, nos. 43 and 44. By contrast, the present model is painted in a more informal idiom, featuring the broad green leaves and trailing flowers also found on the large three footed jug, no. 45, seamlessly interweaving Chinese and Japanese motifs.

As with so many Worcester models of this early period, the precise origins of the shape are difficult to ascertain. The form occurs in early eighteenth century Rouen faience,[19] possibly imitating an earlier French metalwork source. A Chinese *Kangxi* version, issued in both polychrome and underglaze blue, dates from the early eighteenth century, probably influenced by a Meissen model in Bottger porcelain of 1713, modelled by Benjamin Thomae after a silver original by Johann Jacob Irminger, the Saxon Court silversmith. It may be this which is the immediate source of the Worcester jug, as the moulding on the Klepser version, decorated with great restraint, is intriguingly similar to the baroque idiom favoured by Bottger.

cf. Simon Spero, *Worcester Porcelain, The Klepser Collection*, no. 3, colour plate 3.

47. PAIR OF VASES circa 1752-53

MARKS: None
HEIGHT: 7 ins

One of the earliest forms of vase at Worcester, invariably displaying firing blemishes on the underside of the footrim. The superbly balanced form is complimented by an attenuated *famille rose* design, painted in a vibrant palette, which trails rhythmically around the lobed contours. The pattern, subtle and delicately arranged, is far more sophisticated in both design and execution than the more random and spontaneous eruption of tendrils that billow forth on the lobed jug, no. 45. Probably devised in pairs rather than in garniture sets, this model was in production for no more than a year and was not issued in underglaze blue. Its origin is uncertain, although a related shape was made at Saint Cloud in the second quarter of the eighteenth century.

The writhing contours of the rock formations perforated by differently shaped holes, are a recurring decorative idiom on Worcester throughout the 1750s, both in colour and underglaze blue. They mirror motifs on Chinese porcelain depicting the undulating hollowed "scholar's rocks" in Chinese gardens, carefully arranged so as to create a decorative feature. Thus a dramatic phenomenon of nature was introduced into an ornamental garden. The limestone volcanic rocks were themselves often transported long distances, carefully selected for the contours and proportions of their apertures. The Worcester painters had no understanding of the significance of this decorative idiom but nevertheless, it was successfully integrated into their *chinoiserie* style often with great flair and effectiveness.

cf. no. 21, for an interpretation of the writhing rock formations in underglaze blue.

ccf. Simon Spero, *Worcester Porcelain, The Klepser Collection*, no. 2, colour plate 2.

PROVENANCE: *The L L Firth Collection*

48. LOBED BEAKER SHAPED CUP ON THREE FEET circa 1752-53

MARK: None
HEIGHT: 3 ins

A highly inventive and elegant, yet somewhat impractical Worcester form, of which only three examples are recorded, all in the A. J. Smith Collection. The basic contours might have been adapted from Chinese *Kangxi*, whilst the scroll handle and the three splayed feet are suggestive of metalwork. However, in silver, it was pouring vessels such as creamjugs and sauceboats which were supported on feet. No eighteenth century silver models of drinking vessels, beakers, cups or mugs seem to exist in this design. Perhaps the Worcester models were envisaged alongside the rococo teapots on four feet and the equally rare cider jugs, no. 45. If the search for a specific design source is elusive, the inspiration may have been loosely suggested by the series of Augsburg engravings which were circulating around Europe in the 1730s and 1740s.

Yet whether or not this might have been a completely innovative Worcester shape, its decorative impact is striking, and subtly embellished with motifs reflecting the factory's distinctive interpretation of Chinese *famille verte* motifs interwoven with those of the *indianische Blumen* of Meissen. The ladybird in flight, almost appears to have been taken from life. Its purpose is obscure. It may well have been intended for chocolate or conceivably as a novelty for the connoisseur's china cabinet.

As with the moulded cider jug also supported upon three feet, no. 45, there are signs of firing faults and sanding around the base of this beaker, and these problems may have prompted the abandonment of so ambitious a model.

cf. no. 130 in this collection, for the only other two examples of this model so far recorded.

49. BOWL circa 1752-53

MARK: Incised line
DIAMETER: 8 ins

One of only two recorded examples of lotus-moulded bowls, a shape without parallel in other eighteenth century English porcelain. The subtle and innovative decoration integrates elements of Japanese *kakiemon* and Chinese *famille verte,* with a distinct flavour of the *indianische Blumen* of Meissen, to captivating effect. Bowls, in their linear simplicity, reveal little of their time and place. This decoration has a relaxed sophistication analogous with that of Meissen of the 1730s, or even late seventeenth century *kakiemon* porcelain, with its sensitive use of space.

The model, moulded as an opening lotus, harks back to Chinese porcelain of the *Kangxi* period and also to Japanese *Imari* models of the last quarter of the seventeenth century. The overall effect of this allusive form, drawing its artistic origins from so many diverse sources, is of a connoisseur's piece rather than a purely functional vessel, a possibility which echoes through so much of the Worcester production of 1752-53.

The painter has a distinctive style, especially in his treatment of the meandering branches, wispy, not outlined and lacking in solidarity. This artless, loose, idiom conveys a delightful sense of informality and is possibly the work of the same hand as the pair of vases, no. 47, the pair of flared hexagonal bowls, no. 54, the octagonal beaker, no. 57, and the circular stand, no. 61. It contrasts with the heavier, more solid treatment of the lobed beaker on feet, no. 48, and the octagonal coffee cup, no. 56.

cf. Anton Gabszewicz, *Made at New Canton,* plate 44, for an exactly contemporary Bow bowl also painted in the oriental taste, yet utterly different in idiom.

50. COFFEE POT circa 1752-53

MARK: None

HEIGHT: 5⅝ ins

By comparison with the classic "scratch cross" model of the 1753-55 period, no. 100, this rare coffee pot is of smaller proportions and much more closely modelled on a silver original of the 1740s in terms of its contours, the angle of its spout and the shape of its cover. Its paste and hard greyish-toned glaze are also indicative of a slightly earlier date. Indeed, its small proportions have led some authorities to describe it as a chocolate pot.

If the shape is strongly reminiscent of silver, the decoration is a free interpretation of the Meissen *indianische Blumen* of the 1730s, with highly stylised chrysanthemum-like flowers, realised in a bold palette also echoing Meissen.[20] Here is surely incontrovertible evidence of the factory's stated aspiration as a 'porcelain manufactory in imitation of Dresden ware'. Yet even at this early stage of the factory's development, the effect of these two influences, silver and Meissen, disparate yet complementary, is entirely innovative, lending an immediate sense of individuality. Both the vivid palette and the style of decoration were short-lived and mainly confined to larger shapes such as beer jugs.

Two indications of a particularly early period, evident in this rare coffee pot, are the lower handle terminal, separated from the body as if in imitation of the thermal insulating bridge on a silver example, and the particular tone of green.

cf. Simon Spero and John Sandon, *Worcester Porcelain, 1751-1790: The Zorensky Collection*, nos. 1, 2, 3 and 5 for other differing coffee pots of the early 1750s.

51. FLUTED CREAMBOAT circa 1752-53

Mark: None

Length: 4¼ ins

A fluted model on pad feet which is probably the earliest form of creamboat issued at Worcester. It corresponds closely to a Lund's Bristol shape which almost invariably bears the embossed mark *Bristol* or *Bristoll*. The model was in production for no more than a year and very few examples have survived. They characteristically tend to have a slightly greyish cast to their glaze. The decoration, drawn with expressive sympathy for the contours of the shape, interweaves the colours of *famille verte* and Japanese *kakiemon* motifs in a free modification of the *indianische Blumen* style of Meissen.

Comparing and contrasting Worcester creamboats of the 1750s with those of other factories, emphasises the sheer inventiveness of the Worcester designers. Whereas silver sauceboat prototypes presented an abundance of material to inspire imitation, creamboats in silver were generally supported upon three feet, inhibiting simulation. In the absence of metalwork models from which to draw inspiration, Bow, Vauxhall, Derby, Lowestoft and the Liverpool factories tended to adapt scaled-down versions of sauceboats, whereas at Worcester, at least fourteen shapes are recorded in the literature, specifically designed as creamboats. Bow, the main English competitor to Worcester during the 1750s, were particularly unenterprising in their designs for creamboats, most specimens being plain in both their form and their decoration. Imported Chinese creamboats too, were far inferior to those of Worcester, in both design and decoration.

cf. Patricia Begg and Barry Taylor, *A Treasury of Bow,* Exhibition Catalogue 2000, nos. 49, 104, 108, 109 and 120, for a representative range of Bow creamboats.

ccf. Simon Spero, *Worcester Porcelain, The Klepser Collection,* colour plate 8, no. 20, for a Lund's Bristol creamboat of this shape, bearing the embossed mark *Bristoll* overpainted in green.

PROVENANCE: *The H E Marshall Collection*

52. FLUTED CREAMBOAT circa 1753

MARK: None
LENGTH: 4⅜ ins

A rare form of decoration with embossed flowers picked out in colour. An exactly corresponding model in underglaze blue has the moulded decoration left "in the white" and a freely painted interior border. The concept of moulded flowers and sprays in high relief, picked out in colour, is reminiscent of Staffordshire saltglaze. Yet perhaps it is not too fanciful to also suggest faint parallels with the teaplant moulding on triangle period Chelsea, utilising enamel colours in much the same manner. The interior decoration of Chinese emblems and ribbons recurs frequently on sauceboats and creamboats of this period.

Contemporary sources sometimes refer to "butter boats" or merely to "boats", suggesting that the modern description for this shape may be inaccurate. Butter, cheaper than fat, had been for centuries a staple diet for the poor and by the eighteenth century it was used in every branch of cooking. It was added to all varieties of boiled food prior to serving, and melted butter sauces sometimes flavoured with orange, parsley or anchovies, were poured liberally into boiled salads, meat and fish stews, roast meats and vegetables of all kinds. "Boats" and other dishes for melted butter must have been essential. Monsieur Misson, a Frenchman visiting England in the 1690s, wrote in some bewilderment regarding a piece of boiled beef, salted some days beforehand and how he had observed the English "…besiege it with five or six heaps of cabbage, carrots, turnips…swimming in butter…". Alternatively, these elegant and beautifully decorated early Worcester creamboats may have been intended as accessories for the dessert course, in which case they would indeed have been intended to serve cream, as implied by the contemporary description "cream ewer".

cf. cat no. 51, for a slightly earlier and less detailed form of thumbpiece.

53. SUGAR BOWL circa 1753

MARK: None
DIAMETER: 5 ins

A rare form, only one of which is recorded complete with its cover. Sugar was still a luxury at this period and it is likely that many sugar bowls were made in silver rather than porcelain. Indeed, the origin for this beautifully moulded form was probably silver. Sugar boxes were available in Chinese export wares and in Bow, but otherwise few survive from the early 1750s. Single examples are known in Chelsea and Lund's Bristol. Yet this expressive Worcester model, dependant more on its rhythmic moulded ornamentation than on its painted decoration, is the most ambitious vessel of its type in early English porcelain. It exemplifies the enterprising nature of the Worcester production, offering the public a product more innovative than Chelsea and more visually stimulating than either Bow or Chinese importations. At the same time, the factory was coming to pride itself on the durability of its wares, and such problems as the staining in the glaze, evident here, were gradually being eradicated.

Even though the English colonists in the West Indies had turned their plantations over to sugar canes in the 1640s, it remained a luxury until the second half of the eighteenth century. Many sugar canisters were made of silver. Perhaps as a consequence, sugar boxes did not become a regular component of Worcester tea services until about 1760. Indeed prior to this period, the majority of porcelain examples were either Bow or Chinese.

Formerly a monopoly held by apothecaries, sugar was sold by grocers in crystallised cones. It was generally served "ready broke", unlike the French custom for powdered sugar and this necessitated sugar bowls of far greater capacity than contemporary Vincennes or Sevres counterparts.

cf. Simon Spero and John Sandon, *Worcester Porcelain, 1751-1790: The Zorensky Collection*, no. 20, for a sugar box complete with its cover, formerly in the Rous Lench Collection.

PROVENANCE: *The H E Marshall Collection*

54. PAIR OF FLARED DECAGONAL BOWLS circa 1753

MARKS: None

DIAMETER: 2¼ ins

A rare shape, confined to only a year or so of production and otherwise unknown in early English porcelain. The decoration features the Worcester interpretation of Chinese *famille rose* and *kakiemon* motifs, set out in the delicate and distinctive palette of the period. In this early period, the outstanding levels of potting, throwing and firing which distinguished the Worcester production for most of the third quarter of the eighteenth century, had not yet been fully achieved. It is evident that one of these decagonal bowls has suffered distortion in the kiln. Yet the manufacture of beautifully proportioned and decorated small bowls such as these, with no apparent practical function, gives rise to the possibility that a portion of the factory's production of polychrome wares during the early 1750s was intended for primarily decorative purposes. This might also apply to such impracticable seeming pieces as the twelve-sided teabowls and saucers, no. 63, and the quatrefoil lobed coffee cups, no. 130. Porcelain from China, Japan, France and Germany was eagerly collected in the eighteenth century, and it is conceivable that some of these beautifully potted allusive shapes, painted in an entirely innovative idiom, were intended for display in china cabinets rather than for use. If this seems plausible, it would also account for the almost complete absence of blue and white counterparts for so many of the Worcester shapes of the early 1750s, including these decagonal bowls, the hexagonal bottle-shaped vases, no. 69, and the octagonal beakers, no. 57.

cf. The lotus-moulded bowl, no. 49, and the octagonal beaker, no. 57, possibly painted by the same hand.

PROVENANCE: *The Knowles Boney Collection*

55. TWO-HANDLED HEXAGONAL BOTTLE-SHAPED VASE circa 1753-54

MARK: None

HEIGHT: 3¾ ins

One of the rarest forms of early Worcester vase, this is adapted from a Chinese model, made in several sizes. As with the quatrefoil indented example, no. 91, it has a shallow footrim rather than a flat, partially glazed base. The decoration is realised with a delicacy and sense of detail, quite unlike that on the majority of this range of small vases. In this, it resembles the exceedingly rare small scent bottles.[21] The influence is primarily Chinese as interpreted through the prism of Meissen. Somewhat unusually for this early period, there is no hint of the *kakiemon* idiom.

The range of small vases made at Worcester during the early and middle 1750s, echoing earlier eighteenth century Chinese models, had no counterparts in other contemporary English factories. Whilst Bow was primarily concerned with direct competition with the Chinese importations and Chelsea was imitating contemporary Meissen idioms, Worcester seemed to be deliberately harking back to an earlier Meissen style, reinterpreting the *indianische Blumen* of the 1730s. Yet the distinctive and innovative idiom exemplified by this small vase, may also owe something to the more accessible influence of Staffordshire saltglaze stoneware. Small models of this shape and size in Chinese porcelain would have been scholar's vases, perhaps designed to hold a single flower. At Worcester, they are likely to have been intended for a cabinet of curiosities, a decorative vase for the connoisseur.

56. OCTAGONAL COFFEE CUP circa 1753

MARK: None

HEIGHT: 2¼ ins

Octagonal coffee cups are amongst the most common elements of the polychrome Worcester production during the 1752-54 period, equalled only by the ribbed coffee cans, small shell dishes and, more surprisingly, the pedestal sauceboats, no. 88. Yet only three or four octagonal saucers are known to match with the cups. This is particularly odd as the exactly contemporary raised anchor period Chelsea cups and teabowls were invariably matched with saucers.[22] Furthermore, no Chinese saucers are known in this pattern which might have been accompanied by Worcester cups. The cups occur with three different handle forms and were issued, like their Chelsea counterparts, in two sizes. They were perhaps intended to be used alongside the "Octagn" teapots listed in the London wholesale price card, although this reference is probably to blue and white porcelain. The decoration harks back to the secondary motifs flanking *indianische Blumen* patterns on Meissen of the early 1730s with *famille verte* colours interwoven with those of Japanese *kakiemon* porcelain, amid hovering insects.

Whilst surviving coffee cups in polychrome are relatively plentiful, only one example in underglaze blue has been recorded. This is painted in a very primitive manner, suggesting either an inexperienced painter, or one who was finding difficulties painting in underglaze blue. It is therefore likely that the standard of decoration in polychrome was far higher than in underglaze blue. For this reason, blue and white production may have been temporarily abandoned, accounting for the extreme rarity of counterparts to polychrome octagonal cups, twelve-sided tewares, plain creamjugs, no. 66, and even the earliest pedestal sauceboats, no. 44.

cf. Simon Spero, *Exhibition 1999*, cat. no. 32, for the only recorded blue and white Worcester octagonal cup of this period.

PROVENANCE: *The H E Marshall Collection*

57. OCTAGONAL BEAKER circa 1753

MARK: None

HEIGHT: 2⅜ ins

This rare beaker is essentially similar to the more familiar octagonal coffee cup, except that it lacks a handle. Yet the beakers seem invariably to have a drier glaze, lending them a more matt appearance, akin to the twelve-sided teawares. Their function is obscure, although they mirror the exactly contemporary Chelsea octagonal coffee cups, some of which also lack a handle. However, the Worcester decorative idiom on their octagonal teawares could hardly be more different to that of the London factory, so firmly allied to the influence of Meissen. The freer, more inventive and informal Worcester style allowed a far greater measure of individuality and personal interpretation to their designs. . . in this instance, a hybrid amalgam of Chinese and Japanese idioms. Here for example, the alternating panels of insects are far from repetitive. Indeed, in one panel, an elongated beetle-like creature is descending upon his tiny prey in a decidedly menacing manner.

Handleless beakers and saucers appear in silver by about 1710, probably inspired by contemporary *Kangxi* models, no. 129. In English porcelain these shapes were later echoed at Richard Chaffers' Liverpool factory.

cf. John Austin, *Chelsea Porcelain at Williamsburg*, no. 44, for an exactly contemporary Chelsea beaker in the "*red pannel*" pattern.

58. PICKLE LEAF DISH circa 1753

MARK: None

LENGTH: 3⅞ ins

An ivy leaf form initially issued at Lund's factory in underglaze blue and adopted at Worcester in colour from about 1753 to 1755. The shape was also issued in the "smoky primitive" transfer-prints[23] of the same period, but the underglaze blue version[24] was not introduced until about 1755-56, continuing until the end of the decade. Unlike the contemporary shell-shape dishes, this model was produced in only one size, and is somewhat more scarce. Pickle leaves were an important element of the output of nearly all the eighteenth century English factories, but the acids from the pickles tended to eat into the glaze, disfiguring the overglaze colours. Consequently, the vast majority of pickle leaves from the middle 1750s onwards, were in underglaze blue. At factories such as Derby, Lowestoft, Plymouth, Caughley and most of the Liverpool potworks, almost the entire output of pickle leaves was blue and white.

Pickles were customarily served either in small saucers or in leaf-shaped dishes and accompanied cold meat. Chutneys, originating in India, the grandest being "Pickle Lillo" or "Piccalilli", were used to counteract the stale or salty flavour of the meat. Pickling was an English speciality. Herrings, oysters and even salmon was pickled, along with mushrooms, walnuts, onions and nasturtium buds. The relatively shallow contours of most early English pickle leaves suggests that there was little liquid in the relish.

cf. Anton Gabszewicz, *Made at New Canton,* no. 24 for a rare polychrome early Bow pickle leaf.

59. SHELL-SHAPED DISH circa 1753-54

MARK: None

HEIGHT: 3¼ ins.

As with the early ivy leaf pickle dish, no. 58, this shape was issued at Lund's Bristol and was in production at Worcester in colour, from about 1753 to 1755. It was then replaced by an underglaze blue version, also made in three sizes. The form, adapted and simplified from silver models, was nevertheless far more sophisticated than the imported Chinese counterparts which had replaced the *real* shells previously used. The Worcester shells, moulded on their underside, were better potted and decorated than the Chinese and must have seemed a far superior, if far more costly product. Shell-shaped dishes were prominent in the output of Worcester's precursors at Limehouse and Bristol and were later produced at Lowestoft, Caughley and elsewhere, almost invariably in underglaze blue. Small shell-shaped dishes painted in oriental style patterns were also made in Staffordshire saltglaze stoneware. These are impossible to date accurately with any confidence but certainly can be ascribed to the 1750s.

Described variously in contemporary ledgers as "Scallop'd Shells" and "Scallops for Oysters", their abundance in contemporary porcelain echoed the enormous popularity of oysters. Eaten on the half shell, these were consumed in large quantities accompanied by bread and sometimes wine, often as a breakfast dish. Later in the century, Margaret Davis, housekeeper at Saltram House near Plymouth, recorded amongst her purchases "a Hundred of Oysters for 1/-". They were certainly inexpensive throughout the century. Dr. Samuel Johnson fed them to his ailing cat!

cf. Simon Spero and John Sandon, *Worcester Porcelain, 1751-1790: The Zorensky Collection*, nos. 16,17 and 19.

PROVENANCE: *The Wallace Elliott Collection*

60. PAIR OF CORNUCOPIA WALLPOCKETS circa 1754-55

MARK: None

LENGTH: 9½ ins

Worcester wallpockets issued in left and right-handed versions, were made in pairs, five different models being recorded. Two of these models were made in two sizes, corresponding to the price list of the Worcester China Warehouse drawn up in about 1755-56, "Cornucopias 1st & 2nd . . . 2/3d and 2/6d". These were presumably priced per pair, rather than per dozen. All examples were heavily moulded and generally inspired by Staffordshire saltglazed originals. The vast majority were painted in underglaze blue and these examples, in the *indianische Blumen* style, are rarities.

Issued at Bow, Vauxhall, Derby, Lowestoft and Gilbody's Liverpool factory, cornucopia wallpockets had fallen out of fashion by the late 1760s. In eighteenth century porcelain terms, the shape seems to have been peculiar to England. They were made in tin-glazed earthenware, saltglaze stoneware and a little later, in creamware. The precise purpose of these wallpockets is uncertain, but it was probably for either dried flowers or *tole peint* applied with porcelain flowers.

cf. John Sandon, *The Dictionary of Worcester Porcelain Volume I 1751-1851*, p.118, for a later cornucopia wallpocket in different moulding.

61. CIRCULAR STAND circa 1754-55

MARK: None
DIAMETER: 6 ins

This small dish is fluted on the underside, usually a firm indication that its purpose is as a stand for a similarly fluted vessel such as a sugar bowl and cover or a small tureen. However, no such model of this date or with comparable fluted decoration has so far been recorded. The everted rim, lightly fluted, obviates the possibility that this is a saucerdish and sugar bowls and covers were exceedingly rare in the middle 1750s. It is more likely that this dish was intended as a stand for a small tureen, possibly adapted from a Chinese export model. The decoration in the *famille verte* taste interspersed with *kakiemon* motifs, is typical of the period but the paste is unusually creamy in tone, affording a sharp contrast with exactly contemporary "scratch cross" pieces, nos. 99 and 102.

The individual treatment of the stalks, wispy and not outlined, suggests that this is by the same hand as the pair of cornucopia wallpockets, no. 60, the two-handled hexagonal bottle-shaped vase, no. 55, and the lotus-moulded bowl, no. 49.

PROVENANCE: *The H E Marshall Collection*

62. MOULDED SAUCEBOAT circa 1753-54

MARK: None

LENGTH: 9½ ins

One of the most ambitious and extravagantly rococo of all the Worcester sauceboat models, strongly reminiscent of metalwork in its asymmetrical shell moulding, yet with no silver prototype. By comparison with the somewhat restrained approach which Worcester adopted towards the ornate rococo style of the 1750s, unlike that of Chelsea, Bow, Longton Hall and Derby for instance, this shell moulded sauceboat ripples with a flamboyant rhythmic vitality. The temptation to issue the shape in three sizes as with other models, was wisely avoided. Embodying a defining characteristic of early English porcelain, a vividly rococo form with unequivocal silver origins is juxtaposed with decoration adapted from the Chinese *famille rose* style, in itself a relatively unusual Worcester idiom. Yet it is the moulded ornamentation, modelled in high relief, which furnishes the principal visual impact. However, uncharacteristically for a polychrome Worcester sauceboat, the interior conceals a delightful *chinoiserie* landscape scene. The model is also recorded in underglaze blue and with "pencilled" decoration.

This sauceboat model, regardless of its painted decoration, invariably has a distinctly greyish cast to its glaze. This must surely be deliberate, but its purpose is obscure. The porcelain itself has a slightly brittle quality and it is possible that both these characteristics were the unintentional consequence of peculiarities in the firing process.

cf. Geoffrey Godden, *English Blue and White Porcelain,* colour plate 36, for a blue and white example of this model.

NOTES

Chapter 6   The Indianische Blumen Decoration

1.   Spero and Sandon, J (1996), p.20.
2.   Austin, (1977), nos. 61, 62 and 63.
3.   Gabszewicz and Freeman, (1982), nos. 52 and 53.
4.   English Ceramic Circle, (1993), plate XVI.
5.   Sandon, J (1993), p.17.
6.   Barrett, (1966), p.2.
7.   Spero and Sandon, J (1996), p.44.
8.   Delomosne & Son Ltd, (1978), no.6.
9.   Adams, (1987), p.57.
10.   Barrett and Thorpe, (1971), p.21.
11.   Barrett, (1966), p.6.
12.   Spero, *Exhibition Catalogue* (1997), no.16.
13.   H. Sandon, (1969), plate 2.
14.   Spero, *Exhibition Catalogue* (1997), no.16.
15.   Spero and Sandon, J (1996), no.7.
16.   Spero, (1984), Colour plate 1.
17.   Waldron, (1982), p.341.
18.   Austin, (1977), plate 21.
19.   Rondot, (1999), Figs. 5 and 6.
20.   Pietsch, (1993) p.73.
21.   J. Sandon, (1993), p.306.
22.   Adams, (1987), plate VII.
23.   Handley, (1991), p.45.
24.   Spero and Sandon, J (1996), no.537 *(top right)*.

CHAPTER 7 **BIRD DECORATION**

The decorative idiom devised at Worcester to adorn their innovative range of shapes, in their first year of production, was designed to be sufficiently versatile to be accommodated within the rococo-shaped reserved panels of moulded sauceboats and creamboats, potting pots and teawares. At the same time, the style had to be adaptable to the contours of lobed and faceted vases, teapots and creamjugs, necessitating a loose structure which could be modified so as to complement the rhythm of the fluid shapes. This requirement for a composition to flow freely into areas of space and curve around moulded contours, militated against the use of rigid set patterns in the manner of Chelsea, Sevres or imported Chinese wares. From this necessity evolved the airy sense of informality which so characterised this innovative and multi-layered Worcester idiom.

The style, invented in 1752, was a loose association of themes drawn from Chinese *famille verte* and *famille rose*, Staffordshire saltglaze stoneware and the *indianische Blumen* of Meissen. As with the Meissen idiom, the palette interspersed *famille verte* and *famille rose* tones with those of Japanese *kakiemon* porcelain, creating a colour world unencumbered by the need to conform to a conventional house style. Loosely structured compositions were developed, made up of flowering shrubs and branches, decorative rock formations and angular fences, into which could be interposed oriental figures or birds. The freshness and informality of this resourceful and innovative style contrasted with the more precise and repetitive idioms familiar from the imported Chinese wares and from the Bow factory in distant London. This distinctive decorative style permeated the Worcester production from 1752-54 and remained an integral element for a further two years or so.

A recurring motif amongst these earliest Worcester *chinoiserie*s is a crane-like bird, often standing on one leg, his neck arching upwards in quest of a hovering insect, nos. 64 and 71, or alternatively, with head demurely lowered, as if preening itself, no. 69. The bird is usually yellow-breasted but its wings, head and tail feathers vary in tone, corresponding to the overall palette of the decoration, as if in pursuit of camouflage, nos. 63 and 65. This wispy ethereal-looking bird, drawn with more humour than realism, is not to be found in the *indianische Blumen* of Meissen. Its origins are more likely to have had their roots in *famille verte* designs. A distantly related bird was occasionally incorporated into a standard *famille rose* pattern on Bow.[1] This Chinese idiom, strongly represented amongst the importations by the East India Company, was widely imitated at Bow and to a lesser extent at Longton Hall. Worcester avoided this stylised *famille rose* idiom, preferring to tread a more unfamiliar path. However, the crane-like bird also appears occasionally on Longton Hall, in an idiom intriguingly close to that on Worcester, though in a differing palette.[2] Both the Bow and Longton Hall versions of this crane motif date from around 1753-54, but whether they were animated by the Worcester example or drawn from a common oriental source is uncertain.

Whatever its source of inspiration, this crane-like bird, either alert in posture or in more flirtatious mode, appears in some of the most engaging compositions of this early period. It features in three of the six *chinoiserie* patterns associated with the twelve-sided teabowls and saucers, nos. 63, 64 and 65, two in a primarily *famille verte* style, and the third in a fully developed amalgam of Chinese and Japanese *kakiemon* motifs. It also occurs at its most inquisitive, on a moulded sauceboat, no. 71, stretching upwards to investigate a hovering insect and on the superb globular vase, no. 67. The theme is also effective in the moulded reserved panels of sauceboats, no. 70, creamboats and potting pans, no. 68, the versatility of the idiom being readily adapted into differing spaces. The bird itself is sufficiently distinctive in its posture and demeanour as to suggest that it is the work of no more than two different hands. For instance, the crane on the globular vase, no. 67, and that on the delightful bottle-shaped vase, no. 69, certainly seem to have come from the same stable. So too do

No 77 (detail)

the birds on the twelve-sided teabowl and saucer, no. 63, and the teabowl, no. 64. If the cranes themselves are possibly a purely Worcester invention, the flowering branches and foliage which encloses them hark back to the *indianische Blumen* in their contrasting oriental influences.

Bird decoration of a quite separate idiom is embodied in the fine baluster mug, no. 72. Here the bird is perched on a flowering branch, pecking at a tiny insect. The influence of the *indianische Blumen* is betrayed both by the juxtaposition of colours and the palette itself. The overall effect is vastly more sophisticated in both shape and pattern than either contemporary Bow[3] or imported Chinese porcelain. The Japanese *kakiemon* idiom is still more palpable in the beautifully lobed coffee cup, no. 73, and the somewhat crudely decorated plate, no. 75, inferior in quality to both its Bow and Chinese counterparts. Contrasting with these European influences is the superbly potted teabowl and saucer, no. 76, exactly replicating a well known Chinese *famille rose* design. The imposing large jug, no. 77, embodies many of these varied influences interacting so seamlessly on one single piece. A conventional Meissen influence, incorporating both Chinese and Japanese themes, presented in a hybrid *kakiemon* palette, is displayed upon an archetypal George II silver model. Curiously the *indianische Blumen* influence, veiled and intangible to many eyes, is more explicit on the thinly potted, subtly moulded teawares of the middle 1750s, nos. 78 and 79. In their masterly potting, delicate moulding and innovative decoration, they must surely represent the pinnacle of mid eighteenth century teawares, far excelling either Chinese importations or any English counterparts.

If this multi-layered yet subtle and innovative style, developed at Worcester in the early 1750s, may be embodied in one specific shape, it might be the glorious oval potting pan, no. 68. This short-lived model, ostensibly functional in purpose and precursor to a modified and simplified underglaze blue vessel of the 1760s,[4] exemplifies both the inventiveness of this new idiom and the rapidity with which it was brought to perfection. The swirling heavily moulded reserved panels reflect the suppleness of the prevailing rococo style whilst the whimsical decoration mirrors the fashion for *chinoiserie*, tinged with humour yet moderated by the restraining use of a diaper border evoking the Chinese *famille verte*. Whether this potting pan was intended for the enjoyment of the scholarly connoisseur of porcelain or to embellish a particularly exotic table setting for the dessert course, it was a *tour de force*, allying technical excellence and innovative virtuosity in a relaxed and ambient decorative idiom.

63. TWELVE-SIDED TEABOWL AND SAUCER circa 1752

MARK: None

DIAMETER OF SAUCER: 4¾ ins

The earliest form of coloured teabowl and saucer produced at Worcester. A Chinese teabowl and saucer of this same distinctive form, in the Bristol City Museum and Art Gallery, is the likely origin for the celebrated Worcester model. It is from *Jing De Zhen* and dates from about 1680-1720. The decoration is in iron red and gilding and the underside of the saucer was incised in Dresden in 1721, with the code N=6Z ("old Japanese"). It was from the collection of Augustus the Strong, Elector of Saxony and King of Poland, who died in 1733. He assembled an enormous collection of porcelain in his Japanese Palace at Dresden and this was first catalogued in 1721.

This small class of teabowls and saucers was probably made for no more than a year or so. No other twelve-sided forms are recorded to match with the teabowls and saucers although the concept exists in Staffordshire "solid agateware", conceived in the far more practical guise of a faceted teapot.[5]

Characteristics which distinguish this early class include a buff-coloured body with a dryish glaze, less shiny than slightly later wares. Typical flaws include light sanding and a tendency to staining of the glaze. Other examples of this small class of Worcester include the fluted baluster vase, no. 81, the cream jug, no. 66, and the octagonal teabowl and saucer, no. 84.

cf. Henry Sandon, *Worcester Porcelain,* plate 8, for a teabowl and saucer, together with two unglazed wasters from the factory site.

PROVENANCE: *The Charles A King Collection*

64. TWELVE-SIDED TEABOWL circa 1752

MARK: None
DIAMETER: 3⅛ ins

The pattern on this concave fluted teabowl shares several elements with the teabowl and saucer, no. 63, and fits well into the widely fluted panels. Unsurprisingly for so early a Worcester model, the twelve-sided forms tend to suffer kiln imperfections. These include light sanding to the glaze, a characteristic shared with the plain creamjugs, nos. 66 and 108, closely related in both period and decorative style. More seriously from a contemporary perspective, staining and a consequent roughness sometimes affects the glaze, no. 65.

This is one of several of the earliest Worcester forms almost, but not entirely, confined to coloured decoration. Three underglaze blue teabowls are known, one in a private collection in London and another in the Museum of Worcester Porcelain. It is perhaps understandable that the factory soon abandoned underglaze blue production of these complex shapes, so sensitively complimented by their airy *chinoiseries* and subtly blended palette. Not only were the contours of the shape more suited to polychrome decoration, but the cursive rim may have militated against their purpose as conventional drinking vessels, rather than curiosities for the china cabinet.

cf. David Barker and Sam Cole (ed), *Digging for Early Porcelain,* p.75 colour fig. 19, for matching unglazed sherds of this model, from early levels of the factory site.

ccf. Dr. Sam Cole, *Form Versus Function? A Study of some early Worcester tea wares,* The Northern Ceramic Society Journal, Volume 20. 2003-2004.

PROVENANCE: *The H E Marshall Collection*

65. TWELVE-SIDED SAUCER circa 1752

MARK: None
DIAMETER: 4¾ ins

At this early period, Worcester had already evolved a distinctive style combining elements of decorative idioms absorbed from oriental porcelain, Meissen, Staffordshire saltglaze and perhaps even the opaque white glass of South Staffordshire. A small number of set patterns had been developed by 1752-53, many of which were associated with one specific shape. Yet a fairly loose arrangement is evident here, with an element of one pattern being incorporated into a completely different one. Here, a flowering prunus branch, which was soon to expand into an early version of *The Banded Hedge,* is combined with the recurring motif of a crane-like bird standing upon one leg, and a *famille verte* border design. An incipient Japanese idiom has been seamlessly absorbed into a basically Chinese landscape. Yet as with the *indianische Blumen* of Meissen and the long established *chinoiserie* delftware style, these diverse idioms would have been regarded as embryonic design sources rather than utterly separate decorative styles.

cf. nos. 122 and 123, for a more coherent use of the Japanese *kakiemon* style.

66. CREAM JUG circa 1752-53

MARK: None

HEIGHT: 2¾ ins

Early creamjugs of this type share similarities in their paste, somewhat matt glaze, their palette and their decorative style, with the exactly contemporary twelve-sided teabowls and saucers, nos. 63 and 64. They are also linked by their tendency for staining in the glaze, a fault which was almost completely eradicated at the factory by about 1754. Examples vary slightly in the accentuation of their V-shaped lips and were issued with two separate handle forms. Two creamjugs, both in North American collections, have the additional ornament of a masked lip.[6]

As with the octagonal coffee cup, no. 56, one single example of this shape is recorded in underglaze blue. It displays a lack of definition in its decoration and areas of brown staining in its glaze, and would certainly have been viewed as a poor product alongside the aesthetically successful range of polychrome models.

This form of creamjug shares several characteristics with a model from the 'A' marked class, now provisionally ascribed to the first Bow patent and dating from 1745-46. There are similarities in the handle form and overall shape and especially in the accentuated lip, though not with the decoration.

cf. John Mallet, *The 'A' Marked Porcelains Revisited*, front cover, ECC Transactions, vol. 15, part 2, 1994, for an earlier creamjug somewhat analogous in shape.

ccf. Simon Spero, *Exhibition 1998*, cat. no. 34, for the only recorded example of a blue and white creamjug of this type.

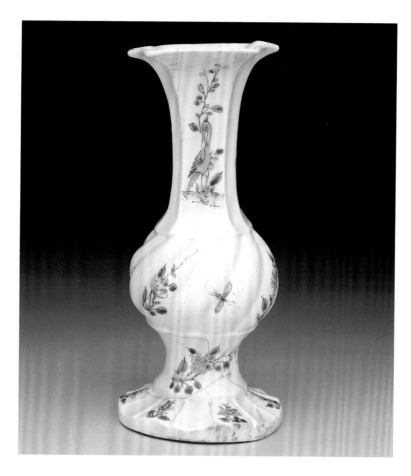

67. GLOBULAR VASE circa 1752-53

MARK: None

HEIGHT: 6½ ins

An enthralling shape, perhaps owing something to metalwork, but fundamentally an imaginative creation by the Worcester factory designers. The upper portion is clearly derived from a Chinese *famille verte* flared vase from a garniture set. Yet incongruously, the central section is palpably European in concept and somewhat reminiscent of George II glass, an impression accentuated by the thinness of the potting. Yet hybrid though this shape might be, its ingenious design would allow it to retain its balance and artistic integrity in either reduced or enlarged proportions, and indeed it is recorded in a larger size.

Its indeterminate genesis is mirrored in the delightful painted decoration, sensitively complimenting the linear complexity of the shape, yet seamlessly integrating Chinese and Japanese motifs. Even the crane-like bird with its demurely oriental demeanour is an entirely fanciful creation, utterly appropriate to its setting. The treatment of the bird, together with the hesitant outline of the flowering stalks, suggest that this vase may have been painted by the same hand as the bottle-shaped vase, no. 69. The bird itself does not occur on contemporary underglaze blue decoration. Nor indeed, do any of the range of allusive moulded models, nos. 67, 68, 69, 91 or nos. 45-47. This serves to emphasise the factory's distinction on both commercial and aesthetic grounds, identifying those shapes more suited to polychrome decoration.

cf. H Rissik Marshall, *Coloured Worcester Porcelain of The First Period*, no. 44, for a tall quatrefoil vase which formed the basis for the upper section of this example.

PROVENANCE: *The Frank Arnold Collection*

68. OVAL POTTING PAN circa 1752-53

MARK: None
LENGTH: 7 ins
WIDTH: 5 ins

The depth, intricacy and detail of this rococo moulding was unequalled in early English porcelain and far beyond the aspirations of Chinese importations. Embellished with *chinoiserie* landscapes within the swirling moulded panels, this potting pan might seem rather an ornate form for so mundane a function. Yet this criteria might apply equally to moulded sauceboats, creamboats and cups of this period, begging the question as to whether these elegant and completely novel vessels were purely functional. Comparable sophisticated models at contemporary factories such as Chelsea, Longton Hall and Derby, would surely have been intended for the dessert course, where utility was secondary to ornament.

The potting pans described in the factory's wholesale price list of about 1755-56 as being issued in three sizes would almost certainly have been blue and white. The heavily moulded coloured version illustrated here, was confined to about 1752-53. From about 1755 onwards, the shape was confined entirely to underglaze blue.[7] According to the Worcester price list, potting pots had covers and potting pans did not. Contemporary recipes made no such distinction, although it is clear that potted meats were sometimes served hot, accounting no doubt for the optional cover.

A recipe for potted swan, by E Smith in *The Compleat Housewife or Accomplished Gentlewoman's Companion*, published in 1753, recommends: "Bone and skin the swan, beat meat with clear fat bacon, cook with bread, drain, squeeze out moisture, cover with clarified butter, next day paper it up". This elegant potting pan might conceivably have been suitable to contain this most distinguished of potted meats.

cf. Simon Spero, *Exhibition 1994,* cat. no. 25, for a small Worcester oval lattice work white tureen and cover, corresponding exactly to the wholesale price list description of about 1755-56 "Potting Pots and Covers white, Oval Basket work … 2/6d".

PROVENANCE: *The H E Marshall Collection*

69. HEXAGONAL BOTTLE-SHAPED VASE circa 1753

MARK: None

HEIGHT: 4⅝ ins

The crane-like bird, head demurely lowered, is one of the most evocative and endearing images on early Worcester porcelain. It recurs on a range of creamjugs, teawares and in the reserved panels of sauceboats and creamboats. In its simplest form, flanked by arching plants, this engaging theme is almost entirely drawn from the imagination of the Worcester designers. Imbued with Chinese and Japanese idioms, it directly imitates neither. In this sense, it embodies the parallels with the *indianische Blumen* of Meissen, wherein Chinese and Japanese motifs were interwoven so as to create an entirely fresh decorative idiom with its own palette, style and *chinoiserie* atmosphere. The bird itself also occurs incorporated into a *famille rose* design on Bow of approximately the same period.[8] Such direct parallels between these two factories during the 1750s are seldom encountered.

The range of small moulded vases, principally devised for decorative purposes, which were such a feature of the early production, were not mirrored elsewhere in contemporary factories. Yet this innovative output was not without its technical handicaps. The most serious of these problems was distortion in the firing which often affected the slightly larger vases, nos. 67 and 125. Even the small hexagonal vases sometimes suffered contortions, twisting their upper sections askew.

70. MOULDED SAUCEBOAT circa 1753

MARK: None

LENGTH: 6¼ ins

A low moulded form which is known in only one size, although the model almost certainly corresponds to the underglaze blue version, listed as "Pannel'd Boats 1st and 2nd", no. 32. The shape was derived from Lund's Bristol, no. 4. The Bristol models are decorated in underglaze blue with two known exceptions: one in the larger size, "in the white"[9] and the other, a single polychrome example, in a collection in London. By comparison with the Lund's sauceboats, the Worcester versions are greyer in their glaze tone, generally more finely and sharply moulded and more sophisticated in their decorative idiom. They are also far less prone to firing faults and potting distortions. These polychrome Worcester sauceboats range in period from about 1753 until 1756, the slightly later specimens having an almost vestigial thumbrest to their handles, by comparison with the well-modelled cursive flourish evident on the present example.[10] The handles on the earlier examples overall, are far more generous in size and afford a more satisfactory balance to the gently curving lip.

The depiction of the bird, characteristically perched upon one leg, displays striking similarities with those on a small class of Longton Hall of almost exactly the same period. The more thickly applied enamels on Longton Hall and the far more vivid palette, especially the tone of green, serves to veil this intriguing if somewhat unexpected correlation.

cf. Simon Spero, *Exhibition 1989 'Twenty Five Years'* 1989, cat. no. 24, for the only recorded undecorated Lund's Bristol sauceboat of this type.

ccf. Bonhams auction catalogue, *The Billie Pain Collection*, 26th November 2003, lot 71, for a Longton Hall conical bowl with comparable bird decoration, though in an entirely different palette.

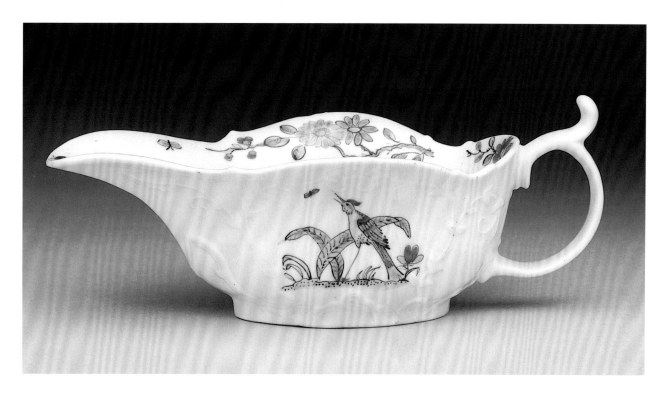

71. MOULDED SAUCEBOAT circa 1753

MARK: None

LENGTH: 6¼ ins

This classic early Worcester model, developed and refined from Lund's Bristol, is a fine example of the sheer novelty of the idiom devised at Worcester within the first year or so of porcelain production. The sophisticated shape evoking but not imitating silver and the intricate moulding in high relief, were both innovative features and embellished a thoroughly functional vessel. Yet it was surely the decorative idiom which must have captured the public imagination. Absorbed within a broad Chinese style, in a highly distinctive palette, is an interpretation and simplification of one aspect of the *indianische Blumen* of Meissen. This specific Meissen idiom of the early 1730s, combined elements of Chinese *famille verte* and *kakiemon* themes, with an element of pure fantasy. The Meissen idiom, often including fanciful birds peering at insects, was never copied. Instead, this invented style was incorporated into the Worcester interpretation of its own *famille verte-rose* creation.

Sauceboats were a prominent feature of most porcelain factory productions from the 1750s until the middle 1780s. Those made at Worcester, Derby, Longton Hall, Vauxhall and sometimes Bow and Liverpool, were generally superior in design to contemporary Chinese models. Mid-eighteenth century cookery books refer to a multitude of sauces, some intended for specific dishes: bread sauce for fowl and game, apple sauce for duck and pork, fennel sauce for fish, alongside the more exotic prune sauce, galentyne sauce, pontiff's sauce and the enigmatic miser's sauce. Yet paradoxically, although the fashion for this myriad of different sauces was introduced by the newly fashionable and often tyrannical French cooks, sauceboats were far less common among the production of the continental porcelain factories.

cf. Simon Spero, *The Bowles Collection of 18th Century English and French Porcelain,* no. 56, for a pair of Bow sauceboats of approximately the same period.

72. BELL SHAPED MUG circa 1753

MARK: Incised cross

HEIGHT: 3¾ ins

A magnificent mug, embodying the remarkable achievement at Worcester, both artistically and technically, in creating subtly designed, superbly potted and delicately painted wares, within two years of the launch of production. In the thinness of its potting, its sleek contours evoking silver, its innovative style of decoration, sparkling palette and sheer practicality, it far outshines its contemporary counterparts, whether Bow[11] or imported Chinese porcelain. From the viewpoint of the discerning consumer, accustomed to the more heavily potted, robust yet relatively crudely painted Bow and Chinese porcelain, this mug must surely have been a revelation. Yet in the context of so technically and commercially successful a product, the Worcester proprietors must have felt dissatisfaction towards the corresponding standard of their blue and white production. The mug, no. 16, for instance is equally well-potted, yet the underglaze blue pattern is not perfectly defined and is blurred in places. Furthermore, the detail and subtlety so evident in the polychrome mug, was beyond the scope of the underglaze blue painters with their background in the mass market delftware industry. For this reason, it is understandable that the factory adopted a short term policy in 1752-53, to concentrate mainly on their polychrome production. During this brief period many of the characteristic models had few, if any, counterparts in underglaze blue.

cf. no. 16, for a rare blue and white mug corresponding in shape and period.

ccf. Anton Gabszewicz, *Made at New Canton*, no. 35 for a Bow baluster mug of corresponding period.

PROVENANCE: *The Lady Corah Collection*

160

73. **LOBED COFFEE CUP** circa 1753

MARK: None

HEIGHT: 2½ ins

Somewhat rarer than the quatrefoil lobed shape, no. 89, this lobed shape is more freely and loosely decorated, almost invariably in this *famille verte* style pattern with its overtones of the Japanese *kakiemon* palette. It displays the Worcester palette of the early 1750s to dazzling effect. The spontaneity of the painting, curving around the beautifully lobed form, uniting oriental motifs with an English shape and handle, must have astonished the public, more used to idioms that were either purely oriental or palpably derived from Meissen. Yet the impression remains that pieces of this kind were probably intended for a more discerning market, perhaps even for porcelain collectors. If this is so, parallels with contemporary Chelsea emerge, although the equivalent Chelsea lobed tewares of the 1752-54 period, adapted from silver models, might seem more suitable as drinking vessels.[12] Furthermore, complete teasets were issued in the Chelsea lobed wares, whereas this Worcester model stands alone, matched with neither saucer nor teabowl.

From about 1754 onwards, the rococo scroll handles which so embellished Worcester coffee cups and creamjugs, no. 89, became gradually simplified, persisting mainly in some sauceboats, creamboats and pleat-moulded teawares, no.135.

cf. John Austin, *Chelsea Porcelain at Williamsburg*, no. 57, for an exactly contemporary Chelsea coffee cup of comparable lobed shape and with a scroll handle.

74. FLUTED CREAMBOAT circa 1753

MARK: None

LENGTH: 4½ ins

This form of fluted creamboat was referred to in the factory's London warehouse wholesale price list as "Cream ewers ribb'd", as opposed to the hexagonal form listed as "pannel'd", no. 109. It shares with the majority of polychrome Worcester creamboats of this period, an interior border of Buddhistic emblems. The exterior decoration, integrating both a Chinese and Japanese *kakiemon* palette, is a little crudely painted and poorly positioned within the finely moulded reserved panel. In this, it has more in common with the decoration on the plate, no. 75, than the lobed coffee cup, no. 73. The well-modelled handle of square section is marginally later in date than the rounded version associated with creamboats on pad feet, no. 51, hexagonal creamboats, no. 109 and mustard pots, no. 96. The handle form was derived from a Limehouse model introduced in about 1746-47. Creamboats (or butter boats) were peculiar to English ceramics, due to the culinary traditions of the eighteenth century. They hardly exist in continental porcelain and are seldom encountered in imported Chinese wares. Yet in early English porcelain, they figure prominently amongst the output of all the major factories and in saltglaze stoneware and early creamware. The shape gradually fell out of fashion during the 1780s.

Although customarily termed creamboats (or "Cream Ewers" in the Worcester price card of 1755-56), this shape may have also been intended for butter which was served in liquid state. Melted butter, often flavoured with parsley, anchovies or even orange, was a popular accompaniment to vegetables. Butter was less expensive than lard.

cf. F Severne Mackenna, *Worcester Porcelain*, plate 4 (e) for an underglaze blue version of this model.

75. PLATE circa 1753

MARK: None
DIAMETER: 9 ins

Loosely adapted from a Chinese *famille verte* model with strong *kakiemon* undertones, and displaying a delft-like influence in its rather crudely executed decoration, this is a rare shape in Worcester, especially in polychrome. Contrary to the prevailing trend in the initial years of production at Worcester, this plate is far inferior to its corresponding blue and white counterpart, no. 22. Yet in plates and dishes, as in teabowls and saucers, Worcester faced fierce competition from Chinese importations, which were serviceable, durable and less expensive. Consequently, the factory chose not to compete seriously in a market so dominated by Chinese porcelain, together with tin-glazed earthenware and Bow porcelain. It is for this reason that the wholesale price list of the London Warehouse omitted any mention of plates and dishes. From this it follows that these shapes are scarce in early Worcester, the polychrome examples especially so. In fact it was not until the late 1760s that Worcester developed a large scale production of dessert wares and was able to compete with Chinese importations in this field.

The few polychrome plates from this era were frequently relatively poorly glazed and sometimes crudely decorated. Either Chinese or delftware plates might have provided a more satisfactory alternative to the contemporary consumer. However, although more expensive, the best Worcester examples outshone their Chinese, delftware and Bow counterparts, in both their palette and in the execution of their decoration.

cf. Anton Gabszewicz, *Made at New Canton*, no. 49, for examples of Bow plates of the 1750s, produced in huge quantities but less expensive than their Worcester counterparts.

76. TEABOWL AND SAUCER circa 1753-54

MARK: None
DIAMETER OF SAUCER: 5 ins

Unlike the majority of patterns of the early 1750s which were interpretations and adaptations of oriental and Meissen themes, this is a direct copy of Chinese *famille rose*. The composition of the different elements of the very detailed design show few variations from piece to piece, nor does the colouring vary as in other patterns of the period. Tearwares, coffee pots and saucerdishes are invariably of comparatively large size, presumably echoing their Chinese originals. Painter's symbols, seldom encountered on polychrome wares of the 1750s, sometimes occur in conjunction with this pattern, perhaps serving to confirm its direct oriental origins.

It is evident from the contours of the coffee pots, the tapering shapes of the teabowls and the overall sophistication of the potting, that particular care was taken with wares painted in this design and certainly, most examples could stand comparison with their similar Chinese counterparts. The pattern was perhaps familiar on Chinese vases and bowls to some English connoisseurs and it inspired both the Worcester designers and their potters to some of their most notable achievements.

cf. Simon Spero and John Sandon, *Worcester Porcelain, 1751-1790: The Zorensky Collection,* nos. 4 and 5, for a saucerdish and coffee pot in this pattern.

77. LARGE JUG circa 1754-55

MARK: Incised scratch and nick marks

HEIGHT: 8⅝ ins

As with coffee pots, early Worcester beer jugs were strongly influenced by slightly earlier George II silver models. The cornucopia moulding on the spout, the scroll handle and the overall contours are all suggestive of a metalwork precursor especially the scrolled lower handle terminal and the delicate moulding below the thumbrest.[13] Yet by comparison with silver, the handle is more generous and the contours of the body slightly exaggerated, perhaps to accommodate the painted ornamentation. The cornucopia moulding too, is far more detailed than on the silver original, probably dating from the middle 1730s. Like the unusual small coffee pot, no. 50, this decoration is an anglicised adaptation of a Meissen idiom of the 1730s, but in this instance, far more freely realised. The pattern, mainly associated with large jugs, is designed so as to curve around the contours of the jug in an engaging if unrealistic manner. As with other shapes from this early period, Worcester beer jugs far excelled both their imported Chinese counterparts and those of most of their contemporary English competitors, in terms of practicability and sheer decorative impact. By comparison with Longton Hall[14] or Derby for example, the Worcester jugs were better potted and had a surer sense of balance and linear vitality.

cf. Dennis G Rice, *Derby Porcelain: The Golden Years 1750-1770,* colour plate G, for an early Derby large jug of approximately similar period.

78. TEABOWL AND SAUCER circa 1755-56

MARK: None

DIAMETER OF SAUCER: 4⅞ ins

The Worcester teabowls and saucers of the middle 1750s far excelled those of all other contemporary factories in the thinness and sheer quality of their potting. Even the imported Chinese teabowls and saucers were hardly superior. To this masterly potting technique was added detailed scroll moulding, an embellishment beyond the scope of the Chinese importations and seldom attempted by contemporary English factories. If one further considers that these teawares had a far greater resistance to the thermal impact of hot liquids than any of their English counterparts, it is readily understandable that Worcester soon became pre-eminent in the production of tea services. By the late 1750s, this moulded decoration on teawares had given way to a series of plain or fluted shapes, less innovative but equally well potted and even sturdier and more resistant to thermal impact.

The decoration, although ostensibly in the manner of Chinese *famille rose*, was also influenced by the delicate Meissen motifs of the 1730s.[15] The scrolling puce border design underlines the European refinements, lending a far greater sophistication to an essentially Chinese idiom.

cf. Anton Gabszewicz, *Made at New Canton*, no. 45, for a Bow saucer of corresponding period, illustrating a far more straightforward and direct treatment of a Chinese *famille rose* design.

79. SAUCER circa 1755-56

MARK: None

DIAMETER OF SAUCER: 4⅞ ins

A thinly potted pleat-moulded saucer painted in a free interpretation of the *indianische Blumen* style of Meissen, popular in the 1730s. The Meissen idiom itself, introduced by J G Höroldt, was a modification of the Japanese *kakiemon* style, intermingled with elements of Chinese *famille verte*. This influence is evident in the orange-red flower-heads[16] which also feature in the border design. However, the pink and green diaper, the partly camouflaged little bird and the moulding in low relief, are all Worcester idioms, themselves adapted respectively from Chinese porcelain and Staffordshire saltglazed stoneware. Thus a truly innovative style was created, as thinly and neatly potted as any Chinese saucer, and far superior in durability and originality of decoration, to contemporary English examples.

This moulding, corresponding to the factory's London Warehouse price card description of "pannelled", was issued mainly on tea and coffee wares. Introduced in about 1754-55, it was used extensively on blue and white wares and remained in production until about 1757-58.

cf. Simon Spero and John Sandon, *Worcester Porcelain, 1751-1790: The Zorensky Collection*, no. 521 (right), for a "pannelled" coffee can painted in underglaze blue.

NOTES

Chapter 7   **Bird Decoration**

1.   Phillips Auction Catalogue (2001), Lot 82.
2.   Bonham's Auction Catalogue (2003), Lot 71.
3.   Gabszewicz, (2000), no.38.
4.   Spero and Sandon, J (1996), no.570.
5.   Wills, (1969), Fig.67.
6.   Spero, (1984), Colour plate 8.
7.   Sandon, J (1993), p.266.
8.   Phillips Auction Catalogue (2001), Lot 82.
9.   Spero, (1984), no.26.
10.   Spero, (1995), no.80.
11.   Dixon, (1962), plate 44B.
12.   Spero, (1995), no.18.
13.   Waldron, (1982), p.340.
14.   Cushion, (1992), p.67.
15.   Pietsche, (1993), no.27.
16.   Pietsche, (1993), no.76.

CHAPTER 8 **PROMINENT FIGURE DECORATION**

The tradition of decorative idioms incorporating Chinese figures prevailed at Worcester from the earliest days of the factory until the late 1770s. Initially, the designs were generally absorbed within landscape scenes and drawn from the imagination, but from the late 1750s onwards, they became either adaptations of Chinese patterns or even direct imitations. Yet this idiom which is so strongly associated with the first two decades of the factory's production and which must assuredly have brought commercial success, was far less prominent elsewhere. At Chelsea, a tiny handful of such designs appeared in the early 1750s, while more surprisingly, the style was sparingly employed at Bow, a far larger concern. When it was used, the oriental figure subjects were highly stylised and most often replicating specific Meissen or Chinese patterns. Vauxhall too tended to avoid this decoration and the few such Derby patterns were invariably direct imitations of Meissen. However, at Longton Hall, a small series of *chinoiserie* designs were developed incorporating Chinese figures, most often decorating mugs. These were spontaneous, highly original and deployed with an eccentricity of palette and representation which somewhat veils intriguing parallels with the idiom devised at Worcester several years earlier.[1] A slightly analogous if more formal version of this style was adopted at the contemporary Liverpool factories of Samuel Gilbody, Richard Chaffers and especially, William Reid.[2] Yet nevertheless, at no other factory of the 1750s was decoration incorporating Chinese figures so prominent as at Worcester.

These *chinoiserie* patterns were fertilised by a multiplicity of disparate sources, including Chinese *famille rose* and *famille verte* porcelain, South Staffordshire opaque white glass, Staffordshire saltglaze earthenware and the *indianische Blumen* of Meissen. This innovative style, associated especially with J E Stadler, combined Chinese *famille rose* and *famille verte* themes with Japanese *kakiemon* motifs, creating a distinctive and idiomatic style which prevailed at Meissen from the middle 1720s through to the early 1730s. More distant parallels can be discerned with both some *Hausmaler* decoration of the same period and with certain pieces from Du Paquier's factory in Vienna.[3]

If the *indianische Blumen* of Meissen served as an influence on the *chinoiserie* style developed at Worcester in the early 1750s, the interpretation of the Chinese figure subjects was very different. The idiom associated with Johann Ehrenfried Stadler, "Master of the Chinese with Fans", is perhaps the closest to the Worcester. Yet his angular figures are more stylised and inhabit a more abstract world of caricature.[4] Individual motifs are juxtaposed so as to create a pattern, almost as one might assemble the props of a stage set. Each element of the design appears to have been composed separately and with the utmost deliberation. Höroldt, who oversaw the work of the painters, compiled a sketch book in 1724-25 of single drawings with Chinese themes, the so-called *Schulz-Codex*. They depict an idealised fairy-tale world of China, inhabited by untroubled and fancifully dressed figures, calmly engaged in fishing, catching birds or insects, merely strolling or standing, holding the inevitable fan. The *indianische Blumen* influence is most evident in patterns depicting single figures in static postures, either pointing or holding fans or parasols, nos. 89 and 91. Yet even in these more repetitive Worcester compositions, there is none of the strict allegiance to a formal house style which characterises the Meissen patterns. Above all, the Worcester *chinoiserie*s lack the self-conscious formality of their Meissen counterparts, whereby every motif is placed with precision and every colour selected with calculated deliberation. The Worcester *chinoiserie*s are more fluid and informal, lending the impression that the painters were allowed a far greater freedom of expression. The landscapes themselves are organic compositions rather than separate motifs assembled in sections and the Worcester figure painting is looser and more relaxed, with a softer palette and far less concern for the areas of white porcelain surrounding the separate motifs. In essence, the concept of the *indianische Blumen* was an ingredient, absorbed into the idiom developed at Worcester, but its spirit was entirely altered.

In some of the earliest Worcester patterns, especially on the twelve-sided teabowls and saucers, no. 80, and the early vases, no. 81, the compositions seem to have been informally created with elements interchangeable between different compositions. Thus, for example, the small boy holding a windmill on the fluted baluster vase, no. 81, reappears in completely different patterns.[5] Similarly, the standing lady on the octagonal teabowl and saucer, no. 84, materialises also on the twelve-sided teabowl and saucer, whilst her young companion, in an attitude of evident consternation, is closely related to the subsidiary figure in the celebrated *Beckoning Chinaman* pattern of the later 1750s. This loose arrangement of composite patterns, briefly employed, was echoed in contemporary underglaze blue landscapes, no. 16. Somewhat random in nature, this practice was abandoned within a year or so in favour of a more conventional adherence to set patterns. These often featured Chinese figures holding fans or parasols, sometimes standing before a fence and flanked by trees, rock formations or vases. The complexity and extent of the secondary decoration was determined by the size and shape of the vessel. On octagonal teapots, coffee cups and bottle-shaped vases, the decorative motifs were necessarily fragmented, whereas on globular teapots, no. 83, bowls no. 86 and sometimes sauceboats, no. 88, an overall continuous landscape was viable. A recurring palette features pink, yellow and brown, a slightly muddy blue and two tones of green. An early tendency for some colours to misfire, no. 84, was swiftly eradicated. It seems likely that the workforce of painters was comparatively small and the same hand may be discerned on different pieces. For instance, the teapot and bowl, nos. 98 and 101, display strong similarities, as do the bottle-shaped vases, nos. 90 and 91. Still more convincingly, the two fine lobed teapots seem to be by the same hand. Here the similarities are striking for a painter working on so irregular a surface.

The earliest pieces, such as the twelve-sided teabowl and saucer, no. 80, the fluted baluster vases, no. 81, and the octagonal teabowl and saucer, no. 84, tend to be decorated with detailed landscapes, elements of which recur in other contemporary compositions. These wares were characteristically prone to such firing flaws as sanding and speckling in the glaze and sometimes staining and discolouration. These faults were rapidly eliminated whilst the quality and thinness of the potting also improved. For the first year or two, the overwhelming majority of pieces were moulded and hand-throwing was only gradually introduced from about 1753-54 onwards, a chronology which contrasts with that of the underglaze blue production. With the introduction of hand-throwing, potting shapes became progressively more functional at the expense of a certain loss of rococo fragility. This increasing emphasis on simplicity and practicality of design over decorative effect, as the production broadened, was mirrored at such contemporary factories as Chelsea, Vauxhall, Derby and Longton Hall. Commercial priorities were paramount. The Collection illustrates this change of emphasis as pieces such as the large jug, no. 103, and the tankard, no. 104, ally the sturdy and rhythmic virtues of practical metalwork models, to those of the connoisseur's china cabinet. Sauceboats were an exception to this gradual shift towards a simplicity of line, retaining their generalised rococo overtones of silver, nos. 95 and 105. Thus, for much of the middle and late 1750s moulded ornamentation was confined principally to sauceboats and creamboats, though it lingered on through some tea services, nos. 78 and 135.

As shapes became more functional, so the Chinese figure subjects gradually lost some of their sense of caprice. The delightful *tableau* of a jaunty chinaman confronted by a coiled serpent, no. 96, and the joyful pair of acrobats balanced beside a *rocaille* table, no. 97, embody this sense of airy frivolity, whilst the vividly decorated creamjug, featuring brightly painted figures with talon-like hands, no. 106, contrasts with the more static treatment of the tightly-grouped family on a slightly later teabowl and saucer, no. 107. Imagination and inventiveness was gradually yielding to commercial reality.

From this chapter, concerned with decoration incorporating Chinese figures, three pieces stand out as being especially striking. The fluted baluster vase, no. 81, painted with such spirit, attention to detail and sense of random activity, presents an engaging and colourful vision of unfathomable oriental activities as seen through European eyes. The tall, extravagantly robed archer, with his vividly be-ribboned parasol, seems oddly equipped for a hunting expedition. His diminutive companion hastens towards him carrying a windmill. Neither seem to have anticipated the possible need for camouflage. More conventional and more directly derivative both in shape and decoration, is the large dish, no. 99. Yet this unique piece is an extraordinary achievement in terms of its potting and its superbly detailed and accomplished decoration, utterly successful in both technical and artistic terms. A *tour de force*, far excelling its Chinese *famille rose* antecedent. Decorative idioms at this initial period of production were unencumbered by the need to conform to set patterns and this allowed a delightful sense of unpredictability, embodied by the octagonal teapot, no. 85. On one side, a Chinese lady coyly extends her fan in the accepted manner of the idiom. Yet on the reverse, her companion stares up in evident astonishment at a sinuous and precipitous rock formation, upon which stands a solitary cow (p.10). The incongruous nature of this *tableau,* with its comical lack of perspective, is illuminated by the sparkling palette, always a focal contribution to the elusive appeal of this seemingly artless decorative style.

No 82 (detail)

80. TWELVE-SIDED TEABOWL AND SAUCER circa 1752

MARK: None

DIAMETER OF SAUCER: 4¾ ins

Even at this initial stage of production, Worcester had developed a coherent *chinoiserie* landscape idiom, allusive, expressive and utterly unlike anything previously seen in European porcelain. The use of the rich green diaper border, echoed in the bushes and trees, adds a fresh dimension to the landscape, emphasising the sharply cursive outlines of the saucer. Six polychrome patterns have so far been recorded on this most idiosyncratic of Worcester shapes, all in the oriental taste, absorbing both Chinese and Japanese motifs. Examples of this shape appear never to bear painted or incised marks.

    This was clearly a somewhat impractical shape for a drinking vessel and it seems unlikely that its Chinese precursor was actually intended for use. Indeed, there are no known teapots, creamjugs or cups to match with these teabowls and saucers. This apparent anomaly may not be quite as puzzling as it first appears. Teabowls and saucers were not a staple element in the output of the early English factories prior to 1753. Chelsea made lobed and octagonal forms, but Limehouse, Lund's Bristol, Derby and Longton Hall all avoided this basic component of the teaservice. Only Bow sought to compete with the superbly potted, relatively inexpensive Chinese importations. The plain circular teabowl and saucer did not emerge elsewhere in England until the early Worcester, Vauxhall and Reid's Liverpool examples of 1753-55.

cf. Simon Spero and John Sandon, *Worcester Porcelain, 1751-1790: The Zorensky Collection,* no. 9, for another pattern associated with this shape.

81. FLUTED BALUSTER VASE circa 1752

MARK: none
HEIGHT: 9 ins

Although echoing oriental decoration, this animated landscape has a sense of fantasy and even caricature, which displays parallels with the *indianische Blumen* of Meissen. The small running figure holding a windmill, arms akimbo, closely resembles a motif on a Meissen pear-shaped ewer painted by Johann Ehrenfried Stadler, who made a speciality of fanciful interpretations of *chinoiserie* themes. His free, loose style, executed in a brilliant palette of elongated figures holding parasols or fans, children flailing toy windmills, tall pine trees, flowering peonies and steep formations of rocks, are all recurring idioms on early Worcester porcelain.[6] Here the decoration is laid out on the faceted shape with the colourfully attired Chinese archer slightly off centre and the barrels and hoops in the foreground, reinforcing the almost skittish sense of parody, with European motifs intruding into the airy *chinoiserie* landscape.

This vase would have formed part of a *garniture de cheminée*, decorating the mantel of the chimney-piece and unlike most Worcester models, is a faithful adaptation of an authentic Chinese shape. One of either five or seven vases, it would originally have had a cover. Whereas the Chinese original would have been used to contain ginger, rhubarb, cinnamon or tea, their European counterparts were purely ornamental. This vase has a distinctly buff-coloured body, linking it to the early class of twelve-sided tewares, no. 80, and the more simply designed creamjugs, no. 66.

cf. Simon Spero, *Worcester Porcelain The Klepser Collection*, colour plate 1, no. 1, for a comparable lobed vase with differing decoration.

82. LOBED TEAPOT circa 1752-53

MARK: None
WIDTH: 7 ins

One of the earliest teapot models issued at Worcester, superbly painted in their newly-invented *chinoiserie* style, loosely interpreting elements of *famille rose-verte* and the Meissen *indianische Blumen*, with an individual idiom drawn from such indigenous sources as tin-glazed earthenware and Staffordshire saltglaze stoneware. From this complex interleaving of complementary influences, has emerged a delightfully airy style, imbued with an element of fantasy and laid out in a sparkling palette. Yet as if not content with this entirely innovative and detailed idiom, the Worcester designers chose to display it on a range of lobed, fluted, hexagonal and quatrefoil shapes. In this instance, the lobed form seems not to have incommoded the painter from creating a fluidly drawn landscape, subtly adapted both to the contours of the shape and to the space available. This same resourcefulness, probably by the same hand, is evident on the fluted baluster vase, no. 81, and the slightly larger teapot, no 83.

As with all the early Worcester models, an overall sense of balance is evident, enhanced by the well-modelled onion-shaped knop. Yet the early period of this superb teapot is disclosed by the light sanding to the glaze, evident on the top of the handle and around the base. This firing blemish recurs on the twelve-sided teabowls and saucers, on vases and other models of this very early class of polychrome wares.

cf. Anton Gabszewicz, *Bow Porcelain The Freeman Collection,* colour plate II for a Bow teapot of the same period, far closer in shape and decoration, to a Chinese original.

ccf. page 171 for the reverse.

PROVENANCE: *The Mrs B B Garstin Collection*

83. LOBED TEAPOT circa 1752-53

MARK: None

HEIGHT: 5¼ ins

WIDTH: 8¼ ins

Even during the initial year or so of production, Worcester offered the public four distinct shapes of teapot, decorated in their innovative *chinoiserie* style: hexagonal, no. 85, plain globular,[7] rococo,[8] and lobed, no. 82. This example, even rarer than no. 82, is an amplified and expanded version of the lobed model. Narrow fluted sections alternate with broad lobed panels, somewhat in the manner of a "ribbed bullet shape" silver kettle of the 1730s.[9] A wider body accommodates an expanded *chinoiserie* scene, whilst the cover becomes more intricate in its design, yet smaller in its proportions. There are faint parallels with the early Derby lobed teapots from the middle 1750s, loosely derived from Meissen, but the Derby decoration, in their "Second Dresden" manner, is far more stylised. This larger lobed model was also issued in *The Banded Hedge*[10] and in underglaze blue, in *The Prunus Fence*. As with all these elaborate moulded shapes, the polychrome versions were issued prior to those in underglaze blue.

Although this landscape shares some general motifs with such underglaze blue patterns as *The Willow Root*, no. 18, there are remarkably few parallels between the polychrome designs of the 1750s and those in blue and white. This strongly suggests that two separate marketing strategies were being independently pursued throughout the decade. A comparison between the Chinese figure on this teapot and corresponding motifs in underglaze blue, nos. 17-19 reveals the far greater measure of detail and definition achieved in polychrome.

Illustrated: Frank Tilley, *Teapots and Tea,* plate XXXIV, no. 107

cf. J L Dixon, *English Porcelain of the 18th Century,* plate 32 (a) for a Derby version of this lobed form, bearing the incised date *1756.*

PROVENANCE: *The H E Marshall Collection*

84. OCTAGONAL TEABOWL AND SAUCER circa 1752-53

MARK: None

DIAMETER OF SAUCER: 4⅝ ins

The earliest polychrome patterns were composite scenes made up from recurring motifs appearing in other contemporary designs. Thus, the Chinese lady appears in a slightly different costume, holding a ceremonial *ruyi* sceptre, on the twelve-sided saucer, no. 80, whilst the running boy, arms akimbo, recurs on the fluted vase, no. 81, and several years later he is regularly summoned by *The Beckoning Chinaman*. Indeed, a strikingly similar figure is present in a fine *chinoiserie* landscape scene on a Meissen ewer painted by Johann Ehrenfried Stadler.

This is probably one of the earliest octagonal teabowls and saucers to have been issued at Worcester, related in its creamy toned paste, matt glaze and palette, to the baluster vase no.81, the twelve-sided teabowl and saucer no. 80, and the creamjug, no. 66. Despite their sophisticated shapes and ambitious *chinoiserie* themes, this distinctive class share a tendency for sanding or speckling in their glaze, a fault evident on this saucer. No other shapes are recorded to go with these teabowls and saucers, and indeed only two examples are known, together with one odd saucer, all originating from the same collection and all decorated in this same *chinoiserie* pattern. Just as the range of lobed and octagonal Chelsea teawares gave way to plain shapes in about 1754-55, so at Worcester did hand-thrown teawares replace twelve-fluted and some octagonal teabowls and saucers.

The *ruyi* was a ceremonial sceptre symbolising notions of wish-fulfillment, social and professional advancement and longevity. The motif recurs on several of the earliest Worcester composite patterns although the painters would have been unaware of its purpose or significance.

cf. Simon Spero and John Sandon, *Worcester Porcelain, 1751-1790: The Zorensky Collection,* no. 137 and 138, for a tankard and a chocolate cup in *The Beckoning Chinaman* pattern.

85. OCTAGONAL TEAPOT circa 1753

MARK: None

HEIGHT: 4¼ ins

The primary decoration, of a Chinese figure holding a fan, flanked by a tree, and flowers issuing from a fence, recurs on many shapes of the early 1750s. Yet on the reverse, (page 10) is a far more whimsical *chinoiserie* landscape, incorporating an improbably gnarled rock formation, surmounted by a windswept pine tree upon which is stranded a lone cow. The precipice upon which the isolated cow stands, is loosely inspired by the Banshi rocks on oriental porcelain, a recurring motif of Chinese chalk cliffs, conveyed here with more humour than realism. This represents an unusually fanciful excursion into the *chinoiserie* style and is not recorded elsewhere. At this early period, patterns on teapots were generally not repeated on the reverse side. The treatment of the small house on the reverse of the teapot and the brush-like trees that surround it, resembles the island landscape on the upper portion of the reverse of the baluster vase, no. 81. The depiction of small tufted rock formations and the drooping fronds are further indication of the same hand, a painter who may also have been responsible for the lobed teapots, nos. 82 and 83, and the teabowls and saucers, nos. 80 and 84.

Octagonal Worcester teapots were produced for only three years or so, from about 1752-54 in polychrome. The even rarer blue and white version, no. 29, differing in shape, spans about 1754-56 and is referred to in the factory's warehouse wholesale price list as "octagn" at 30/- per dozen, exactly twice the cost of a globular teapot. This striking differential in price emphasises both the variety which the factory sought to offer the public and the relative affluence of a proportion of their customers. Unlike the characteristic curved spout associated with these teapots, the blue and white version followed the Chinese model, having a straight spout.

cf. page 10 for the decoration on the reverse.

PROVENANCE: *The H E Marshall Collection*

86. LOBED BOWL circa 1753

MARK: None

DIAMETER: 7¾ ins

Bowls were a speciality in Chinese porcelain, expertly potted, competently painted and imported into England in the eighteenth century in vast quantities. This example is closely adapted from a Chinese model, except that the lobing is perpendicular rather than tapering. The English factories were generally reluctant to embark upon direct competition with the Chinese and throughout the 1750s this was avoided at Chelsea, Longton Hall and Derby. Bow, with their mass market strategy, attempted to match all importations, but their potting of teawares and bowls, especially larger bowls, was markedly inferior to that of the Chinese examples.

At Worcester, from about 1754 onwards, the superb standards of hand-throwing, together with the beneficial soapstone recipe, encouraged the production of finely potted bowls of all sizes, although no large scale attempt was made to compete with the importations of plates, dishes and tureens until the 1770s.

Initially however, Worcester bowls, as with teawares and sauceboats, were moulded. Larger bowls presented problems for the potters and lobed surfaces created difficulties for painters. These handicaps are evident in this rare bowl, yet despite a certain lack of fluidity in the figure painting, the effect of the river landscape on the reverse and the arching pine tree is delightful. A more familiar version of this standard early Worcester pattern, painted on a plain surface, is the teapot and cover, no. 98.

Punch bowls, termed at Worcester "Quart Basons", were made at most of the eighteenth century factories. Most often an after dinner drink, punch was made from five basic ingredients: rum or brandy, boiled water, spices (particularly nutmeg), lemons, oranges, and limes, with the addition of sugar. Worcester "basons", sturdy and resistant to thermal changes, were particularly well-suited to this purpose.

PROVENANCE: *The Ron Wallman Collection*

87. LOBED CREAMJUG circa 1753

MARK: None

HEIGHT: 3¼ ins

A vibrant and allusive press-moulded form, probably intended to match with the early lobed teapots, no. 82. The shape has its clear origins in a silver prototype but a more immediate influence may be from a Staffordshire saltglaze stoneware model, strikingly similar in shape, size and with a similar, if slightly simplified handle. Saltglaze stoneware, especially if undecorated, is notoriously difficult to date with accuracy, but it does seem likely that some complex moulded models of the late 1740s and early 1750s served as the inspiration for Worcester counterparts. To this slender and highly tactile profile has been added a delightful *chinoiserie* design, brimming with humour and vitality and laid out in a brilliant palette. The effect of the decoration is more sophisticated and less stylised than the Chinese, yet more relaxed and informal than Meissen. Similarly, the engaging contours and proportions far excel any Chinese creamjug, yet are less severe and angular than the Meissen creations of the early 1730s. The model, with its strong rococo overtones, is almost exclusively associated with *chinoiserie* designs, whether in polychrome, underglaze blue or purple-puce *camaieu*. A rare exception is of European figures, no. 133.

The decoration strongly resembles that on the lobed teapots, no. 82 and 83, and may be further linked to a series of pieces from this period, nos. 81, 84 and 85. This suggests that perhaps only one or two hands were responsible for the earliest decoration in this idiom.

cf. Geoffrey Godden, *English Blue and White Porcelain,* plate 169 for this model decorated in a underglaze blue.

88. PEDESTAL SAUCEBOAT circa 1753

MARK: None

LENGTH: 8¾ ins

If one can judge from the surviving output – not always a secure premise – sauceboats comprised a startlingly high proportion of the Worcester production of the early 1750s. Yet by comparison with so many shapes of this period, they were conspicuously robust, especially this model, supported upon a pedestal foot. Issued in three sizes and originating in Bristol, no. 6, these sauceboats spanned a period from about 1752 until 1758, being described in the London Warehouse price list as "Sauce-boats, high footed 1st 2nd and 3rd . . ." of which this is the largest size. The shape was issued in polychrome and underglaze blue in three sizes and with overglaze transfer-prints only in the two smaller sizes.[11] It was press moulded in two sections and therefore, the moulded sides did not necessarily correspond with one another. For all its metalwork overtones, no precisely comparable silver counterpart seems to exist.

The model was issued in conjunction with a wide range of designs, almost all oriental in style. The largest size, with its more capacious reserved panels, tended to be particularly finely decorated, especially in the sloping interior border. In essence, this most archetypal of early Worcester sauceboats is a modification and pragmatic simplification of the Lund's Bristol model and its Worcester counterpart, no. 44. The Worcester sauceboats at about 5 shillings a pair, were slightly more expensive than their exactly contemporary Bow counterparts at 4 shillings a pair. Yet they were far more sophisticated in form and decoration and far more durable. To put these costs in context, a rural labourer of the period earned approximately 7 shillings a week and a pair of silver sauceboats cost about £8.

cf. Simon Spero, *The Bowles Collection of 18th Century English and French Porcelain*, no. 56, for a pair of approximately contemporary Bow sauceboats.

89. QUATREFOIL LOBED COFFEE CUP circa 1753

MARK: None

HEIGHT: 2¾ ins

An enchanting Worcester form in which a linear rococo vitality is matched in perfect harmony with airy *chinoiserie* motifs. These cups, issued without saucers, were produced at Worcester in considerable numbers, yet for a very brief period. They embody the inventiveness by which a truly innovative style was devised through disparate strands of influence. The quatrefoil shape was freely adapted from Meissen and softened in impact by its more flared contours. More distantly, the shape may even hark back to the Chinese *Fujian* beakers of the late seventeenth century. The scroll handle acts as a balance to the overall shape and was suggested by rococo silver. The decorative motifs integrate the *indianische Blumen chinoiserie* style of Meissen with Chinese *famille rose* idioms, interpreted in the delicate manner of such *chinoiseries* on South Staffordshire opaque white glass.[12] For all these disparate influences, the effect is utterly different from the more formal Meissen style and perhaps has more in common with comparable motifs on Dutch delft. The shape is recorded in two polychrome patterns[13] and with two handle forms. Two blue and white examples are known, far less successful in their decorative impact, lacking the warmth and definition of the sparkling Worcester palette.[14]

For all its visual allure and elegance of form, this is hardly a practical drinking vessel and seems not to have been designed with utility as its main priority. Perhaps as with other allusive and sophisticated shapes of this period, its primary purpose was decorative, designed to appeal to the connoisseur collector.

cf. John and Margaret Cushion, *British Porcelain*, p. 126 for a Derby interpretation of this quatrefoil shape, so much simplified as to be hardly recognisable.

ccf. Bernard Watney, *English Blue & White Porcelain of the 18th Century*, plate 23A for this model painted in underglaze blue.

90. HEXAGONAL BOTTLE-SHAPED VASE circa 1753

MARK: None

HEIGHT: 4½ ins

Derived from early eighteenth century Chinese models, this form of vase was in production at Worcester from about 1753 until about 1756. It was issued in at least ten patterns of which none were in underglaze blue. In keeping with the origins of the shape, almost all these patterns are in the oriental taste. Although the most common form of vase at Worcester during the middle 1750s, only one single example is recorded from elsewhere, that being a raised anchor period Chelsea example, somewhat larger in size. However, press moulded vases of this shape were also made in Staffordshire, in saltglaze stoneware.

This pattern is chiefly associated with small vases and displays remarkably little variation in either its components or its palette, even the tiny pair of birds being a consistent feature. However, a closely related pattern depicts an almost identical Chinese figure of indeterminate sex, with arms folded, indicative that it might be the companion vase. Themes depicting a single Chinese figure beside a fence, flanked by floral sprays occur both on Chinese porcelain and on Meissen of the early 1730s, painted in the reserved panels of vases attributed to J E Stadler.[15]

cf. no. 91 for a smaller vase with lug handles in an almost identical version of this pattern, probably painted by the same hand.

PROVENANCE: *The John Broad Collection*

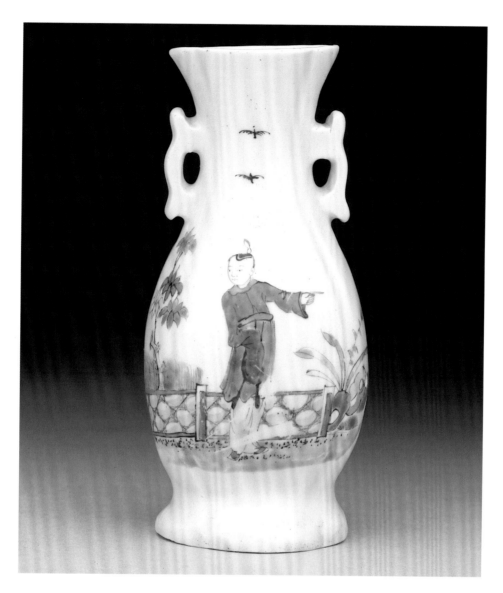

91. TWO-HANDLED VASE circa 1753

MARK: None
HEIGHT: 4 ins

This is smaller than the hexagonal model, far rarer, and was restricted to a shorter period of production, probably of less than two years. However, it shares at least three of the patterns associated with the hexagonal form and was also directly copied from a Chinese model. Although the painted design is basically Chinese, the floral branches on the left are more Japanese in palette, a further instance of the Worcester inclination to integrate disparate oriental motifs. Unlike the flat, partially unglazed underside of its hexagonal counterpart, this indented quatrefoil shape has a shallow footrim.

The distinctive shape is otherwise unknown in early English porcelain aside from several far larger Chelsea and Worcester examples of the early 1750s, and a magnificent early Bow model of similar proportions painted in the *famille rose* style, in the Boston Museum of Arts.

None of the range of Worcester vases of the 1750s appears to be marked in any way, either with incised or painter's symbols.

cf. Anton Gabszewicz, *Made at New Canton,* plate 37, for a Bow vase of approximately corresponding period, also painted in the Chinese taste.

92. LOBED CREAMJUG   circa 1753-54

MARK: None
HEIGHT: 3¼ ins

Unlike the slightly later blue and white versions, the polychrome lobed creamjugs were issued in only one size and remained in production for about three years. They were succeeded by a slightly larger and more heavily moulded model, also echoed in underglaze blue.[16] A more simplified version of this graceful rococo shape was made at Limehouse in about 1746-47.[17]

Although this lobed cursive form, with its rococo scroll handle made in two sections, is redolent of the 1750s, it is significant that it was mirrored at no other contemporary porcelain factory with the exception of Vauxhall and to a lesser extent, William Reid's Liverpool factory. The specific shape itself was not made at the London factory, but Vauxhall did convey much the same decorative flair, expressed in their mastery of moulded ornamentation.[18]   This use of moulding was avoided elsewhere. The apparent dichotomy is perhaps explained by the phosphatic body utilised at Bow and William Reid's Liverpool factory, and the glassy recipes of Chelsea, Longton Hall and Derby, being less suited to press moulded decoration. Thus, the Worcester soapstone formula contributed directly to the individuality of Worcester shapes of the 1750s, by comparison with most other factories of the period.

Although many of the polychrome idioms followed a different path to those in underglaze blue, there were sometimes striking parallels. Here, not only does the central Chinese figure resemble that on *The Lange Lijzen* bottle, no. 19, but the tufted bush to her left bears comparison to that in the exactly contemporary underglaze blue pattern. This cross fertilization of idioms is also evident in the drooping reeds to the right of the figure, echoed on the blue and white mug, no. 18.

cf. Anton Gabszewicz, *Made at New Canton,* plate 42, for rare Bow cream jug exactly contemporary in period.

93. OCTAGONAL TEAPOT circa 1753-54

MARK: None
HEIGHT: 4¾ ins

The origin of the octagonal teapots, produced at Worcester between 1752 and about 1754, presents an intriguing conundrum. Octagonal and hexagonal teapots were being imported from China in the mid seventeenth century. Francis Hayman's painting of *Jonathan Tyers and Family,* 1740, shows the family taking tea. The porcelain tea service is Chinese, yet the hexagonal teapot is redware and almost certainly, oriental. Octagonal teapots were made in silver during the 1720s. Yet it is likely that inspiration for the Worcester octagonal teapots emanates from Staffordshire. Hexagonal and octagonal teapots in imitation of the red stoneware of *Yi-hsing* were being made by the Elers brothers at the beginning of the eighteenth century, with panels containing oriental scenes in relief.[19] A more immediate inspiration may have been the Staffordshire lead-glazed redware from Samuel Bell's Pomona Works of the 1740s. Teapots share similarities with Worcester in their spouts, moulded panels, overall shape and in the lion or *Dog of Fo* knop, which also appears on Worcester versions. A further possible source may have been the hexagonal saltglazed stoneware teapots of the 1740s, closely resembling the Worcester model and often having *chinoiserie* figures, trees and birds moulded within reserved panels. The Worcester designers created a more vivid effect by replacing the moulding within the panels with brightly painted *chinoiserie* scenes.

cf. M Mellanay Delhom, *English Pottery The Mint Museum,* no. 187 for a plain white hexagonal saltglazed stoneware teapot and no. 188 for a saltglazed blockmould for a hexagonal teapot.

PROVENANCE: *The Major Galloway Collection*

94. OCTAGONAL COFFEE CUP circa 1753-54

MARK: None

HEIGHT: 2½ ins

Octagonal forms at Worcester were almost invariably associated with decoration in the oriental style. In this instance, alternating panels depict an oriental vase of flowers, a Chinese figure and an elongated spray in the Worcester adaptation of the *indianische Blumen* style. Coffee cups in this recurring pattern have no saucers, neither are teabowls known. This anomaly contrasts with the exactly contemporary Chelsea output of octagonal tewares. Yet whereas Chelsea harked back to the Meissen forms of the 1730s and 1740s, Worcester octagonal forms were influenced by those of Chinese *Kangxi* porcelain, itself copying the shapes of Japanese *kakiemon* models. These comprised teapots, teabowls and saucers but no coffee cups, vessels which were unknown in Chinese domestic use. If this class of Chinese porcelain, by now collected in England, lacked coffee cups, it might have made sound commercial sense for Worcester to provide their own. The few patterns in octagonal wares for which teabowls and saucers were provided, tended to be those closely imitating Chinese designs, nos. 113 and 128.

As with so much early Worcester in this idiom, a basically Chinese influence has been interwoven with flowerheads in the Japanese *kakiemon* palette. Yet if no distinction was made between *famille verte* and *famille rose* motifs, the introduction of *kakiemon* colours would hardly have seemed in any way incongruous.

cf. John C. Austin, *Chelsea Porcelain at Williamsburg* plate 44, for an exactly contemporary Chelsea octagonal beaker and saucer.

95. SAUCEBOAT circa 1753-54

MARK: None

LENGTH: 6⅛ ins

One of the rarest of all the early Worcester sauceboat shapes, this model seems invariably to occur in conjunction with particularly clear and inventive moulding, most often featuring a generous fan-shaped central reserved panel. It is also characterised by a distinctive angular handle with an accentuated cursive thumbrest. The shape originated in Lund's Bristol, only three examples being known. At Worcester it was issued in both polychrome and underglaze blue for a brief period of about 1753-54. Although visually a most satisfying form, its handle is a little impractical, lacking the typical sturdiness of the more familiar cursive loop handle. It is this which may account for the short life of the model. As with all Worcester sauceboats, this has no metalwork precursor.

In this instance, the Chinese figure is a little too large for the panel and appears cramped, slightly spoiling the effect. The hand may be gainfully compared with that on the bowl, no. 101, and probably the rococo creamjug, no. 92.

cf. Geoffrey Godden, *English Blue and White Porcelain,* plate 132 for a blue and white Lund's Bristol version of this model, one of only two known. This was formerly in the Bernard Watney Collection.

ccf. Anton Gabszewicz, *Made at New Canton,* plate 40, for a contempory Bow sauceboat on lion paw feet, illustrating a far more direct approach to both a silver influence and a Chinese idiom, yet characteristically lacking any moulded ornamentation.

96. MUSTARD POT circa 1753-54

MARK: Painted arrow and amulet in red

HEIGHT: 2¼ ins

This is the second of two examples recorded of one of the most engaging and humorous *chinoiserie* scenes on early Worcester. A Chinaman is nonchalantly warding off a threatening snake with a wand-like spear, whilst holding up one finger as if to silence the serpent's hissing. From his jaunty demeanour, it is apparent that he is blithely unaware of the stealthy approach of a second snake. The expression and body language of the Chinaman and the contorted hoop-like posture of the serpent, lend the scene a whimsical atmosphere of pure fantasy.

The shape of this mustard pot may have been adapted from contemporary silver, although wet mustard pots for prepared mustard were uncommon in silver until the 1760s. Prior to this period, mustard was generally used as a spice and sprinkled from a caster. The handle was directly derived from that of a contemporary hexagonal Worcester creamboat, itself echoing a Limehouse model, no. 109. The cover would have been slightly domed with a simple pear-shaped knop. As with silver models, porcelain wet mustard pots are exceedingly rare in the period prior to 1760, whether in polychrome or underglaze blue. Only at Bow[20] was there a serious attempt to compete with the large scale importations of Chinese mustard pots, although they were also issued in saltglazed stoneware, costing three shillings each in 1749.[21] When the shape did finally achieve commercial popularity in English porcelain in the 1770s at Worcester, Lowestoft and Caughley, it was principally confined to decoration in underglaze blue transfer-prints.

cf. Simon Spero, *Worcester Porcelain The Klepser Collection*, nos. 9 and 197 for a similar polychrome mustard pot and a contemporary blue and white model.

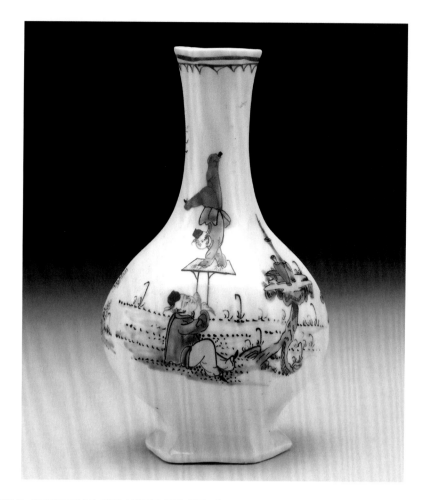

97. HEXAGONAL BOTTLE-SHAPED VASE circa 1753-54

MARK: None

HEIGHT: 4½ ins

This decoration embodies the playful, whimsical humour of the Worcester interpretation of the *chinoiserie* style of the 1750s. Here, in a pattern probably derived from a printed source, a pair of acrobats practice beside an organic table, fashioned from a tree stump, upon which are perched exotic refreshments. The reverse is more prosaically decorated with houses surrounded by a fence. Patterns incorporating acrobats are recorded on mid eighteenth century Chinese porcelain.

The range of Worcester vases, well represented in the A. J. Smith Collection, were like their Chinese precursors, purely ornamental. The majority of models date from the 1752-54 period, a phase of production when the factory's priority was not to compete directly with the utilitarian Chinese wares being imported in vast quantities. Instead, the intention was to employ the skills of their mould makers to create luxury products, superior to the Chinese in terms of ornamentation. This accounts for the emphasis on sauceboats, creamboats and pickle dishes, all of which were novelties in terms of their design and far more decorative than their humdrum Chinese counterparts. Thus the Worcester production at this period would have been seen as a luxurious alternative to the less expensive but more mundane Chinese importations.

Unlike the majority of patterns on these bottle-shaped vases, *The Acrobats* seems to have been a pattern specifically devised for this shape. However, according to W.B. Honey, this distinctive design was also used on South Staffordshire opaque white glass of the middle 1750s, an intriguing correlation.

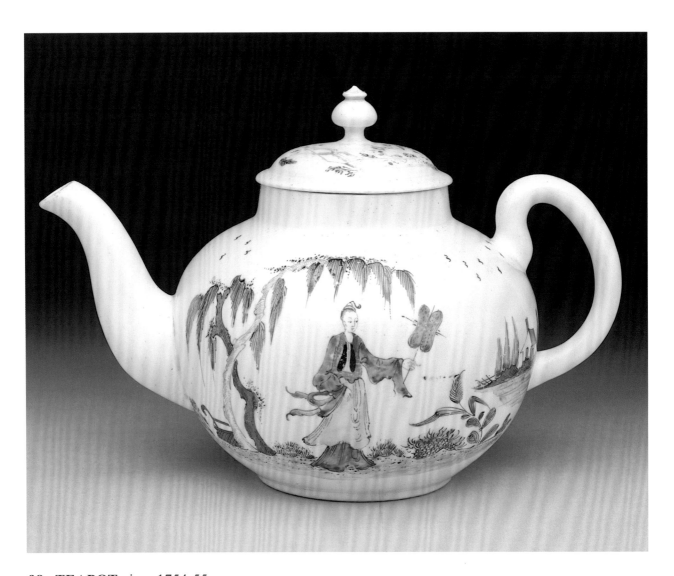

98. TEAPOT circa 1754-55

MARK: None

HEIGHT: 5¼ ins

Issued in two sizes, this plain hand-thrown shape was an alternative to the lobed and octagonal models. It was the progenitor of the classic globular teapot which became the benchmark for all others in the second half of the eighteenth century. As with teabowls and saucers, Worcester teapots afforded the enormous advantage of being able to withstand the impact of boiling water, a recurrent predicament at such factories as Bow, Chelsea, Derby, Lowestoft and Longton Hall, where there was no access to the soapstone formula.

This large teapot has allowed the painter to expand the landscape, lending the Chinese lady a more windswept appearance than on other interpretations, nos. 101 and 102, extending one of the trees so as to arch over her head. The pattern itself has been popularly named "the snake in a basket", so called after the receptacle to the left of the pine tree. Yet on this teapot it is clear that the eponymous serpent is in reality a curved ladle. This was probably the first of all the polychrome landscape patterns in English porcelain, aside from Bow, to appear on plain hand-thrown teasets. It contrasts with the series of Worcester Chinese figure patterns of the late 1750s and beyond where the figures are depicted as the primary feature rather than a component of a landscape scene, no. 107.

cf. Robin Emmerson, *British Teapots and Tea Drinking*, plate 12, no. 182, for a Derby teapot of approximately corresponding period, far more vulnerable to abrupt thermal changes.

99. LARGE CIRCULAR DISH circa 1754

MARK: None

DIAMETER: 12¼ ins

Underside

A remarkable dish copied directly from a Chinese *famille rose* original in both shape and pattern. The design is executed with a delicacy and an attention to detail which does abundant justice to the oriental original. The arrangement of the complex border design is particularly effective. The central pattern also appears on large hexagonal vases with Chinese *kylin* handles. These too were copied at Worcester during the middle 1750s.[22] Adaptations of Chinese shapes were commonplace at the factory during the 1750s, but exact copies, far less so. Here, even the lotus leaf underside of the dish has been precisely replicated. The firing faults which characterised the early jugs and beakers on feet, nos. 45 and 48, are evident in what is probably the most ambitious surviving example of Worcester flatware of the entire decade. For so challenging an undertaking, it is extraordinarily successful, both technically and artistically. Decoration in this idiom was unique to Worcester at this time.

The greyish-toned glaze and relatively muted palette suggest that this dish belongs to the "scratch cross" class, nos. 101 and 103, although it far outshines other specimens of this group in both the refinement of its decoration and in its artistic aspirations. As with other contemporary shapes, including vases, bowls and some tewares, it is difficult to suppose that this dish had a function. It is surely a cabinet piece, mirroring the purpose of its Chinese counterpart.

cf. no. 100 for a "scratch cross" coffee pot painted with elements of the pattern on this large dish.

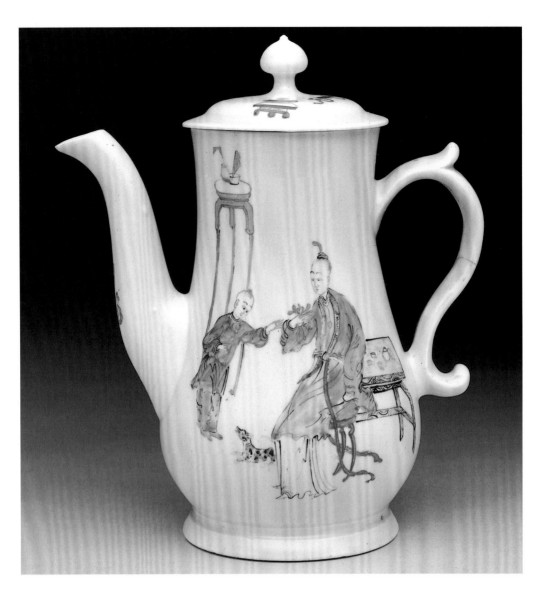

100. COFFEE POT circa 1754-55

MARK: Incised scratch
HEIGHT: 7 ins

Worcester was the first English porcelain factory to introduce coffee pots as a regular component of their production. In the period prior to about 1755, Bow coffee pots seem not to have been issued on a consistent basis, and at Chelsea they were restricted to the "teaplant" and strawberry leaf models of the triangle period (1745-49). From about 1755 onwards, coffee pots were incorporated into the production at Vauxhall, Derby and especially Liverpool, though not at Chelsea and seldom at Longton Hall.

The earliest Worcester coffee pots were adaptations of silver models with flattened covers, curved spouts and scrolled handles applied with a thumbrest. By 1760, they had become taller with more domed covers.[23] With their sophisticated contours and associations with silver, early Worcester coffee pots afforded a far superior alternative to the imported Chinese models, equally robust but lacking elegant contours and linear vitality. This classic "scratch cross" pattern with its languid figures and elongated furniture was ideally suited to the embellishment of large jugs, tankards and coffee pots. The design was not issued on the conventional range of teawares.

cf. Simon Spero and John Sandon, *Worcester Porcelain, 1751-1790: The Zorensky Collection*, nos. 1, 2, 3 and 5 for a discussion about early Worcester coffee pots.

101. BOWL circa 1754-55

MARK: Incised line
DIAMETER: 6 ins

As with their teawares, Worcester was particularly skillful in the potting of bowls. "Basons" are listed in a surviving price card for the factory's London Warehouse at London House, Aldergate Street, in four sizes: quarter pint, half pint, pint and quart. The largest of these cost over four times the price of the quarter pint "bason". Throughout the 1750s and beyond, the production of polychrome bowls was far smaller than that of blue and white, a proportion not mirrored in the output of teawares. At this early period, bowls tended to be sold separately rather than as a component of a tea service.

Naturally, patterns on bowls were laid out more expansively than on other shapes where space was more restricted. Sometimes subsidiary motifs were added or elements of the pattern expanded. Here, for example, the standing lady stretches out her arm, holding a fan, as if about to conduct an orchestra. Her coiffure, flowing sash and facial expression suggest that this bowl was painted by the same hand as the teabowl and saucer, no. 102, the sauceboat, no. 95, and possibly the teapot, no. 98. The pattern appears on the widest range of polychrome shapes of any Worcester design of the middle 1750s, including teawares, coffee cans and wine funnels.

cf. Bernard Watney, *Liverpool Porcelain,* plates 1a, 1b and 1c for comparable Chinese figures on pieces from William Reid's factory dating from the middle 1750s.

102. TEABOWL AND SAUCER circa 1754-55

MARK: None

DIAMETER OF SAUCER: 5 ins

This is the earliest established polychrome pattern on Worcester teawares. It is also the first pattern to appear on plain hand-thrown teawares, as opposed to the twelve-fluted or octagonal models. Until about 1753-54, the crucial and highly profitable market for teawares had been dominated by Chinese importations. Of the first English factories, only Bow attempted to compete with these mass-market importations and despite every effort, they were quite unable to even distantly emulate the staple Chinese production of teabowls and saucers. Even by the middle 1750s, only Bow, Vauxhall and Worcester were making plain hand-thrown teawares. Of these, Worcester was by far the most proficient in the thinness of their potting, the enterprise of the decoration and the sturdiness of their product. This ascendancy in the production of tea services, rooted in their soapstone recipe and superb potting technique, prevailed for a quarter of a century. Only at Vauxhall and Philip Christian's Liverpool factory, was a comparable thinness of potting achieved, in both instances nourished by the indispensable soapstone recipe.

Aside from its practical function, the fan in Chinese art was a symbol of "goodness". The painter of the Chinese figure on the teabowl seems to have been unaware of this as the fan is painted upside down.

cf. John and Margaret Cushion, *British Porcelain*, p.110, for a finely potted Christian's Liverpool teabowl and saucer in underglaze blue.

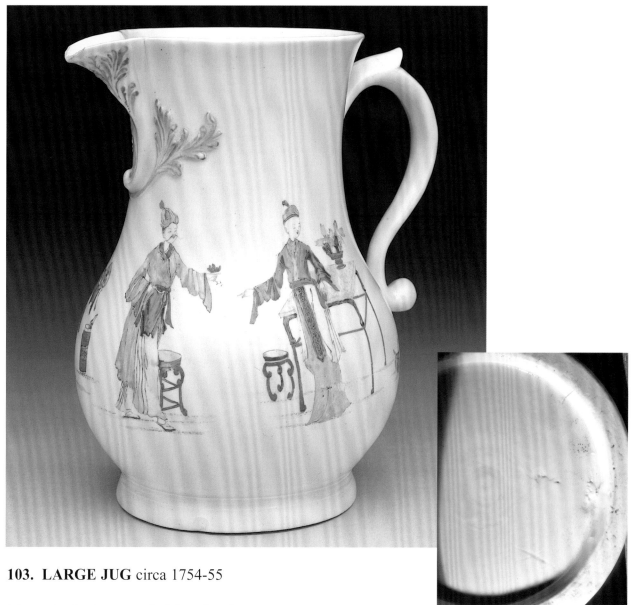

Detail of base showing incised marks

103. LARGE JUG circa 1754-55

MARKS: Incised cross and nick to footrim

HEIGHT: 7¼ ins

A classic Worcester model of the middle 1750s, loosely adapted from a silver original introduced in the 1720s and remaining popular in a variety of styles for nearly fifty years. Features such as the cornucopia moulding on the lip, the lower handle terminal, the residual thumbrest and the graceful baluster outline, were all derived from George II silver models.[24] The cornucopia moulding around the lip, augmented with leaf moulding picked out in puce, is an embellishment not encountered in silver but possibly derived from salt-glazed stoneware. The model was issued in two sizes and also available in underglaze blue.[25] In silver, jugs of this type were generally used for wine, but in porcelain they were more likely to have been intended for either beer or cider.

Chinese figure subjects, often associated with this subdued palette with its tendency to misfire, were mainly issued on tall slender forms such as coffee pots, large jugs, tankards and sometimes vases. This group of patterns contrasts with the brilliant palette used on the slightly earlier *indianische Blumen* mugs, sauceboats and teawares, no. 88. and the teawares of the later 1750s, nos. 106 and 107.

cf. Peter Waldron, *Antique Silver,* 110b for a silver beer jug of baluster form, with a cornucopia lip, dating from 1725.

195

104. TANKARD circa 1754-55

MARK: Incised line

HEIGHT: 4¾ ins

This belongs to a small class of tankards with flared bases and strap handles, characterised by a grey-toned glaze and a less bright and vibrant palette than on other contemporary wares. The decoration is invariably adapted from a standard pattern on Chinese wares and overall, these tankards stand slightly apart, even from comparable "scratch cross" models, no. 103. This has led some authorities to doubt their Worcester origins.[26] However, despite these discrepancies, there are compelling Worcester characteristics in terms of shape, handle form and style of decoration. A related pattern, more elaborate but sharing the same basic elements, occurs on South Staffordshire opaque white glass of the same period.

Beer was brewed in hundreds of varieties in the eighteenth century. A Royal edict of 1637 had forbidden home brewing in order to facilitate taxation. This proved impossible to enforce and was later revoked. By the beginning of the eighteenth century, at least half of the beer consumed in England was home brewed. Some was strong, but "small beer" for servants and children had an alcohol content of as little as 2.3 per cent. Beer mugs and tankards became a speciality at all of the English porcelain factories, usually surpassing Chinese importations in the sophistication of their patterns, contours and potting characteristics.

cf. Delomosne & Son Ltd, *Gilding the Lily,* plate 11, for an opaque white glass vase with comparable decoration, attributed to South Staffordshire and dating from the middle 1750s.

105. TWO-HANDLED SAUCEBOAT circa 1755

MARK: None

LENGTH: 6½ ins

The oriental figures painted within moulded reserved panels and the green diaper border are rare features. Two-handled Worcester sauceboats are almost invariably associated with European decorative motifs, unless they are painted in underglaze blue, no. 33. In this instance, the interior is also decorated with Chinese figures. Two-handled sauceboats were very popular in continental porcelain and it is possible that for all its metalwork overtones, the Worcester model was somewhat influenced by the Meissen version of the 1740s. This smallest of the three sizes issued at Worcester, tends to have thumbrests formed as flattened oval pads, a device adapted from silver models of the 1720s.[27] This contrasts with the more conventional curved thumbrest associated with the middle size, no. 33, and the elaborate monkey-head on the largest size.[28] The floral and shell-moulded decoration and the ribbing on the handles, are features which distinguish these Worcester sauceboats. Yet the various silver models, most often dating from the 1720s and 1730s are surprisingly plain, apart from their scroll handles. Thus, if the moulded ornamentation was not a purely original invention, its inspiration was probably derived from Staffordshire saltglaze rather than from silver.

cf. Simon Spero, *Exhibition 1996*, no. 5, for a remarkable early Bow model far more closely resembling a silver prototype.

No 106 (reverse)

106. CREAMJUG circa 1755-56

MARK: None
HEIGHT: 3¾ ins

An exuberant pattern, characterised by a loose, relaxed and vivacious style of painting, realised in a distinctively bright and well-contrasted palette. The composition itself, animated and atmospheric, displays Worcester *chinoiserie* at its most evocative. Even the wispy willow tree and the trousered ornamental rock formation on the reverse, contribute to the *tableau vivant*. The pattern, confined to teawares and mugs[29] in three sizes, was short-lived but invariably painted with great panache, featuring expressive faces and gestures and curiously talon-like hands.

By the second half of the 1750s, Worcester creamjugs were becoming progressively simpler in design, both in terms of their overall shapes and their handle forms. A plain hand-thrown model was introduced with a grooved loop handle. The shape was to remain essentially unchanged for almost twenty years - a more thinly potted and elegantly finished alternative to the rather basic imported Chinese model. In this instance, the jug has a rolled foot, an embellishment briefly employed on the two sizes of creamjug issued during the 1755-58 period and characterised by their especially neat potting, slender contours and narrow lip.

cf. Delomosne & Son Ltd, *Gilding the Lily,* plate 6, for related decoration on an opaque white vase dating from the middle 1750s and possibly made in South Staffordshire.

ccf. page 198 for detail of the decoration on the reverse.

PROVENANCE: *The McEwen Collection*

107. TEABOWL AND SAUCER circa 1758-60

MARK: None

DIAMETER OF SAUCER: 4¾ ins

This Chinese figure pattern affords an illuminating contrast with the slightly earlier teabowl and saucer, no. 102. The more crowded composition containing four figures reflects a change of emphasis in this idiom. As imitations of Chinese export patterns began to replace innovative *chinoiserie* landscapes, the figures gained more prominence and were no longer just one element in a landscape scene. The figures became more stylised and the palette altered, the characteristic tones of green, puce and brown disappearing completely. Even so, points of reference remain with the earlier pattern, no. 102. The left hand figure holding a stylised fan has now joined a family group and the so called "snake in a basket" is now clearly revealed as a ladle protruding from a square receptacle. The decoration, if more static and one dimensional, remains effective and the Worcester potting is still in a class of its own, by comparison with other English porcelain of the period. The indented rim, a device copied from the Chinese and used during the late 1750s and early 1760s, adds further interest to this bustling scene.

cf. no. 102, for a comparison with a slightly earlier Chinese figure subject.

PROVENANCE: *The Selwyn Parkinson Collection*

NOTES

Chapter 8   **Prominent Figure Decoration**

1.   Pierce, (1988), no.149.
2.   Watney, (1997), plate 1b.
3.   Savage, (1958), plate 67B.
4.   Pietsche, (1993), nos. 59 and 60.
5.   Spero and Sandon, J (1996), no.137 (lacking his windmill).
6.   Jarry, (1981), Fig.100.
7.   Spero and Sandon, J (1996), no.6.
8.   Spero and Sandon, J (1996), no.7.
9.   Waldron, (1982), p.317.
10.   Spero, (1984), Colour plate 5.
11.   Spero and Sandon, J (1996), no.488.
12.   Delomosne & Son Ltd, (1978), no.10 *(right).*
13.   Spero and Sandon, J (1996), no.21.
14.   Branyan *et al.*, (1989), p.42.
15.   Jarry, (1981), Fig.101 *(bottom).*
16.   Reynolds, (1988), no.495, for a larger heavily moulded creamjug.
17.   English Ceramic Circle, (1993), plate XII.
18.   Spero, (2003), plate 43.
19.   Wills, (1969), p.65.
20.   Spero, *Exhibition Catalogue* (2002), no.9.
21.   Edwards, (2003), *"1 Stone Mustard Pot - 3 -".*
22.   Marshall, (1954), no.64, p.125.
23.   Spero, (1984), Colour plate 17.
24.   Waldron, (1982), no.1108, p.340.
25.   Watney, (1973), plate 24A.
26.   Boney, (1957), plates 26b, 27a, 28, 29c and 29d.
27.   Waldron, (1982), no.433.
28.   Spero, (1984), Colour plate 15.
29.   Honey, (1977), plate 81C.

CHAPTER 9 ORIENTAL LANDSCAPES

It seems probable that during the early and middle 1750s, there was a coherent artistic and commercial policy to confine the more established *chinoiserie* landscape idiom to underglaze blue decoration, apart from those designs incorporating prominent figure motifs (Chapter 8). Consequently such characteristic landscapes as nos. 27-29, 32 and 33, have relatively few counterparts in polychrome. This practice was no more than a continuation of the procedure distinguishing between a "porcelain manufactury in imitation of India China Ware", as promulgated at Bristol, and the newly stated purpose of a "porcelain manufactury in imitation of Dresden Ware", adopted at Worcester. In this sense, the underglaze blue idiom developed at Bristol, itself evolved from Limehouse, was expanded and perfected at Worcester. The "imitation of Dresden" designation, applied only to the innovative series of polychrome patterns.

This small section of the Collection is concerned with those polychrome pieces least related to any kind of Meissen influence. At Bow, and to a far lesser extent at Longton Hall, the principal alternative influence was that of Chinese *famille rose*. This style, imitated so assiduously at Bow, was assimilated into the developing Worcester idiom in such a way as to become almost inconspicuous, merely one of several thematic elements fully absorbed into an entirely new *chinoiserie* idiom. On the early creamjug, no. 108, for instance, the palette is not principally *famille rose*. In the same way, the wine funnel, no. 110, and the coffee can, no. 111, both display *famille rose* colours, but they are absorbed into a fresh innovative palette rather than echoing an established oriental pattern. Only on the hexagonal creamboat, no. 109, and the landscape saucer, no. 116, is the decoration more or less completely free of this pervasive Meissen influence. Perhaps this landscape style, with its associations with imported Chinese porcelain and tin-glazed earthenware, was considered insufficiently original for the more cultivated market for which it was intended. The Worcester factory may not have envisaged a specific two-tier market in the manner of Bow, yet there was almost certainly an anticipated distinction between their polychrome and underglaze blue productions in terms of the projected consumer. It is surely significant that so many characteristic shapes of this early period had few if any counterparts in underglaze blue. Small bottle-shaped vases, no. 69, twelve-sided teabowls and saucers, no. 63, plain creamjugs, no. 66, quatrefoil lobed cups, no. 89, and the heavily moulded oval potting pans, no. 68, provide just a few such examples. In the same way, decorative idioms were generally devised for either polychrome or underglaze blue, but seldom for both. One exception perhaps proves the rule. The coffee cup, no. 112, painted in a polychrome variation of an underglaze blue pattern, no. 17, stands out as being atypical. In fact its slightly coarse decoration may even suggest that of an inexperienced hand, more accustomed to the differing technique of painting in underglaze blue.

A small number of recurring patterns from this early period seem to be close interpretations of existing Chinese designs although somewhat altered in palette. These include a *famille verte* design issued in differing colours, nos. 113-115, and *"The Stag Hunt",* widely imitated at many English factories throughout the second half of the eighteenth century, no. 118.

As with the decoration, several diverse influences informed the Worcester shapes. The hexagonal creamboat, no. 109, harks back to an earlier Limehouse model,[1] the wine funnel, no. 110, and the lobed creamjug, no. 118, evoke associations with George II silver, whilst the ribbed coffee can, no. 111, perhaps the archetypal shape of this early period, was possibly developed from a Fulham stoneware model made by Dwight, some seventy years earlier.

108. CREAMJUG circa 1752-53

MARK: None

HEIGHT: 2¾ ins

This is the earliest form of creamjug made at Worcester and the forerunner of the classic "sparrow beak" shape which became the standard model at the factory until the end of the eighteenth century. In its contours, design and practicality, it was far superior to either its imported Chinese or Bow[2] counterparts. Issued with two different handle forms, this scrolled type and a simpler rolled form, it was a beautifully balanced shape. Within a year or so, these handles had given way to a sturdier grooved handle, no. 106, which served as a crucial improvement to a definitive porcelain shape. The contrast with the almost contemporary lobed form with its exuberant rococo handle, no. 92, is remarkable in vessels of the same period, serving the same function and decorated to an equally high standard, often in the same idiom.

The patterns associated with this model were invariably painted in the oriental taste, most often Chinese. *Famille rose* idioms interpreted through the Meissen *indianische Blumen* style, were painted in a delicate palette, creating a subtle yet delightfully spontaneous composition. Unlike their lobed rococo counterparts, no. 87, patterns tended to concentrate on birds and *famille rose* and *famille verte* motifs, rather than on figure subjects.

cf. Simon Spero and John Sandon, *Worcester Porcelain, 1751-1790: The Zorensky Collection*, nos. 12-14, for three creamjugs of this class with contrasting decoration.

109. HEXAGONAL CREAMBOAT circa 1753-54

MARK: None
LENGTH: 4⅝ ins

A hexagonal form introduced at Worcester in about 1753, which continued in production in a slightly simplified form, with a scroll handle, until the middle 1760s.[3] The model is an almost exact replica of a Limehouse creamboat, also with a geranium-moulded lip and an angular handle.[4] It is distinguished by superb moulding and such ornamental embellishments as the bosses on the handle terminals, evoking associations with silver, and the moulded scrollwork on the thumbrest. The bosses on the terminals served the dual purpose of disguising the mould line and obscuring any firing cracks or flaws. The shape probably corresponds to the "Pannel'd Ewers" described in the price list of the London Warehouse in about 1755-56, although this would have referred to the blue and white version, introduced in about 1754-55. Hexagonal creamboats were issued with four different handle forms and were probably sold by retailers in pairs.

The archetypal underglaze blue landscape of the middle 1750s, issued on moulded sauceboats and creamboats, no. 32, was seldom echoed on their polychrome counterparts. More often, the factory's designers considered that bird and figure patterns were more suited to the brilliant *indianische Blumen* palette which they had devised, nos. 71 and 74.

Most silver creamboats were supported upon three feet and unlike sauceboats, there are seldom even approximate correlations between porcelain and silver vessels.

cf. Hilary Young, *English Porcelain 1745-95,* fig. 13, for a comparison between a similar hexagonal Worcester creamboat and a silver-gilt example made by William Bagnall, London, 1755-56.

110. WINE FUNNEL circa 1754

MARK: None
HEIGHT: 4 ins
DIAMETER: 3⅝ ins

Only fourteen coloured examples of this rare shape are known to have survived, together with a handful of underglaze blue models, no. 25. They occur in two slightly differing versions of this flowering peony and rockwork pattern and with a Long Eliza holding a fan, no. 101. One further pattern is recorded of rococo scrollwork in puce *camaieu*. The polychrome examples had a very brief period of production from about 1754 until 1756. The underglaze blue version was reintroduced fleetingly in about 1768-70, in a larger size.[5] The extreme rarity of this shape is accounted for by its fragility and a realisation that porcelain was not an ideal material for the function of a wine funnel.

The purpose of a wine funnel was to decant wine from one vessel into another. Bottles of wine were "binned" or stacked on their sides for long periods, causing an accumulation of sediment. This necessitated decanting prior to the consumption of the wine. Port was especially popular in the eighteenth century, both because it was less heavily taxed than French wines and because it had more patriotic associations than claret following a trade agreement with Portugal in 1703, the Methuen Treaty.

cf. Simon Spero and John Sandon, *Worcester Porcelain, 1751-1790: The Zorensky Collection,* no. 34 for the alternative polychrome pattern on wine funnels and no. 651 for the later model transfer-printed in underglaze blue.

111. COFFEE CAN circa 1754

MARK: None
HEIGHT: 2 ins

This coffee can probably corresponds with the factory's London Warehouse price list of about 1755-56, describing coffee cans as "ribb'd" and selling at 8/- per dozen. Significantly, no mention is made of saucers and indeed no examples are known today. This reference was almost certainly to the blue and white coffee cans of this shape,[6] which invariably seem to be a year or two later in date and of slightly smaller proportions than their polychrome counterparts. The present example is more finely and more ambitiously decorated than normal.[7] The reeded or ribbed surface must have created difficulties for the painter and consequently most decoration is relatively crude by the standards of the time. Yet the sophisticated shape, the thinness of the potting and the complex scroll handle, afford a remarkable contrast with the forthright simplicity of both the Chinese importations and the contemporary Bow coffee cans decorated in a comparable *famille rose* idiom. The vastly superior Worcester product would certainly have warranted a higher price and the comparison mirrors the differences in commercial objectives with the mass market enterprises of Bow and Chinese export porcelain.

The model, unique to Worcester, was in production from about 1754 until about 1756, the coloured versions being generally earlier in date than those in underglaze blue. The shape itself perhaps harks back to a model made by Dwight in stoneware at his Fulham factory during the late seventeenth century. There are similarities in the ridged or ribbed moulding and the flared rim.

cf. Anton Gabszewicz, *Bow Porcelain*, no. 27, for a Bow coffee can in the *famille rose* taste, dating from the same period, robustly potted but far less ambitious in both its design and its decoration.

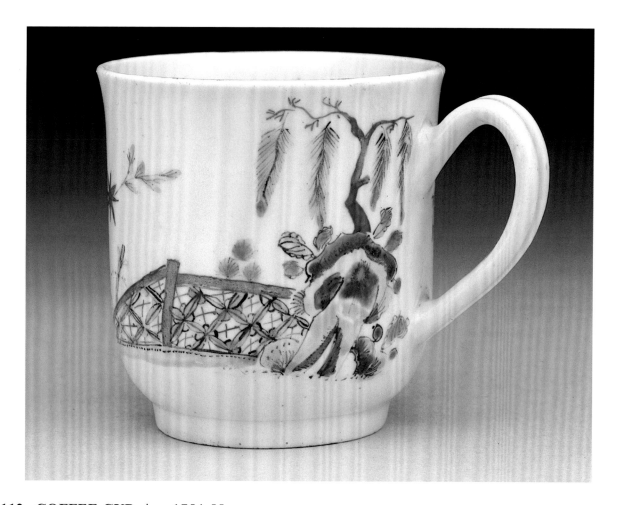

112. COFFEE CUP circa 1754-55

MARK: Incised line
HEIGHT: 2⅜ ins

A classic outline for a Worcester coffee cup of the middle 1750s , cleanly yet robustly potted, with a slightly flared rim and generously grooved handle, in every respect superior to its imported Chinese counterpart. The pattern incorporating a bird and insects within a fenced garden, is painted in a slightly less bright palette than usual for the period. The greyish toned glaze, characteristic of the "scratch cross" class, reinforces this slightly muted effect. Against this background, the tones of green especially, appear a little dull. It could be argued that the idiom looks more successful in the guise of underglaze blue, realised in such patterns as *The Zig-Zag Fence* or *The Rock Warbler*, with both of which it shares elements. More specifically, this pattern closely resembles *The Willow Root* nos. 17 and 18, an extremely unusual example of an early design being issued in both underglaze blue and polychrome. Despite the advantage of a colourful palette, this version paradoxically lacks both the clarity of line and the rythmic spontaneity of the blue and white version.

This is one of a range of Worcester coffee cups, almost invariably painted in Chinese patterns, for which no teabowls and saucers can be matched. Chinese teabowls and saucers were superbly potted, but the coffee cups were far inferior to contemporary Worcester. Furthermore, Chinese cups were significantly more expensive than teabowls because of their inconveniently fragile handles: 2d or 3d, by comparison with 3d for a teabowl and saucer. Bow coffee cups cost 6d, "deft" cups 1½d, whilst an invoice for Worcester porcelain from John Taylor, a pottery and porcelain dealer of Pall Mall, dated 31st May 1753, included "3 Dozen blue handle cups . . . £1 7s 6d".

cf. nos. 17 and 18, for the underglaze blue version of this pattern.

113. OCTAGONAL COFFEE CUP AND SAUCER circa 1754-55

MARK: None
DIAMETER OF SAUCER: 4½ ins

Both this pattern and *The Red Bull*[8] were issued with deep saucers accompanied by octagonal cups and teabowls and a little later, with shallower saucers matched only by octagonal teabowls, no. 115. The pattern is one of the most brilliantly coloured of the 1750s and in its earlier form, features vivid turquoise rockwork, a colour more associated with Staffordshire saltglaze. The design itself, as with so many from this period, is an adaptation of the Chinese *famille verte*, interpreted through the *indianische Blumen* of Meissen. It occurs also on hexagonal and circular bowls, octagonal teapots and on shell-shaped dishes.

This deep form of saucer has no counterpart in underglaze blue and only one single octagonal coffee cup of this class is recorded. Thus, this deep saucer and its corresponding octagonal teapot represent two more Worcester models of the early 1750s deemed more suited to the polychrome idioms of the time than to underglaze blue decoration.

cf. Simon Spero and John Sandon, *Worcester Porcelain, 1751-1790: The Zorensky Collection*, no. 16, for a shell-shaped dish in this pattern.

PROVENANCE: *The H E Marshall Collection*

114. BOWL circa 1755

MARK: None
DIAMETER: 5 ins

One of the relatively few standard or recurring polychrome patterns to be issued during the initial three years of production of a conventional range of shapes, most often hexagonal, but sometimes fluted or plain. The precise palette varied slightly according to the period but the arrangement of the design remained fairly consistent. As with so much Worcester decoration of the middle 1750s, the idiom was an amalgam of Meissen and Chinese, in this instance *famille verte*. This example displays the brilliance of the Worcester palette and its subtly matched colours to vivid effect.

With their mastery of hand-throwing, Worcester could match the Chinese in both thinness of potting and robust durability of teawares and especially bowls. From the middle 1750s, the factory was able to set a benchmark for fine potting beyond the scope of all their English competitors and this technical excellence prevailed throughout the following two decades.

cf. Anton Gabszewicz, *Made at New Canton,* plate 44 for a Bow bowl of approximately corresponding period also painted in the Chinese taste, less well potted and far less enterprising in its decorative idiom and palette.

PROVENANCE: *The Selwyn Parkinson Collection*

115. OCTAGONAL TEABOWL AND SAUCER circa 1755

MARK: None

DIAMETER OF SAUCER: 4¼ ins

By comparison with the octagonal coffee cup and saucer, no. 113, this example is slightly later and the saucer is both more shallow and slightly smaller in diameter. Yet significantly, the palette is more subtle, with a rich tone of green replacing the earlier turquoise and a far more sensitive arrangement of the treatment of the composition. Here is an instance of a refinement of an earlier version of a pattern, lending it more clarity and a more sympathetic combination of colours. The treatment of the branches and foliage, with dotted outlines, perhaps links this decoration with a range of slightly earlier pieces, such as the pair of lobed vases, no. 47, and the octagonal beaker, no. 57.

The deep form of octagonal saucer, echoing those of Chelsea during the early 1750s, nos. 84 and 113, was replaced in about 1754, by a shallower model, far closer to that in Chinese porcelain. This shape, though relatively uncommon, was issued in several polychrome patterns and also in underglaze blue no. 38. The blue and white version remained in production into the early 1760s, issued in at least four patterns, one of them transfer printed. However, it seems that no octagonal cups were issued to match with the teabowls and saucers.

cf. Robin Emmerson, *British Teapots and Tea Drinking,* plate 13 for an octagonal teapot in this pattern.

116. SAUCER circa 1755-56

MARK: None
DIAMETER: 4⅞ ins

In many respects the elements and composition of this pattern, and the manner in which it is painted, has more in common with "pencilled"[9] and underglaze blue designs. Indeed the outlines here are "pencilled" and the serene atmosphere evoked is shared by such underglaze blue patterns as *The Patty Pan Angler*, no. 28. The Chinese fishermen, the highly stylised riverbank and the delft-like expression of perspective are all reminiscent of contemporary blue and white designs, whilst the curious aerial-like structure surmounting the distant hut, resembles that on "pencilled" patterns.[10] The faintly crab-like rock formation in the foreground too, is reminiscent of the "writhing rocks" on the blue and white plate, no. 21.

Another unusual feature is the atypical palette with its prominent tones of yellow and grey. The pattern also has the distinction of being one of the first to employ the factory's standard elements of a "full" tea service, including a sugar box and cover, a teapot stand and a spoontray, although no tea canister has been recorded. These accessories to the basic Worcester tea service did not become regularly available until the greatly broadened production of teawares in the middle 1760s.

cf. Simon Spero and John Sandon, *Worcester Porcelain, 1751-1790: The Zorensky Collection,* nos. 60 and 63 for "pencilled" designs in this idiom.

117. SAUCEBOAT circa 1755-56

MARK: None

LENGTH: 7⅛ ins

Issued in two sizes, this subtle and rhythmic model spans a period from about 1753-1758 and was also produced in underglaze blue.[11] In this instance, the creamier body and strong colours are suggestive of a date in the middle, rather than early, 1750s. The shape was copied by Samson of Paris in underglaze blue in hard paste porcelain, during the late nineteenth century.[12]

In the quality of its detailed moulding and in its decoration and palette, it far excels any imported Chinese sauceboats. In its robust design and construction, it was far less vulnerable to damage than contemporary sauceboats made at Chelsea, Bow, Longton Hall or Derby. Only at Vauxhall was a soapstone recipe used at this period, ideal for the manufacture of sauceboats, as it was for teawares. It was consequently no coincidence that Vauxhall was the single factory to rival Worcester in both the quality and variety of its range of sauceboats.[13]

"The Stag Hunt" pattern, first issued at Worcester in about 1752-53,[14] was used at a range of factories including the Liverpool classes of Richard Chaffers and Samuel Gilbody, Derby, Lowestoft and Chamberlain's Worcester and on Chinese porcelain decorated in England. A group of pieces in this pattern are in the *Zorensky Collection*, nos. 7, 55, 56 and 58.

cf. Simon Spero, *Worcester Porcelain The Klepser Collection*, cat no 27, for a sauceboat of this shape and pattern, but with more detailed moulding.

ccf. no. 120 for a slightly earlier version of this model.

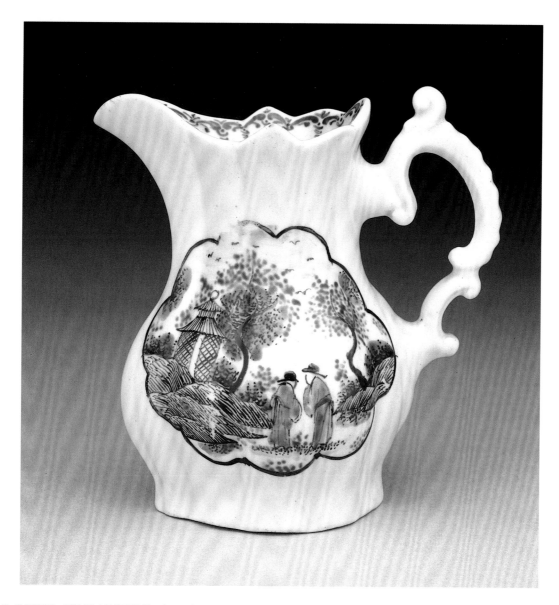

118. LOBED CREAMJUG circa 1755-56

MARK: No mark
HEIGHT: 3 ins

This creamjug, one of the most tactile and visually stimulating models created at Worcester had its origins in a silver shape of the 1740s. It was also the source for a Staffordshire saltglazed version inspired by the complex rococo contours and detailed moulding of metalwork. Worcester adapted the saltglaze model, altering and sharpening up details in the modelling, especially in the handle. The superb quality of the factory's press moulding, together with the slightly opacified glaze, created a jug superior to its saltglaze predecessor, having the additional asset of polychrome decoration. This was almost invariably in the prevailing Chinese taste, with distant undertones of the Meissen *indianische Blumen* and executed with wit and vitality. In this way, through the filter of four separate layers of influence, silver, saltglazed stoneware, Chinese and Meissen, a truly innovative product evolved, beguilingly fragile to the eye, yet durable enough to remain commercially successful for at least five years.

cf. Bernard Watney, *Liverpool Porcelain*, colour plate 2C, for a creamjug showing the reverse of "The Stag Hunt" pattern.

NOTES

Chapter 9   **Oriental Landscapes**

1.   Godden, (2004), Colour plate 28.
2.   Gabszewicz, (2000), no.42 for an exactly contemporary Bow creamjug.
3.   Spero and Sandon, J (1996), no.117.
4.   Godden, (2004), Colour plate 28.
5.   Spero and Sandon, J (1996), no.651.
6.   Spero and Sandon, J (1996), no.521 *(left)*.
7.   H. Sandon, (1969) plate 7.
8.   Spero and Sandon, J (1996), no.501.
9.   Spero and Sandon, J (1996), no.60.
10.   Spero, *Exhibition Catalogue* (2003), no.31.
11.   MacKenna, (1950), Fig.18.
12.   Godden, (2004), plate 701.
13.   Spero, *Exhibition Catalogue* (1999), no.30.
14.   McNeile, (1990), p. 16.

CHAPTER 10 *KAKIEMON* DECORATION

The Worcester approach to the Japanese *kakiemon* idiom was entirely different to that of any other mid eighteenth century factory. At Chelsea the style was a crucial element in their output from the late 1740s until about 1753, when it was abruptly terminated, never to reappear. Patterns were copied either directly from available Japanese sources or from accurate Meissen versions. Not only was the *kakiemon* palette closely imitated, but many of the Chelsea shapes echoed the Japanese models which had not been imported into England since the 1720s. To all but the most practised eye, the Chelsea versions were indistinguishable from their Japanese or Meissen precursors. The Bow production by contrast, concentrated on a narrower range of patterns but a far larger overall output, spanning a longer period of some eighteen or so years. By far the most prominent of these was *The Quail* or *Partridge* pattern which remained conspicuous until the middle 1760s. Bow favoured the Meissen versions of *kakiemon* patterns and was far less enterprising in both their palette and their arrangement of the compositions. They were also less concerned to match *kakiemon* patterns to appropriate shapes. Neither Vauxhall nor Longton Hall made substantial use of the idiom and Derby, for all its explicit Meissen associations, avoided the *kakiemon* palette almost entirely.

The earliest Worcester essays into the *kakiemon* style were painted with great flair and an imaginative juxtaposition of the various elements of the designs. This is exemplified by the glorious fluted baluster vase, no. 119, with the suppleness of the composition arranged to maximum effect as it curves rhythmically around the lobed contours. The treatment of the pair of moulded sauceboats, no. 120, although clearly reflecting *kakiemon* themes, echoes the graceful fluidity of the most inventive *indianische Blumen* compositions, nos. 46 and 49. More conventional interpretations of *The Banded Hedge* pattern, nos. 121-123, seem to mirror Meissen rather than Japanese progenitors, with far less concern for the fidelity of the palette. By the later 1750s, the bright tones of yellow, orange and even turquoise, as on the deep pickle leaf, no. 126, were used essentially for decorative effect, anticipating the *Rich Kakiemon* patterns of the 1770s.[1] In other instances, *kakiemon* motifs and colours have been so integrated into a style developed from Meissen as to be indistinguishable, no. 124.

Just as the Worcester palette was seldom faithful to its *kakiemon* counterpart, the shapes too seldom if ever reflected those of Japanese porcelain. Chelsea models were carefully selected so as to be appropriate for their *kakiemon* designs whereas little effort was made at Worcester to correlate shape with decoration. Shapes were randomly drawn from Chinese porcelain, nos. 119 and 121, freely adapted from silver, nos. 120 and 122, or even from models of their own invention, no. 126.

The original market for imported Japanese *kakiemon* wares had been among the aristocratic and wealthy classes. It may have been for this reason that the revival of this allusive and subtle style was concentrated upon the London factories rather than in the provinces. At Bow, it was one element of a mass market production, gradually focusing on one popular design: *The Quail* pattern. Conversely, the idiom was always a peripheral element in the Worcester *ouevre* throughout the 1750s and 1760s, being used principally for decorative effect in a manner which culminated in the series of *Rich Kakiemon* patterns of the 1770s. Only at Chelsea was the *kakiemon* idiom faithfully replicated, being directed at a more discerning public who were perhaps more conscious of its exotic origins.

It may be that there are parallels between the Chelsea production of imitations of *kakiemon* wares, no longer available through importation and the Worcester copies of *Kangxi* porcelain, an importation also curtailed. This class of Worcester stands apart from the mainstream production in both being a direct imitation rather than a decorative interpretation, and in correlating the specific *famille verte* decoration with shapes which were appropriate to both palette and period, nos. 127 and 128. From a purely business standpoint this would have made sound commercial sense, for neither Chelsea nor Bow supplied the more cultivated connoisseur market, now denied access to importations of *Kangxi* wares, no. 129.

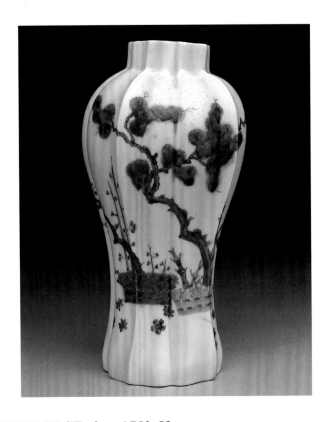

119. FLUTED BALUSTER VASE circa 1752-53

MARK: None
HEIGHT: 8¼ ins

A fluted baluster shape differing slightly from the taller faceted vase, no. 81. Painted in the *kakiemon* taste, this version of a late seventeenth century Japanese *Banded Hedge*[2] pattern has become far more dramatic in its palette than either its *kakiemon* or its more conventional Worcester counterpart, no. 123. As with the exactly contemporary raised anchor Chelsea versions,[3] the gnarled pine has assumed a startlingly verdant foliage, originating at Meissen. Winding around the reverse is a long-tailed phoenix, also decorated in a vibrant style. Whilst the idiom is Japanese, the rhythmic lobed contours are Chinese in inspiration. Yet the palette, the placing of the decorative elements and the expansiveness of the arrangement of the composition, lend it a panache utterly characteristic of early Worcester. The blue branches, anomalous to English eyes, were typical of Japanese *kakiemon* wares.[4]

Somewhat unexpectedly, vases featured conspicuously in the initial output of most of the early English porcelain factories, especially Bow, Derby, Vauxhall and even Chelsea. Perhaps there was a sense that they embodied the public's image of Chinese porcelain. Yet whereas Bow, Vauxhall and Derby vases of the early 1750s are almost invariably simple in design and usually unmoulded, Worcester vases were characteristically lobed, faceted, quatrefoil, no.81, or heavily moulded, no. 67, and occur in a broad range of graceful and ambitious models, all derived from earlier Chinese prototypes.

Illustrated: F Severne Mackenna, *Worcester Porcelain,* plate 3, no. 6

cf. Ayers, Impey and Mallet, *Porcelain for Palaces*, plate 337 for a Bow vase of approximately the same period, decorated in a more conventional *kakiemon* pattern.

PROVENANCE: *The H W Hughes collection*
The Frank Arnold Collection

216

120. PAIR OF MOULDED SAUCEBOATS circa 1753

MARK: None

HEIGHT: 6¾ ins

By comparison with the slightly later model, no. 117, these sauceboats have a very white shiny glaze, almost giving the impression of being opacified. They vary slightly from the later model in their length, the contours of their lips and in the details of their moulding.

The sinuous floral decoration, faintly in the manner of the *indianische Blumen* of Meissen, is more freely executed than was customary in the Worcester interpretation of *kakiemon* themes. The colours too, appear unusually brilliant against the very white porcelain body. From these details of paste, glaze and palette, it may be argued that these sauceboats are amongst the earliest examples of Worcester decorated in the *kakiemon* style. They also display a greater measure of individuality of interpretation and composition than is evident in the shell-shaped dish, no. 122, the pickle leaf, no. 126, or the hexagonal bottle vase, no. 121. Most unusually for a Worcester sauceboat of the 1750s, there is no border pattern on the interior.

The high cost of silver in mid eighteenth century England, relative to porcelain, the prevailing taste for rococo ornamentation and the vogue for a myriad of differing sauces, created a keen demand for porcelain sauceboats mirroring in their contours the luxury associations of silver. This was reflected in the output of the earliest factories in the 1740s and 1750s, alive to the commercial possibilities of this market, unsatisfied by either the unenterprising Chinese importations or the aesthetic limitations of earthenware models. At Limehouse, Bow, Vauxhall and the Liverpool factories of Samuel Gilbody and William Reid, a range of rococo shapes were devised, resonant of earlier silver models. Yet most of these were adaptations of specific silver models of the 1730s and 1740's. By contrast, Worcester sauceboats were generally more original in their design, conveying the spirit and luxury associations of rococo silver in the intricacy and imaginative detail of their moulded ornamentation.

cf. Geoffrey Godden, *English Blue and White Porcelain,* plate 49, for a blue and white Bow version of this model, dating from the middle 1760s.

121. HEXAGONAL BOTTLE-SHAPED VASE circa 1753-54

MARK: None
HEIGHT: 4½ ins

By comparison with the slightly later versions of *The Banded Hedge*, no.126, this is painted in more sombre colours, far more faithful to the Chelsea, Meissen and even *kakiemon* palette. Its origins may even relate to Chinese porcelain decorated in England. The right hand "Wheatsheaf", in reality a bundle of millet or rice, is painted in green rather than in turquoise and there are fewer highlights in bright yellow. The phoenix in flight, also somewhat more subdued in its plumage, appears on the reverse.

These little vases, well represented in the A. J. Smith Collection, are among a wide range of polychrome models of the 1752-55 period, vases, bottles, beakers, bowls and ewers, which have no counterparts in underglaze blue. Yet from the second half of the decade onwards, the vast majority of shapes were issued both in colour and blue and white, a change of emphasis which reflected both an alteration in commercial priorities and the significant widening of the factory's production.

cf. the deep leaf shaped dish, no. 126, for a slightly later version of *The Banded Hedge*, in a brighter, more decorative palette.

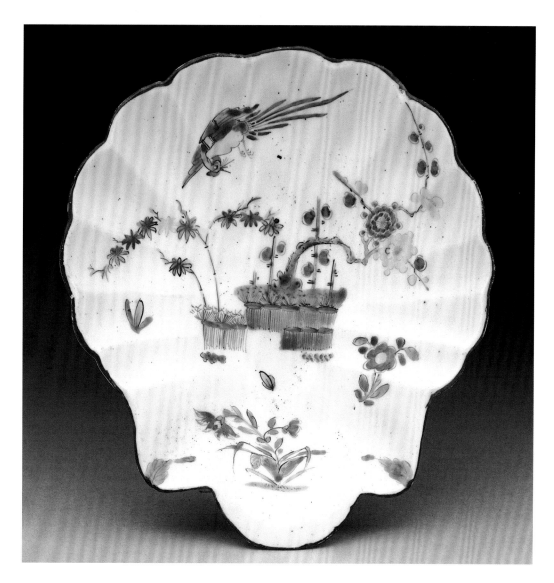

122. SHELL- SHAPED DISH circa 1754-55

MARK: None
HEIGHT: 5¼ ins

Whereas all the principal English factories of the eighteenth century, with the exception of Longton Hall, produced blue and white pickle leaves and shell-shaped dishes in substantial numbers, only Worcester and Bow attempted a large scale replication of this output in polychrome. Bow concentrated on directly competing with Chinese imports, largely utilising their own *famille rose* idiom. Characteristically, Worcester rose to the challenge more obliquely, supplying a product which was both more sophisticated in form and more imaginative in decoration. Their shell-shaped dishes, whether blue and white or polychrome, emphasised the associations with silver in their finely moulded undersides. In underglaze blue, they were issued in four sizes but the far rarer polychrome examples were confined to only two.

The Banded Hedge pattern was a colourful interpretation of a Japanese *kakiemon* theme perhaps viewed through the prism of Meissen, with flowering chrysanthemums, bamboo and a long-tailed phoenix in flight. It embodies elements of the symbolic "Three Friends", a recurring design on Chelsea, Bow and Worcester, but without the pine tree, emblematic of longevity.

cf. John Austin, *Chelsea Porcelain at Williamsburg,* no. 38, for a teabowl and saucer in a differing version of the pattern, in a slightly more subdued palette.

123. OVAL POTTING PAN circa 1754

MARK: None
LENGTH: 6⅝ ins
DIAMETER: 5 ins

The decoration of banded hedges with a phoenix in flight on the reverse, is in the Japanese *kakiemon* taste, although the direct influence was almost certainly that of Meissen.

Potting pans decorated in polychrome were almost entirely confined to Worcester and Derby,[5] all known Worcester examples being of oval form. Underglaze blue versions, most often unmoulded, were issued in various sizes at Limehouse, Bow, Worcester, Lowestoft, Derby, several Liverpool factories and elsewhere. The Worcester London warehouse wholesale price list reference to potting pots in three sizes, is almost certainly to circular examples, painted in underglaze blue. These had almost entirely replaced Worcester's oval shape by the early 1760s. Potting pots had no covers, nor did the majority of potting pans.

Potted meat, fish and especially game, was an effective method of preserving food during the winter months when fresh meat was scarce. Hannah Glasse in her widely popular recipe book of 1747, *The Art of Cookery Made Plain and Easy,* gave advice on how "To save potted Birds that begin to go bad". Meat, fish and even cheese, was baked in butter, sealed with a layer of clarified butter and stored in potting pans, where it could be preserved for up to a year. These dishes were popular amongst the lighter choices in the second course of dinner, served either hot or cold.

cf. Anton Gabszewicz, *Bow Porcelain, The Freeman Collection,* no. 108, for a blue and white Bow oval potted meat dish.

124. TANKARD circa 1756-57

MARK: None

HEIGHT: 5½ ins

A large tankard presenting a perhaps inexperienced painter with an expansive canvas upon which to express himself. This was achieved with more enthusiasm than subtlety. The detailed *kakiemon*-style theme has been handled boldly, but without any understanding of the idiom. The composition, crudely realised, is so crowded and compressed that the structure of the design has been overwhelmed by its greatly enlarged elements. All sense of space and proportionate fidelity has been dissipated. The two birds, for instance, have expanded to alarming proportions and their plumage has become indistinguishable from their surroundings. It is significant that the tankard has suffered chips to the base and glaze faults to the handle during the process of manufacture. It was perhaps for this reason that an apprentice painter was allowed to try his hand on a finished piece of porcelain. Comparisons are instructive between this tankard and the treatment of comparable decoration on a large jug, no. 77. The handsome jug is decorated in the extrovert Worcester interpretation of the *kakiemon* style, executed with equal spirit yet with a much greater appreciation of space, and contour.

Tankards of this shape, with generously curved handles and slightly flared bases, were issued in three sizes from about 1755 to 1758, occurring in polychrome, underglaze blue and in such overglaze transfer-prints as *The King of Prussia*. Slightly earlier precursors of this cylindrical model, with less angular handles and more splayed bases, are nos. 18 and 104 in this Collection.

cf. no. 77, for a comparison with more accomplished decoration in this idiom.

PROVENANCE: *The H Clark Collection, Morton Hampstead*

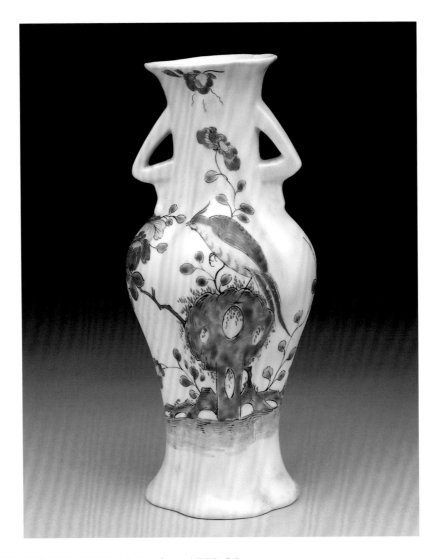

125. QUATREFOIL LOBED VASE circa 1755-56

MARK: None

HEIGHT: 6½ ins

A colourful pattern freely adapted from a late seventeenth century Japanese *kakiemon* design depicting a long-tailed richly plumaged phoenix or *Ho-ho* bird perched upon a scholars rock.[6] Introduced in the middle 1750s, the pattern was issued in four versions. Following its early treatment, it reappeared in the late 1760s on a white ground in both dessert wares and fluted tewares.[7] Thereafter, it was transformed into one of the factory's *Rich Kakiemon* range, either within underglaze blue bands or upon a "wet blue" or *gros bleu* ground.[8] Over the years, the pattern has come to be associated with the artist Sir Joshua Reynolds, perhaps through subsequent ownership. Versions of the earlier interpretation of the pattern were used at Chelsea[9] and Vauxhall[10] in the early and middle 1750s.

The shape was loosely derived from Chinese porcelain although the triangular handles were a Worcester invention. The model first appeared in about 1753 and remained in production until the end of the decade. It was one of the relatively few Worcester shapes of the 1753-55 period decorated in oriental themes which survived until the end of the decade, attired in the new European floral idiom.[11]

cf. Simon Spero, *The Bowles Collection of 18th Century English and French Porcelain*, no. 7, for a Chelsea lobed beaker in this pattern.

126. DEEP PICKLE LEAF circa 1757-58

MARK: None
HEIGHT: 6 ins

A deep form of pickle leaf issued for a brief period, which has an exact counterpart in underglaze blue[12] almost invariably decorated with floral motifs in the Meissen style. This reinforces the impression that *The Banded Hedge* was derived from Meissen rather than from Chelsea or from the original Japanese *kakiemon* porcelain. By comparison with the hexagonal bottle-shaped vase, no. 121, the pattern has become more colourful, a bright turquoise replacing the more sombre tone of green and yellow highlights illuminating the floral motifs. This represents a movement away from the relatively faithful Meissen interpretation of the pattern, towards the *Rich Kakiemon* style developed in the 1770s, loosely utilising *kakiemon* themes to create a purely decorative idiom, intricate, colourful but far removed from any recognisable Japanese style. By about 1760, the extensive range of Worcester pickle leaf dishes and shells was almost entirely confined to underglaze blue decoration.

cf. Simon Spero and John Sandon, *Worcester Porcelain, 1751-1790: The Zorensky Collection*, nos. 297, 298, 300 and 302 for examples of the factory's *Rich Kakiemon* style.

127. DECAGONAL BOWL circa 1754

MARK: None
DIAMETER: 5⅛ ins

Whereas the Chelsea production of the early 1750s was firmly rooted in an earlier Meissen idiom, the Bow factory concentrated principally on imitating and competing with contemporary Chinese importations. Worcester on the other hand sought either to develop their own innovative style drawn from several influences, including *famille rose* and *famille verte* idioms, or else, to directly copy early eighteenth century Chinese porcelain. Direct imitations of patterns as here, were unusual, but a whole range of shapes were produced, otherwise unknown in early English porcelain, all evoking *Kangxi* or early *Chien Lung* models. These included octagonal and decagonal bowls, small bottle-shaped vases, no. 121, fluted baluster vases, no. 119, twelve-sided tewares, no. 63, and garnitures of quatrefoil vases, all shapes free from either Meissen or contemporary imported Chinese influences. This was partly designed to set the Worcester production apart from contemporary porcelain and offer the public something entirely new, echoing Nicholas Sprimont's aspirations at Chelsea, achieved by different means. It may also have been designed to provide collectors and connoisseurs with fine porcelain in the style of earlier Chinese wares, no longer available through importation.

128. OCTAGONAL TEABOWL AND SAUCER circa 1753-54

MARK: None

DIAMETER OF SAUCER: 4½ ins

Unlike the majority of early Worcester patterns, this was derived directly from a Chinese *famille verte* original from the *Kangxi* dynasty, no. 129. Porcelains of this type were highly prized in Europe and imported into England in the early eighteenth century. By the middle of the century they were less readily available, perhaps accounting for Worcester's uncharacteristic decision to imitate Chinese porcelain directly. Although almost certainly not replacement pieces, these were very faithful copies in terms of shapes, patterns (made by copying the "Precious Objects" and Buddhist symbols in the Hundred Antiques), even the border designs being accurately reproduced. In production for only about two years, they were issued in octagonal teapots, coffee cups, teabowls and saucers and flared octagonal and decagonal bowls, no. 127, all exceptionally well potted for their period. Octagonal cups were occasionally printed in outline and coloured in by hand.

The parallel production of octagonal wares at Chelsea during the same period, were less thinly potted and invariably harked back to Meissen of the 1720s and 1730s for their decorative inspiration.[13]

cf. Joseph Handley, *18th Century English Transfer-Printed Porcelain and Enamels*, no. 4.1a, p. 127, for an octagonal coffee cup in this pattern with printed outlines.

129. CHINESE HEXAGONAL BEAKER circa 1700-1720

MARK: Square within two concentric circles

HEIGHT: 2¼ ins

A *Kangxi* beaker painted in the *famille verte* style featuring in its principal palette, a dark tone of green, blue, yellow, purple and red, with an inner hatched border. This style was popular with English collectors in the first half of the eighteenth century but by the 1750s, it was no longer readily available. Worcester, with their ability to pot thinly and reproduce colours accurately, found an eager market for a range of octagonal and hexagonal shapes mainly depicting Buddhist symbols and most often in this exact pattern. In certain respects, it could be argued that the Worcester imitations were superior. The palette was brighter, the colours less muddy and the characteristic roughness of glaze around the rims on Chinese wares, was entirely avoided.

Beakers of this hexagonal form were made in silver with matching saucers in England in about 1710. Their Chinese prototypes of much the same period would have been highly prized by contemporary collectors and connoisseurs in Europe.

cf. no. 128.

NOTES

Chapter 10   *Kakiemon* **Decoration**

1.   Spero and Sandon, J (1996), nos. 296-298.
2.   Ayers, *et al.,* (1990), no.121.
3.   Adams, (2001), Fig.7.19, p.82.
4.   Ayers, *et al.,* (1990), no.135.
5.   Brayshaw Gilhespie, (1961), nos. 33 and 34.
6.   Ayers, *et al.,* (1990), no.136.
7.   Ayers, *et al.,* (1990), no.348.
8.   Spero and Sandon, J (1996), no.310.
9.   Adams, (2001), Fig.3.25 *(left).*
10.   Spero, *Exhibition Catalogue* (1993), no.11, *(and front cover).*
11.   Spero and Sandon, J (1996), no.79.
12.   Branyan *et al.*, (1989), p.274.
13.   Adams, (2001), Fig.7.16.

CHAPTER 11 **EUROPEAN DECORATION**

It is evident from previous chapters that the overwhelming proportion of Worcester during the initial five years or so of production was decorated with oriental themes; Chinese, sometimes Japanese, and often surveyed through the filter of the Meissen *indianische Blumen*. An exactly contemporary factory, Derby, termed ". . . the second Dresden", also concentrated exclusively on Meissen idioms. Yet whereas at Worcester, it was the *chinoiserie* style of the 1720s and early 1730s which became the starting point of a new idiom, Derby sought a more conventional source, imitating the contemporary Meissen themes of the 1740s and early 1750s. These purely European motifs of flowers, figures and sometimes landscapes, reflected current Meissen decoration, highly fashionable yet expensive. As at Chelsea, the Derby production was greatly concerned with figure models, also exclusively derived from Meissen. The Bow output by contrast, was far greater in volume and combined a Meissen influence, especially in its figure production, with a more conservative emphasis on oriental themes, imitated rather than interpreted. The principal competition was overtly perceived as being the Chinese importations, a conviction made explicit in the factory's nomenclature of "New Canton".

From this it is clear that Worcester deliberately sought to offer the public something different from what was available in Chinese importations, contemporary Meissen or other English porcelain. As a consequence, purely European themes played little part in the early output and examples are scarce. The beaker shaped cups on splayed feet, no. 130, are two of only three such models recorded. Their delicate floral painting, almost botanical in style, is in the Meissen taste, perhaps demonstrating an awareness of the prevailing idiom on the contemporary raised anchor period wares at Chelsea. The analogy may be taken further. As with some Chelsea, these two elegantly designed cups lend an impression of being intended for a luxury market, possibly even for a porcelain connoisseur's cabinet. Certainly, in their graceful contours, accomplished potting, subtle floral painting and contrasting rococo scroll handles, they are unlike anything seen before in English porcelain. If they were indeed conceived as curiosities, perhaps even created to a specific commission, it would account both for their extreme rarity and for their apparent incongruity within the mainstream Worcester production of the early 1750s. The octagonal teapot, no. 131, is also a hybrid which fits uneasily into the factory *oeuvre* in terms of its decoration, interweaving associations with redware, Chinese porcelain and Meissen. Like the beaker shaped cups, this intriguing piece may have more in common with the luxury output of the still enigmatic 'A mark' class or with Gouyn's St. James' wares, than with the fundamentally utilitarian emphasis of most English porcelain from the middle 1750s onwards.

Decoration featuring prominent European figures is relatively scarce on English porcelain. The overall style had its genesis in Meissen and was imitated at Chelsea during the raised anchor and early red anchor periods. The specific idiom employed at Worcester during the middle 1750s may have had its roots in the Chinese porcelain, chiefly coffee cups, decorated in independent ateliers in London. These pieces depict figures in contemporary dress, either promenading or clustered together as if engaged in conversation. The compositions are often arranged in such a way as to suggest a printed source. Similar patterns were issued at Derby in the 1753-56 period, particularly on vases, two-handled salts and small punch cups applied with *Tau*-shaped handles. At Worcester the idiom occurs in a slightly uncharacteristic palette and upon shapes with European rather than oriental associations. The compositions are ideally suited to being accommodated within the reserved panels of sauceboats, nos. 132 and 136, and moulded tewares, no. 135. In fact, the idiom seems to occur exclusively in conjunction with moulded, lobed and decagonal shapes, most of which have associations with silver. The style itself, distinctive and reflective of contemporary paintings, uses trees and sometimes buildings with which to frame the conversing figures. It evokes the landscape decoration on Birmingham enamel boxes of an exactly similar period and it is tempting to speculate upon a connection in this particular context.[1]

A defining characteristic of early Worcester porcelain, evident almost throughout this Collection, was for oriental decorative themes to embellish essentially European shapes. This was clearly a premeditated marketing strategy. In much the same way, the short-lived idiom featuring European figures in contemporary dress, seems only to have been employed in conjunction with models specifically associated with silver.

No 135 (detail)

130. TWO BEAKER SHAPED CUPS ON THREE FEET circa 1752-53

MARKS: None
HEIGHTS: 2¾ ins and 3 ins

Two outstanding and utterly atypical pieces which beg several questions. The hexafoil shape supported on three splayed feet, for all its loose silver associations, appears to have no discernible precursor. Only one other example of this beguiling yet slightly impractical shape has been recorded, no. 48. It perhaps belongs to the small class of rococo forms on feet, issued in about 1752-53, comprising teapots,² large jugs, no. 45, and these beaker-cups, possibly intended for chocolate. Coffee pots, teapots, and jugs on splayed feet recur frequently in eighteenth century German porcelain, but no model resembling these Worcester cups has been identified. The sensitively painted and subtly detailed floral decoration too, has no counterpart in the Worcester *oeuvre* of the early 1750s. It is revealing to compare the colourless glaze on these two examples with the more greyish tone of the *famille verte* style cup, no. 48, a distinction which recurs throughout the production of the early 1750s.

In considering the conundrum presented by these untypical yet extremely sophisticated pieces, it might be helpful to seek parallels in other mid eighteenth century English factories. Highly ambitious and refined "luxury wares"³ were produced in the early years of several factories, including triangle period Chelsea⁴ and the 'A mark' class, now provisionally ascribed to the first Bow patent and dated to the mid 1740s. Even at Derby, the initial output was of figures and vases. Hence, there was a precedent for an enterprising output, as the early porcelain makers perceived the market as one for "luxury wares" rather than as competition for the sheer utility of the mass importations of Chinese porcelain. Yet there were inherent hazards to this adventurous *modus operandi*. The larger of these cups, for all its sleek contours and refined decoration, has firing faults in its interior, concealed in a green wash, and a firing crack to one splayed foot. Ambitious shapes such as these and the large jug, no. 45, must surely have been particularly vulnerable to kiln wastage and it is hardly surprising that this early essay into a high rococo style was so short-lived.

cf. Simon Spero and John Sandon, *Worcester Porcelain, 1751-1790: The Zorensky Collection,* no. 7, for rococo moulded teapot on four splayed feet decorated in *"The Staghunt"* pattern.

131. OCTAGONAL TEAPOT circa 1753-54

MARK: None
HEIGHT: 4½ ins

A very uncharacteristic style of decoration for this early period, combining *bianco sopra bianco* with carefully painted insects in the manner of Meissen. A direct Meissen influence, so prominent on contemporary Chelsea, Longton Hall and Derby, is seldom explicit on Worcester of the early 1750s. The octagonal shape is usually seen in conjunction with a small, somewhat impractical triple twig handle. However, some models have a lion knop, derived originally from the "Dog of Fo", a Chinese lion associated with Buddha.[5] This form of knop was widely used on Staffordshire redware and saltglazed teapots, and intriguingly, on teapots from the 'A mark' class, provisionally attributed to the first patent at Bow, of about 1744-45.

By the middle 1750s, Worcester had established a pre-eminence in the market for tewares. Their products were better potted, more practical, more durable and sturdier, than those of any of their English competitors. Furthermore, they far excelled even the Chinese importations in elegance of design and sophistication of decoration. As their commercial ascendancy in this market became more assured, their output increased. Yet, the range and variety of teaware shapes which had characterised the initial five years of production, narrowed. Shapes became progressively simplified with less use of moulded ornamentation. From the dazzling and innovative range of teapots of the early 1750s, a plain globular shape, no. 98, emerged as a triumph of utility of design over originality of shape.

cf. Robin Emmerson, *British Teapots and Tea Drinking,* plate 18, no. 27, for a Staffordshire hexagonal lead-glazed teapot of about 1740.

132. MOULDED SAUCEBOAT circa 1753-54

MARK: None
LENGTH: 9½ ins

Judging from the surviving examples, this model had a very brief period of production. Almost all known specimens are polychrome, aside from a "pencilled" example formerly in the Knowles Boney and Montagu Collections and one single underglaze blue sauceboat, remarkable in its visual impact. This was formerly in the possession of H. Marden King.

By comparison with the *famille rose* model, no. 62, the moulding on this sauceboat has been accentuated by being picked out in colours. The European figure decoration closely follows that on the lobed cream jug, no. 133, the decagonal bowl, no. 134 and the moulded teabowl and saucer, no. 135. In all instances, this distinctive decorative idiom is confined to moulded and faceted forms. As at Derby, it is never extended into the detailed and less stylised landscape developed at Chelsea during the early 1750s.[6]

During the initial twenty five years of production, Worcester devised at least twenty-four sauceboat models, nearly all of which had moulded ornamentation. This far exceeded in detail and intricacy the moulding of any other factory, and the depth of the embossed designs effectively concealed any distortions in the biscuit firing. All these diverse and varied models are suggestive of silver, yet none are exact imitations. During the 1750s, only Vauxhall matched the range, variety and sheer multiplicity of choice afforded by Worcester sauceboats.

cf. Joseph Handley, *18th Century English Transfer-Printed Porcelain and Enamels*, colour plate V (and front cover), for an almost contemporary Vauxhall sauceboat, far more closely based upon a specific silver model.

ccf. Geoffrey Godden, *English Blue and White Porcelain,* colour plate 37, for a blue and white version of this model.

133. LOBED CREAMJUG circa 1753-54

MARK: None

HEIGHT: 2¾ ins

Decoration with prominent European figures is very uncommon on early Worcester porcelain. The idiom is more familiar on contemporary Staffordshire saltglazed earthenware. Yet although the fundamental influence in decoration in this style derives from Meissen, the parallels here are with London decoration on Chinese porcelain and on the figure painting on early Derby vases,[7] baskets and small salts of the 1753-56 period. A further influence is from South Staffordshire or Birmingham opaque white glass. A faceted tall narrow glass scent bottle, formerly in the H E Marshall Collection is decorated with an almost identical figure in a tricorn hat and with stockinged legs. The Worcester style, limited to this same brief span, is associated with heavily moulded sauceboats, no. 132, decagonal bowls, moulded teawares and two-handled sauceboats, no. 136. It rarely occurs in conjunction with unmoulded shapes. Such a practice seems perverse, compounding the technical difficulties of painting in this detailed European idiom, on a moulded or cursive surface. No such demands are associated with contemporary Chelsea, Derby or Chinese porcelain decorated in this style, yet most often with plain unmoulded contours.

Curiously, although surely deliberately, the lobed, decagonal and heavily moulded examples of this idiom tend to have a distinctly greyish cast to their glaze, a characteristic shared with their exactly contemporary Derby counterparts.

cf. Dennis G Rice, *Derby Porcelain: The Golden Years 1750-1770,* fig. 120, for a pair of early baskets with comparable decoration.

134. DECAGONAL BOWL circa 1753-54

MARK: None

DIAMETER: 5⅛ ins

European figure subjects, rare in early Worcester, occur almost entirely in conjunction with moulded ornamentation, usually being contained within reserved panels of sauceboats, no. 136, or teawares, no. 135. Less often, they appear on ribbed or lobed shapes, no. 133, but very seldom on plain shapes such as this bowl. Octagonal, and the far rarer decagonal shapes were made in Chinese porcelain and in silver,[8] but the interior border design here suggests that the general inspiration was that of Meissen. In the decorative idiom, as in the faceted contours, there are parallels with both Meissen and Chelsea. Yet in this instance, the Worcester interpretation of the style was both static and unimaginative. There is little variation in the pattern regardless of the shape upon which it occurs. The contrast with the superb Chelsea interpretation of this Meissen idiom, almost entirely free from repetition, is startling.[9] However, it is possible that the influence was tempered by that of London decoration on Chinese porcelain,[10] a far more stylised version of the genre.

cf. F. Brayshaw Gilhespy, *Derby Porcelain*, fig. 42, for a related style of almost contemporary decoration on a pair of salts.

PROVENANCE: *The H E Marshall Collection*

135. MOULDED COFFEE CAN AND SAUCER circa 1755-56

MARK: None
DIAMETER OF SAUCER: 5 ins

This is by far the most expansive Worcester excursion into the European landscape style, brought to such distinction at Meissen and later employed so successfully at Chelsea. Even at its best, Worcester could hardly compete with the superb landscape painting of Chelsea during the early 1750s, far less with that of Meissen. Yet here, Worcester exemplified resources beyond the scope of Chelsea and scarcely within that of Meissen. The thinness of the potting and the durability of the soapstone body was comparable to imported Chinese porcelain and the decoration far superior. Furthermore, the delicate and detailed moulded border to the saucer and the feather moulding on the coffee can, with overtones of decoration found on silver, provided a commodity which combined utility and innovative decoration far in advance of any other porcelain available in England at this time. The scroll handle on the coffee can, reminiscent of silver, occurs mainly on coffee cans and coffee cups and to a lesser extent on teacups, in conjunction with feather or "pannelled" moulding. The moulding itself and the shape, is echoed in contemporary Doccia porcelain.

   Unlike the creamjug, no. 133, and the decagonal bowl, no. 134, this coffee can and saucer are components of a conventional tea and coffee set, although no corresponding coffee pot has been recorded. A matching teapot is in the Zorensky Collection, no. 43.

cf. Simon Spero, *The Bowles Collection of 18th Century English and French Porcelain*, nos. 14-18, for landscape painting on Chelsea of a corresponding period.

136. TWO-HANDLED SAUCEBOAT circa 1755-57

Mark: None

Length: 6⅕ ins

European figures, a rare form of decoration on early English porcelain, are associated with moulded ornamentation on Worcester, and most especially on two-handled Worcester sauceboats. The theme corresponds approximately to contemporary idioms favoured at Derby, on Chinese porcelain decorated in London and to that on Birmingham enamel snuff boxes.[11] The puce scrollwork around the border is a distinctive feature associated with this style of decoration.

Two-handled sauceboats were not a staple component in the output of early English factories. They appeared briefly at Chelsea during the raised anchor period and still more fleetingly, at Longton Hall in about 1753-54. Aside from this, porcelain examples tended to be either Worcester or Bow. Yet as with so many porcelain models, the Worcester version was far more original in its form. The Chelsea version was directly inspired by a Meissen two-handled creamboat of the 1730s, whilst Longton Hall directly copied a Meissen sauceboat supported on an oval base, also dating from the 1730s. By contrast, the Bow two-handled sauceboats of the 1750s and early 1760s were far plainer, resembling the imported Chinese models with which they competed. The Worcester model had a far more convoluted and allusive genesis. Adopting the loose framework of a delftware design,[12] with moulded scroll handles inspired by silver models of the 1720s and 1730s,[13] the shape is lent far greater sophistication by its moulded cartouches and shell-moulded lips. This innovative use of moulded ornamentation was adapted from Staffordshire saltglazed stoneware and created a highly original shape, far superior to any of its ceramic competitors and invariably decorated to a high standard. This example is the smallest of the three sizes, issued between the middle 1750s and about 1758.

cf. Anton Gabszewicz, *Bow Porcelain*, no. 68, for a pair of slightly earlier sauceboats in the Imari style, far plainer in design.

NOTES

Chapter 11   European Decoration

1.   Watney and Charleston, (1966), plates 92 and 93.
2.   Spero and Sandon, J (1996), no.7.
3.   Spero, (1988), no.59 for a similarly decorated cup from the St James' factory.
4.   Adams, (2001), Fig. 3.19.
5.   Emmerson, (1992), no.29, p.119.
6.   Spero, (1995), plate 15.
7.   Barrett and Thorpe, (1971), plate 29.
8.   Waldron, (1982), no.903.
9.   Spero, (1995), no.20.
10. Tapp, (1938), plate 17, Figs. 39-40.
11. Charleston and Towner, (1977), no.237.
12. Savage and Newman, (1974), p.255.
13. Waldron, (1982), no.433.

CHAPTER 12 "PENCILLED" AND TRANSFER-PRINTED DECORATION

Although integral elements in the Worcester production from about 1755, "pencilled" and overglaze transfer-printed decoration stand apart from the polychrome output at Worcester in the minds of many collectors, particularly those concerned principally with the earliest years of the factory. This preference throws into sharp relief the compelling appeal of the Worcester palette, as devised in the early 1750s, both the colours themselves, and the manner in which they were juxtaposed. The enthusiasm with which this most distinctive of decorative styles is collected, perhaps conveys an insight into its impact on the mid eighteenth century consumer, beguiled as much by its airy sense of caprice and engaging colours, as by its notional domestic function. At any event, both "pencilled" and transfer-printed decoration were peripheral to the formation of the A. J. Smith Collection and the few examples in this chapter were assembled to exemplify these two techniques which evolved during the middle 1750s alongside the *chinoiserie* idiom and which became particularly associated with the Worcester factory.

The technique of "pencilling", using a small pointed brush or "pencil", was used to create detailed patterns in monochrome, usually in either black or puce *camaieu*. The effect when employed in black, resembled an engraving, with some areas being shaded and others more sharply delineated. The superb saucerdish, no. 137, represents this technique at its best, the ample canvas enabling the painter to compose a fluid landscape, expanding such features as the fretwork fence and the slanting pine tree which seems to have been permitted a spiralling existence of its own. The generous space has also allowed for the appearance of a second Chinese figure, leaning comfortably against the fence and observing the *chinoiserie tableau*. Here, in its monochrome purity is an essentially English expression of *chinoiserie*, unalloyed by the colours of *famille verte, famille rose* or the *indianische Blumen* and conveying a more intricate if less vivid atmosphere than the kaleidoscopic series of images in Chapter 9. The pair of "Fig Leaves", no. 138, also represent the factory's monochrome decoration at its most effective, echoing the gentle and allusive Italianate landscape idiom at Chelsea during the early red anchor period.[1] The floral painting affords an illuminating contrast with that on the creamjug, no. 149, and the two baluster mugs, no. 148.

The development and perfection of the technique of overglaze transfer-printing on porcelain was perhaps the most significant single contribution to the commercial success of the Worcester factory and to the English porcelain industry as a whole. It provided a relatively simple, cost effective form of decoration, widening artistic parameters, extending commercial opportunities and initiating new markets.[2] Yet this crucial aspect of the Worcester production from the middle 1750s onwards, lies outside the scope devised for the A. J. Smith Collection. With characteristic judgement he chose to represent overglaze transfer-printing in black by one extreme rarity, no.140 with direct links in its shape to the mainstream thematic emphasis of the Collection.

It might well have seemed logical to utilise the innovative technique of overglaze printing to facilitate the decoration of polychrome *chinoiserie*, landscape and figure patterns, combining the detail and sense of perspective permitted by the print, with the vibrant palette which had proved so successful during the early 1750s. Yet this artistic compromise diminished the effect of both decorative idioms. Figure patterns, no. 141, lacked the fluid rhythms of hand painting and the palette was unsuited to the incorporation of black outlines. Consequently, as the late 1750s yielded to the following decade, these two decorative techniques were used separately, both with conspicuous artistic and commercial success.

137. SAUCERDISH circa 1756-57

MARK: Painter's symbol
DIAMETER: 8 ins

A magnificent example of Worcester *chinoiserie* decoration at its most sensitive and allusive. The unusually large proportions of the dish have enabled the painter to expand the composition so as to position the various elements of the design in an expressive manner. The pine tree, with its gnarled serpentine branches curving upwards, adds a real flavour of the *chinoiserie* spirit, accentuated by the fretwork fence. Leaning upon the fence, a second Chinese figure, augmenting the conventional pattern, surveys the scene attentively. The painter has conveyed a wonderfully detailed dimension to this engaging landscape by means of a lightly charged "pencil" or brush, revealing subtleties such as the Chinaman's wispy moustache and beard, his loose fitting gown and even the tiny tassels on his parasol. His use of space adds a sense of depth and perspective to this enchanting *tableau* which artfully succeeds in conjuring up a European vision of Cathay.

This is an expanded version of one of the half dozen or so black "pencilled" patterns, originating from Chinese designs derived from European prints.

cf. Simon Spero and John Sandon, *Worcester Porcelain, 1751-1790: The Zorensky Collection*, no. 150, for a more conventional version of this pattern, in a more heavily charged brush and compressed uneasily onto a teabowl and saucer. Also nos. 60-62 and 149-51 for a range of other "pencilled" decoration.

138. PAIR OF "FIG LEAVES" circa 1757-58

MARKS: None

DIAMETER: 7½ ins

Worcester "fig leaves" confined to the 1756-58 period are invariably associated with decoration of the highest order. Here, an Italianate landscape with ruined columns echoes a Chelsea idiom of about 1753-54, painted in the manner of Jefferyes Hamett O'Neale. The floral style too, is reminiscent of Chelsea.[3] Yet the Worcester treatment is more fluid and romantic and the emphasis is purely decorative, contrasting with the more precise and allusive Chelsea idiom. Nevertheless, the parallels are intriguing. The employment of detailed moulded ornamentation was a feature which set the Worcester style apart from both Chelsea and Meissen. Superimposed within the subtle moulding on these dishes is a reserved panel modelled as an unrolled scroll, a delightful conceit without precedent in English porcelain.

These innovative dishes foreshadow both the series of leaf-shaped dessert wares which distinguished the Worcester production throughout the 1760s[4] and the range of patterns "pencilled" *en camaieu* in tones varying from rose-pink, puce and lilac, to carmine, mauve and purple.[5] The majority were either moulded teawares and "Blind Earl" dishes painted in a *chinoiserie* landscape, no. 151, or mugs painted in Italianate ruined landscapes.[6]

cf. Simon Spero, *Exhibition* 2003, cat. nos. 10, 11 and 12 for three examples of the Chelsea style in purple-puce *camaieu* in the manner of J H O'Neale.

139. TEABOWL AND SAUCER circa 1758-60

MARKS: None

DIAMETER OF SAUCER: 5¼ ins

This belongs to a small group of patterns, mainly dating from the late 1750s and early 1760s, which are painted or "pencilled" in one colour. The majority of these are in black, no. 137, whereas this design varies from a purple *camaieu,* to a puce, carmine or pink. Generally speaking, the less bright tones are earlier. Almost entirely confined to teawares and "Blind Earl" dishes, the pattern occasionally occurs on leaf dishes, tall Chelsea ewers and creamboats. It is subject to slight variations, especially to the border design.

Most of these delightful *camaieu* patterns are of *chinoiserie* landscapes, in this instance the source possibly being from a Chinese version of a European print. Particular care was associated with this puce *camaieu* idiom. The painting tends to be highly detailed and some teawares, as here, have an indented outline and a border design moulded in low relief. This combination of sophistication of shape and pattern, and functional utility, was without parallel in the porcelain available elsewhere in England during the third quarter of the eighteenth century.

cf. Simon Spero and John Sandon, *Worcester Porcelain, 1751-1790: The Zorensky Collection*, no. 148, for three variations of this pattern, of different periods and in differing tones of puce.

241

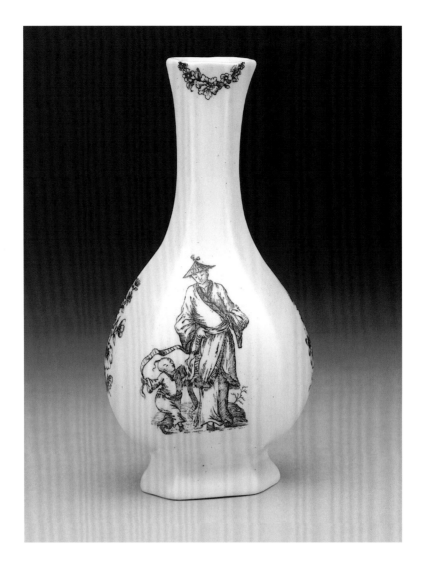

140. HEXAGONAL BOTTLE-SHAPED VASE circa 1753-54

MARK: None

HEIGHT: 4⅝ ins

The development at Worcester of the newly invented technique of overglaze transfer-printing on porcelain, from about 1753-54 onwards, was a crucial and far-sighted commercial and artistic decision with momentous consequences for the economic prosperity of the factory throughout the subsequent two decades. The large-scale exploitation of the process proved extremely profitable, shrewdly assisted by an astute choice of printed subjects.

This hexagonal vase is a shape not conventionally associated with printed decoration and indeed only three examples are known, all in this same design. Yet during the initial period when the technique was first being developed commercially, it was naturally used on the contemporary range of models, including pedestal sauceboats, hexagonal creamboats, pickle shells and small ivy leaf dishes, together with plain hand-thrown tewares. It was also reasonable to try to absorb the new technique into the prevailing *chinoiserie* idiom of the middle 1750s, though subjects with prominent oriental figures were more often confined to polychrome or underglaze blue decoration. The source of the print itself is unknown, although it may share the printed origins of the related "Dry-edge" Derby figural group emblematic of "Feeling" from a set of the Chinese "Senses".[7]

cf. John Mallet, *Agostina Carlini, Modeller of "Dry-Edge" Derby Figures, British Ceramic Design 1600-2002*, plate 6.

141. OCTAGONAL COFFEE CUP AND SAUCER circa 1754

MARK: None

DIAMETER OF SAUCER: 4½ ins

The Red Bull pattern, transfer-printed in outline and hand painted, was derived from a Chinese *famille rose* design of the *Yongzheng* period and remained popular at Worcester from its introduction in about 1754, until the middle 1760s. It was issued on lobed teapots, both types of octagonal teabowls and saucers and on plain tewares. It occurs on a wide range of shapes including tewares, wet and dry mustard pots,[8] hexagonal and plain bowls, small hexagonal bottle-shaped vases, leaf-shaped dishes, finger-bowls and stands and even large vases. It was the earliest of the printed patterns to be incomplete without hand painting and is unknown in purely transfer-printed outlines. The device proved so successful and the pattern so popular, that it endured well into the 1760s, by which time other designs in the idiom had fallen entirely out of fashion.

cf. *Simon Spero and John Sandon, Worcester Porcelain, 1751-1790: The Zorensky Collection*, no. 501, for a finger bowl in this pattern.

142. TEABOWL AND SAUCER circa 1760

MARK: None

DIAMETER OF SAUCER: 4⅝ ins

The technique of transfer-printing on porcelain, first developed at Worcester, was introduced in about 1753 and almost entirely executed in monochrome. However, a small range of patterns was issued with additional polychrome decoration, principally on teawares and mugs. All these patterns were in the Chinese taste and mainly restricted to the late 1750s. The most common were *The Red Bull* pattern, and this delightful scene depicting a pair of geese confronted to their evident consternation by an enormous spray of peonies in *famille rose* colours. It is not clear why this pattern required additional painted decoration but perhaps it appeared too sombre in monochrome. A contemporary Longton Hall version was decorated purely in colours, and substantially the same design hand-painted, was reissued at Worcester in the 1770s, adapted from a Chinese original.

The technique of Chinese scenes in printed outlines, filled in with polychrome enamels was also utilised at Bow in the later 1760s with far less satisfactory results.

cf. Bernard Watney, *Longton Hall Porcelain*, plate 60A, for a hand-painted version of this pattern on a cylindrical mug.

NOTES

Chapter 12   "Pencilled" and Transfer-Printed Decoration

1.   Adams, (2001), Fig. 8.19.
2.   Spero and Sandon, J (1996), Chapter 13.
3.   Austin, (1977), plate 75.
4.   Spero and Sandon, J (1996), nos. 136, 208 and 257.
5.   Spero and Sandon, J (1996), no.148.
6.   Spero and Sandon, J (1996), no.73.
7.   Young, (1999), plate 15.
8.   Spero, *Exhibition Catalogue* (2002), no.22.

THE POST 1756 WARES

The sweeping changes to the decorative idioms used at Worcester from about 1756 onwards, are evident in the small group of later pieces in the Collection, so utterly different in character and spirit to those in previous chapters. Whereas in the early 1750s the factory had harked back to a Meissen idiom of the 1720s and 1730s, infused with disparate oriental motifs, a new style now emerged, unambiguous and up-to-date, reflecting a recognisably contemporary Meissen decorative idiom. Gone was the *indianische Blumen* style and the *chinoiserie*s lingered on only in "pencilled" and transfer-printed decoration. The palette, which so distinguished the earlier idiom, was also altered, both in tone and in the juxtaposition of colours. Decorative styles became explicit rather than obliquely allusive. Meissen themes remained a primary influence, expressed far more directly, as in the *deutsche Blumen*, now reflected in the fashionable Chelsea taste no. 148. Shapes became more simplified, shorn of their rococo overtones and elaborate moulded ornamentation. This more fluid style persisted only in sauceboats, leaf dishes and some creamboats. Otherwise, clean contours, simpler outlines and a pragmatic emphasis on practicality of design, were clear priorities.

This abrupt change of emphasis seems to have been initiated in about 1756-57, coinciding with the opening of the factory's London warehouse, the successful artistic and commercial development of overglaze transfer-printing, an overall widening of production and an increasing awareness of the styles fashionable in London, especially those at Chelsea. No other English factory could match the toughness, durability and thinness of the Worcester tewares, an ascendancy due to the expertise of their potters and the possession of the crucial soapstone formula. With the fashionable new European decorative idioms derived from Meissen, these tewares could not only excel Chinese importations in the quality of their potting, but in their decoration too. Where idioms remained in the Chinese taste, they were more directly influenced by themes recurring on imported wares. Novelty had given way to a more explicit competition.

Elsewhere, Bow was maintaining a large scale two-tier production, incorporating a continuing emphasis on domestic wares in the oriental taste, with an expanding production of figures. Derby too, were launching a figure production alongside their range of dessert wares, also in the Meissen taste. At Longton Hall, figures were also prominent in a distinctive output featuring dessert wares and tewares in an often eccentrically anglicised Meissen idiom. Vauxhall, together with the early Liverpool factories by contrast, concentrated chiefly on decoration in the Chinese taste, with an emphasis on underglaze blue decoration. With the onset of the gold anchor period, Chelsea was moving towards a Sevres style and had more or less abandoned the *deutsche Blumen* of Meissen. Consequently in about 1756-57, there was an opportunity in the market for high quality domestic wares reflecting the taste for contemporary Meissen motifs. This perhaps provided the incentive for the Worcester decision to initiate so radical an alteration to the decorative idiom which they had established to such innovative effect four years earlier. There were recent precedents for this abrupt change in style. Nicholas Sprimont's range of Japanese *kakiemon* patterns and shapes, introduced in 1750 as "A Taste entirely new" was abruptly superseded in 1754, never to reappear, by both a fresh porcelain recipe and a completely different decorative idiom drawn from the *deutsche Blumen* style. This new Chelsea recipe was suited to the production of plates and dishes, but far less so, for other domestic wares, such as teapots, jugs and vases. Consequently, it in turn was discarded two years later in favour of a more glassy recipe, facilitating the production of vases, large figures and other models in the more highly gilded and opulent designs which had developed at Sevres. But Chelsea were concerned exclusively with a far narrower and more elevated market and lacked both the motivation and the technical expertise to capitalise on the large scale demand for high quality domestic wares in the prevailing Meissen taste.

As the Worcester output widened both in scale and variety, a series of skilfully designed and highly practical shapes were developed which became not only the finest and sturdiest of their kind available in England, but also a template which served to inspire models made elsewhere. The baluster mug, no. 148, first issued in about 1756-57 in three sizes, is associated with the celebrated *"King of Prussia"* transfer-print, most often incorporating the date *1757*. These elegantly designed and superbly potted mugs, technically superior to the earlier versions, nos. 16 and 17, remained in production for at least fifteen years, imitated at such factories as Derby, Plymouth, Champion's Bristol[1] and Caughley. So too were the new range of coffee pots, teapots, creamjugs and other components of a tea and coffee service, first issued at this period. From both a practical and commercial standpoint, this fundamental change of direction in marketing strategy was a necessary and far-sighted business and artistic decision which contributed significantly to the factory's prosperity and financial stability into the 1770s. It should not be forgotten that during this period, four contemporary factories, Longton Hall, Vauxhall and the Liverpool factories of William Reid and Samuel Gilbody, all succumbed to the hazards endemic to the English porcelain industry. Furthermore, the early 1770s witnessed the most severe financial recession for nearly fifty years.

The pieces in this small section of the Collection, relating chiefly to the late 1750s, vividly illustrate the radical change of style devised in about 1756. This is strikingly evident in a comparison between the creamjug, no. 144, and its rococo predecessor, no. 92, separated in period by only five years. The baluster mugs, nos. 72 and 148, both fine examples in their way, also seem worlds apart. It is no wonder that many collectors draw a distinction between the two phases of production. A. J. Smith admired this slightly later period, yet considerations of budget and space obliged him to concentrate his resources. The pair of "fig leaves", no. 143, are the outstanding pieces in this section of the Collection. Superbly painted in the Meissen taste, moulded in low relief, a skill unsurpassed at any other factory, they embody the highest aspirations of the Worcester designers as the factory entered a new phase of its development.

143. PAIR OF "FIG LEAVES" circa 1756-58

MARKS: None

DIAMETER: 7¼ ins

This shape, unique to Worcester, probably corresponds to the factory's London warehouse price list of about 1756, describing "Fig Leaves . . . 4/-, 12/-" per dozen, available in two sizes. The prices almost certainly relate to blue and white fig leaves,[2] the smaller size being a pickle leaf dish and the larger size being for dessert. Polychrome examples were issued only in the larger size and in almost all instances, their decoration was inspired by Meissen. The moulded decoration, always of superb quality and minute detail, is executed in low relief and was possibly influenced by Staffordshire saltglazed stoneware. These "fig leaves" are invariably painted to the highest standards of the period, whether floral, "pencilled" in either black or purple *camaieu,* or decorated with figure subjects. They represent the onset of a new polychrome idiom at the factory, approaching themes influenced by Meissen in a far more explicit manner. In this instance, Meissen motifs of the 1740s have been imitated with both accuracy and flair. The floral decoration has been placed around the borders, both in appreciation of the moulding and of their notional function in the dessert course. "Fig leaves" were the earliest and the most accomplished of the series of leaf-shaped and moulded dessert dishes which were a speciality at Worcester from about 1756 until the late 1760s.

cf. Simon Spero, *Worcester Porcelain The Klepser Collection,* no. 41, colour plate 14, for a "fig leaf" dish with "pencilled" decoration.

144. CREAMJUG circa 1758

MARKS: None
HEIGHT: 3 ins

A deliberate copy of an oriental pattern designed to accompany Chinese teabowls and saucers.[3] The creamjug conforms precisely to a model issued in about 1756-58, with a rolled base, no. 106. Yet the atypical palette with its extensive use of black and brown and its idiosyncratic depiction of trees and bushes, reveal this to be an accurate imitation of a Chinese pattern, rather than a *chinoiserie* design devised at the factory. The Chinese excelled in the manufacture of teabowls and saucers of almost eggshell thinness, highly translucent and superbly potted. Yet the corresponding teapots, creamjugs and coffee cups, alien shapes to the Chinese, were heavily potted, sometimes clumsy in design and had a regrettable tendency for the glaze to shear off leaving an uneven rough or "fritted" rim.[4] Worcester on the other hand, were expert in their hand-thrown teapots, creamjugs and coffee cups. Hence the demand for Worcester shapes to accompany Chinese teabowls and saucers.[5]

In this instance, by comparison with an imported Chinese model, the Worcester creamjug is more thinly potted, more sophisticated in outline, far better glazed and has a delicate yet robust grooved handle, superior to that of its Chinese counterpart.

cf. Simon Spero and John Sandon, *Worcester Porcelain, 1751-1790: The Zorensky Collection*, no. 135 for a Worcester coffee cup and a Chinese teabowl and saucer of about 1735, painted in this same oriental pattern.

ccf. Geoffrey Godden, *English Blue and White Porcelain,* colour plate 2 (bottom left) for a slightly later Chinese creamjug.

145. BALUSTER VASE circa 1758

MARKS: None
HEIGHT: 6¼ ins

The Mobbing Birds, one of the most dramatic Worcester patterns of the late 1750s, is depicted here in more subdued style. Confined entirely to vases, usually of baluster form and to plates, it depicts a long-eared owl, drawn here with a distinct lack of ornithological accuracy, flanked by two birds, one of which has adopted a threatening posture. The atmosphere of frenzied activity often associated with this pattern is replaced here by a sense of caricature. A Meissen influence is evident in both shape and decorative idiom, yet the pervasive humour is entirely indigenous. A related pattern was issued at Chelsea in the 1756-58 period, also on vases. At least four different hands are associated with this design, but its traditional attribution to the painter James Rogers is unconvincing.

Unlike the other two components of the garniture, this baluster model, intended to be complete with a high-domed cover, was discontinued in the early 1760s. Some examples were decorated in underglaze blue, also with bird designs in the Meissen taste, no. 41. Yet if both shape and decoration in vases of this type are evocative of Meissen, the immediate source of influence was more likely to have been that of Chelsea.

cf. Simon Spero and John Sandon, *Worcester Porcelain, 1751-1791: The Zorensky Collection,* nos. 76 and 77, and Margaret Legge, *Flowers and Fables,* no. 137, for a red anchor period Chelsea vase of this shape decorated in a comparable idiom.

146. OVOID VASE circa 1758-60

MARKS: None
HEIGHT: 7 ins

Part of a garniture set of five (or seven) vases, comprising two ovoid, two of flared beaker shape and one of baluster form, no. 145.[6] All would have been originally intended to have covers except for the flared beaker form. These models, inspired by Meissen and Chelsea precursors were introduced at Worcester in about 1757-58 and remained in production until the early 1770s, although the central baluster model seems to have been abandoned some years earlier. They represent a shift away from the ambitious moulded complexity of the earlier Worcester models with their oriental associations to the plainer outlines favoured at Meissen in the 1740s and mirrored at Chelsea during the red anchor period, c1754-58.

The floral decoration is far less characteristic and presents an instructive contrast to that of the two bell-shaped mugs, no. 148 and the creamjug, no. 149, decorated in the factory's mainstream floral idiom. Both the delicate palette and the style of painting are reminiscent of the floral bouquets on South Staffordshire opaque white glass of the middle 1750s.

cf. Delomosne & Son Ltd. *Gilding the Lily,* plate 4, for a rectangular opaque white glass tea canister with related floral decoration, dating from the middle 1750s and probably made in South Staffordshire.

147. TWO-HANDLED SAUCEBOAT circa 1758-60

MARK: None

LENGTH: 7½ ins

Two-handled sauceboats were introduced into the Worcester production in about 1754-55 and were included in the factory's London Warehouse wholesale price list of about 1755-56.[7] Issued in three sizes, of which this is the middle, they were intended for use in pairs. They remained in production until the late 1750s, although the somewhat ungainly largest size was discarded a little earlier.[8] By 1760 the shape, with its rococo overtones, had fallen out of fashion. Only at Bow did it linger on for several years.[9] The Bow model, far plainer in form and unmoulded, was issued in only one single size.

By the late 1750s, a European floral style adapted from Meissen and Chelsea had replaced the Chinese themes prevailing earlier in the decade. This new loose floral idiom was ill suited to an essentially rococo shape and blends less harmoniously with the intricate moulding and the complexities of the overall contours. Hence, this new style is associated mainly with plain hand-thrown shapes although it appeared on some feather moulded tea and coffee wares to delightful effect.

cf. no. 33, for a blue and white example and nos. 105 and 136 for two slightly earlier smaller sauceboats.

148. TWO BELL-SHAPED MUGS circa 1758-60

MARKS: None

HEIGHT: 3½ ins and 5½ ins

Issued in three sizes, 5½ inches, 4½ inches and 3½ inches, this classic shape evolved from the earlier baluster mugs of 1753-55 which were more directly influenced by silver models, no. 16. This simplified adaptation with its elegant, clean contours was introduced in about 1756-57 alongside a cylindrical alternative, also available in three sizes. Such was the success and durability of these new shapes that they remained in production until the late 1770s, almost unaltered except for a modification to the grooved handle. By comparison with the imported Chinese mugs,[10] they were far more sophisticated in their shape and handle form, better glazed and finished and had more stylish decoration. And crucially, they were equally sturdy. Indeed these two shapes served as the basis for models used at Derby, Champion's Bristol, Caughley and elsewhere.

The floral decoration, typical of the late 1750s, was loosely derived from the *deutsche Blumen* of Meissen,[11] adapted through the filter of the red anchor period Chelsea style. However the Worcester palette was fuller, brighter and more varied than that of Chelsea and the porcelain body itself, more robust and durable.[12] Far closer to contemporary Meissen motifs, this style presents an illuminating contrast to the floral idiom freely adapted from the *indianisch Blumen* of the 1720s and 1730s, embodied in the pair of wallpockets, no. 60.

cf. Simon Spero and John Sandon, *Worcester Porcelain, 1751-1790: The Zorensky Collection*, p. 372 for a discussion about the evolution of the Worcester bell-shaped (or baluster) mug in the third quarter of the eighteenth century.

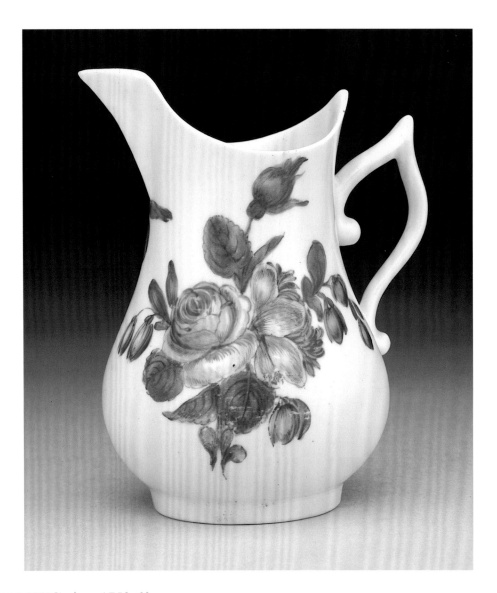

149. CREAMJUG circa 1758-60

MARK: None

HEIGHT: 3¾ ins

A relatively short-lived shape intended to match with the pear-shaped teapots with faceted spouts[13] and the bell-shaped coffee cups, also with *Tau* handles.[14] This distinctive angular handle was freely adapted from Meissen,[15] the distant source for all three Worcester shapes. A similar handle form occurs on Derby bell-shaped[16] and quatrefoil coffee cups, also derived from Meissen and first issued a year or so prior to the Worcester version. The creamjug shape, striking in its contours but perhaps a little impractical, was discarded several years before the related teapots and coffee cups.

The decoration associated with this distinctive model was invariably of high quality, whether polychrome, "pencilled" *en camaieu,* transfer-printed or in underglaze blue. Indeed particular care was taken with the decoration on all of these models alluding to earlier Meissen forms. This example is decorated with flowers, with a large insect on the reverse, in the strong thickly applied colours resembling those used on contemporary early gold anchor period Chelsea.[17] Although probably in production for only two or three years, this model was issued in both polychrome and underglaze blue and was especially associated with overglaze transfer prints.

cf. Simon Spero and John Sandon, *Worcester Porcelain, 1751-1790: The Zorensky Collection*, nos. 94 and 124 for a teapot and a coffee cup which would have been matched with this model of creamjug.

150. COFFEE POT circa 1768-70

MARKS: None

DIAMETER: 8¼ ins

One of thirteen[18] recorded versions of *The Quail* pattern on Worcester. The design originated in Japanese *kakiemon* porcelain in the late seventeenth century and it was extensively imitated in England during the 1750s and 1760s, especially at Chelsea, Bow and Worcester. Owing to their size, the quail were mistaken for partridges and the English adaptations became progressively more remote from their Japanese origins, especially during the 1770s. In this instance, the two black quail have been abducted from a Chinese *famille rose* version and all traces of *kakiemon* motifs eliminated. The palette, the composition and the slightly unsophisticated style of decoration strongly suggests that this coffee pot was decorated outside the factory.[19]

The graceful shape, only distantly influenced by silver, evolved from the Worcester coffee pots of the 1750s, becoming progressively simpler in its contours. Covers became more domed, spouts more curved and a floral finial replaced the pear-shaped knop. By comparison with earlier examples, nos. 50 and 100, Worcester coffee pots from the 1760s onwards, became significantly taller and more capacious. This specific shape, introduced in the late 1750s, remained in production almost unaltered, until the middle 1770s, becoming the model for coffee pots made at Lowestoft,[20] Caughley,[21] Plymouth,[22] Bristol and elsewhere.

cf. Simon Spero and John Sandon, *Worcester Porcelain, 1751-1790: The Zorensky Collection*, nos. 124, 194, 294, 295, 300 and 469 for other versions of *The Quail* pattern.

151. "BLIND EARL" DISH circa 1770-72

MARK: None

DIAMETER: 6 ins x 5⅝ ins

A sweetmeat dish painted in two shades of green with characteristic shadowing and moulded with rose leaves and buds. Known as the "Blind Earl" pattern after the Earl of Coventry who reputedly lost his sight in a hunting accident, it was ordered from the factory as a porcelain design which he could feel. However, it first appeared in English porcelain at Chelsea in about 1755, many years prior to the accident. The dessert dish, introduced at Worcester in the late 1750s, was produced in a large range of patterns, polychrome, transfer-printed, "pencilled" *en camaieu rose* and in underglaze blue.

   This example was decorated in the London atelier of James Giles. Clues to its attribution include a frilled tulip, a convolvulus with tendrils, a spray of daisy-like flowers and an overall looseness of the decoration. The shape probably corresponds to pieces in the Christies sale of March 1774, ". . . Part of the stock in trade of Mr James Giles . . .". The fifth day's sale of Friday March 25, lot 69, refers to "a desert service with embossed rose bud enamel'd . . .". On the second day's sale, lot 47 was listed as "a desert service enamelled in green flowers and gold edge . . .".[23] Decoration in monochrome green was a speciality of the Giles atelier.

   A service of this precise pattern was ordered from the factory in about 1770 by Sir John Horner of Mells in Somerset. He was reputedly a descendant of "Little Jack Horner", celebrated in the traditional nursery rhyme.

cf. Simon Spero and John Sandon, *Worcester Porcelain, 1751-1790: The Zorensky Collection*, nos. 87, 119, 125, 208, 411, 418 and 623 for other examples of the "Blind Earl" moulding and also no. 432 for a plate with related Giles' decoration.

NOTES

Chapter 13   **The Post 1756 Wares**

1.   Spero, *Exhibition Catalogue* (2002), no.18.
2.   Spero and Sandon, J (1996), no.539.
3.   Spero and Sandon, J (1996), no.135.
4.   Charleston and Towner, (1977), nos. 213 and 214.
5.   J. Sandon, (1993), p.112.
6.   J. Sandon, (1993), Colour plate 59.
7.   Young, (1999), plate 65.
8.   J. Sandon, (1993), p.351.
9.   Begg and Taylor, (2000), plate 130.
10.   Coke, (1983), plate 18.
11.   Savage, (1958), plate 21 for the style which inspired Chelsea and Worcester.
12.   Spero, (1995), no.26.
13.   Spero and Sandon, J (1996), no.93.
14.   Spero and Sandon, J (1996), no.124.
15.   Pietsch, (1994), no.95.
16.   Brayshaw Gilhespy, (1961), Colour plate VI.
17.   Spero, (1995), no.47.
18.   Girton, (2004), p.49.
19.   Girton, (2004), p.46.
20.   Godden, (2004), plate 362.
21.   Godden, (2004), plate 582.
22.   Watney, (1973), plate 93c.
23.   Spero and J. Sandon, (1996), no.432.

GLOSSARY

Atelier - A studio or workshop

Banded hedge - A decorative subject associated with porcelain painted in the Japanese *kakiemon** style

Camaieu - Painted decoration in monochrome*, usually three-dimensional

Cartouche - A term generally used to describe an oval frame decorated with scrollwork

Chinoiserie - European decoration inspired by oriental sources, especially Chinese

Coffee can - A straight-sided cylindrical cup, generally about 2½ inches high and shaped like a mug

Delftware - Tin-glazed earthenware

Deutsche Blumen - A naturalistic style of flower painting originating at Meissen

Diaper - An ornamental diamond or lozenge* pattern; intersecting criss-cross

Dutch jug - Large jug moulded with overlapping leaves, some with mask spouts, 1750s - 1780s. Probably of German origin.

Export china - Porcelain made specifically for the export market, usually oriental

Faceted - Connected plain surfaces as in hexagonal or octagonal forms

Famille rose - The palette of enamel colours used in China from c.1730s including a prominent rose pink

Famille verte - The category of Chinese decoration characterised by a brilliant transparent green enamel and associated with the *Kangxi* period (1662-1722)

Feather moulding - An embossed pattern derived from silver

Festoon - A garland of flowers, leaves or drapery, hanging in a natural curve and suspended from either end

Finial - the knop or lifting handle on the lids of such objects as teapots and coffee pots

Fire crack - Damage sustained during the process of manufacture

Fluted - Moulded vertical stripes or ribs

Garniture de cheminée - A set of three, five or seven porcelain vases used to decorate the mantel shelf or chimneypiece

Glaze - A coating of glass applied to the porous body of porcelain in order to seal it against the penetration of liquids

Hausmaler - German term applied to a painter of glass or ceramics who worked either at home or in a studio rather than a factory

Ho-ho bird - A phoenix incorporated into several *kakiemon** patterns

Indianische Blumen - A style of floral decoration based on the Japanese *kakiemon** but incorporating elements of Chinese famille verte*, introduced at Meissen in the early 1720s

Iron-red - An orange-red colour made from a base of ferric oxide

Japan patterns - A series of designs on English porcelain inspired by Japanese Imari wares

Jet-enamelling - An 18th century term used to describe the process of overglaze* transfer-printing in black on Worcester

Kakiemon - A Japanese potter associated with a distinctive style of decoration originating in the late 17th century and much imitated in Europe

Lobed - Shaped with projections of rounded form

Long Eliza - A Chinese figure painted in blue, resembling a "tall lady", from the Dutch *Lange Lijzen*

Lozenge - A decorative form resembling that of a diamond

Monochrome - Decoration in one colour

Ogee - A shape of a handle or fluting formed in a double curve as in the letter "S"

Osier - A willow twig used in basketry, simulated in moulded designs on porcelain

Overglaze - Decoration, either painted or transfer-printed, applied on top of the fired glaze

Palette - A group of colours peculiar to an artist or a factory

Paste - The composite material from which porcelain is made, also called the body

Pencil - A very fine brush used for making extremely thin lines, often used in monochrome* decoration, hence "pencilled" decoration

Polychrome - Decoration in two or more colours

Potting pan - An oval pot or tub for serving potted meat

Prunus - A white plum blossom. Utilised as a decorative motif in underglaze* blue, also in enamels and relief moulding

Quatrefoil - A shape having four equal lobes or foils

Relief decoration - Decoration which projects from the surface of the porcelain

Reserve - A portion of the ceramic surface left free of the surrounding ground colour

Rococo - A style in art inspired by asymmetry and the shape of sea shells, popular from the 1740s to the 1770s

Saucerdish - A shallow dish of saucer shape, usually a component of a tea service

Scalloped - Having a continuous series of segments of circle resembling the edge of a scallop shell

Silver-shape - A form adapted from, or suggested by, a silver original

Slop-bowl - A small bowl or basin for the dregs of tea from a teabowl or teacup. A component of a tea service

Smoky primitive - Early overglaze* transfer prints. Technically unsophisticated

Soaprock - A granite rich in steatite which has decomposed into an almost crumbly mineral, used as a principal ingredient in Worcester porcelain

Soft paste - So-called artificial porcelain, made without kaolin. Standard porcelain body used in England from the 1740s until the 1760s

Sparrow beak - A pouring lip resembling the pointed beak of a sparrow, associated particularly with milk or creamjugs

Spoontray - A narrow tray on which a hot or wet teaspoon was placed when not in use - a component of a "full" tea service

Strap handle - A loop handle which is flat on each side, like a narrow strap. Associated particularly with tankards, large jugs and some coffee cups

Tart pan - A shallow circular pot probably used for pâté or jelly

Teabowl - A cup without a handle for drinking tea in the Chinese style

Throwing - The process of shaping a ceramic vessel on a rotating potter's wheel

Underglaze - Decoration applied to a ceramic body before glazing, usually in blue

Wall-pocket - A flower vase made to be attached to a wall, often loosely termed a cornucopia as most examples were of this shape

Waster - A broken or defective pot cast aside upon a waster heap at some stage during the process of manufacture

Wigornia - The Roman name for the settlement on which the city of Worcester now stands Associated with moulded decoration on Worcester creamboats of the early 1750s

Wheatsheaf - A popular name for the banded hedge* motif after *kakiemon* *

BIBLIOGRAPHY

E. Adams, *Chelsea Porcelain* (London, 1987)

E. Adams, and Redstone, D., *Bow Porcelain* (London, 1981)

R.R. Angerstein, *Illustrated Travel Diary, 1753-55* (London, 2001)

J.C. Austin, *Chelsea Porcelain at Williamsburg* (Williamsburg, VA, 1977)

J. Ayers, O. Impey and J.V. Mallett, *Porcelain for Palaces: The Fashion for Japan in Europe 1650-1750*, (British Museum Exhibition Catalogue, London, 1990)

D. Barker, and S. Cole (eds.), *Digging for Early Porcelain: The Archaeology of Six 18th-century British Porcelain Factories* (Exhibition Catalogue, Stoke-on-Trent, 1998)

F.A. Barrett, *Worcester Porcelain and Lund's Bristol* (2nd edition, London, 1966)

F.A. Barrett, and A.L. Thorpe, *Derby Porcelain* (London, 1971)

P. Begg, and B. Taylor, *A Treasury of Bow* (Box Hill, 2000)

S. Benjamin, *English Enamel Boxes* (London, 1978)

K. Boney, *Liverpool Porcelain of the Eighteenth Century and Its Makers* (London, 1957)

Bonham's Auction Catalogue, *The Billie Pain Collection* (26 November 2003)

G. Bradley, (ed.) *Ceramics of Derbyshire 1750-1975* (Tiverton, 1978)

L. Branyan, N. French and J. Sandon, *Worcester Blue and White Porcelain, 1750-1790* (2nd edition, London, 1989)

F. Brayshaw Gilhespy, *Derby Porcelain* (London, 1965)

R.J. Charleston, (ed.) *English Porcelain, 1745-1850* (London and Toronto, 1965)

R.J. Charleston, and J.V.G. Mallett, 'A Problematic Group of Eighteenth Century Porcelains', *ECC Transactions*, Vol. VIII, part 1, 1971, pp.80-121

R.J. Charleston, and D. Towner, *English Ceramics 1580-1830,* (London , 1977)

G. Coke, *In Search of James Giles* (Wingham, 1983)

S. Cole, 'Potters' Incised Marks on Early Worcester Porcelain', *Antique Collecting*, June 1995

C. Cook, *Supplement to the Life and Work of Robert Hancock* (London, 1955)

— *The Life and Work of Robert Hancock* (London, 1948)

J. Cushion, and M., *A Collectors' History of British Porcelain* (Woodbridge, 1992)

M. Delhom, *English Pottery* (Charlotte NC, 1982)

Delomosne & Son Ltd., *Gilding the Lily* (Exhibition Catalogue, London, 1978)

J.L. Dixon, *English Porcelain of the Eighteenth Century* (London, 1953)

D. Edwards, 'English White Salt-glazed Stoneware for the American Market', *ECC Transactions* Vol. 18, part 2, 2003, pp.315-334

R. Emmerson, *British Teapots and Tea Drinking* (London, 1992)

English Ceramic Circle, *Limehouse Ware Revealed* (London, 1993)

A. Gabszewicz, *Made at New Canton* (London, 2000)

A. Gabszewicz, and G. Freeman, *Bow Porcelain; The Collection formed by Geoffrey Freeman* (London, 1982)

C. Girton, *The Two Quail Pattern,* (Buckingham, 2004)

G. Godden, *English Blue and White Porcelain* (Woodbridge, 2004)

— *Eighteenth Century English Porcelain: A Selection from the Godden Reference Collection* (St Albans, 1985)

J. Handley, *18th Century Transfer-Printed Porcelain and Enamels* (Carmel,1991)

W.B. Honey, revised by F.A. Barrett, *Old English Porcelain: A Handbook for Collectors* (3rd edition, London, 1977)

F. Hurlbutt, *Bristol Porcelain* (London, 1928)

O. Impey, *Chinoiserie: The Impact of Oriental Styles on Western Art and Decoration* (London, 1977)

M. Jarry, *Chinoiserie,* (New York, 1981)

P. Langford, *A Polite and Commercial People; England 1727-1783* (Oxford, 1992)

F.S. MacKenna, *Worcester Porcelain - The Wall Period and its Antecedents* (Leigh on Sea, 1950)

H.R. Marshall, *Coloured Worcester Porcelain of the First Period* (London, 1954)

J. McNeile, 'The Stag Hunt Pattern 1745-1795', *ECC Transactions* Vol. 14, part 1, 1990, pp.12-23

D.C. Pierce, *English Ceramics: The Frances and Emory Cocke Collection* (Atlanta, 1988)

Phillips Auction Catalogue, *The Watney Collection. Part 1* (22 September 1999),

— Auction Catalogue (12 December 2001)

— Auction Catalogue (11 September 1991)

U. Pietsch, *Early Meissen Porcelain* (Lubeck, 1993)

J. Poole, 'Ceramics in the Household of the 4th Duke of Bedford – Bills and Other Evidence', *ECC Transactions* Vol. 18, part 1, 2002, pp.122-168

R. Porter, *English Society in the Eighteenth Century* (London, 1982)

W. Pountney, *Old Bristol Potteries* (Bristol, 1920)

D. Reynolds, *Worcester Porcelain in the Ashmolean Museum,* (Kineton, 1988)

D.G. Rice, *Derby Porcelain: The Golden Years 1750-1770* (Newton Abbot, 1983)

P. Riley, 'A Review of Wigornia Cream Jugs', *ECC Transactions*, Vol. 13, part 3, 1989, pp.166-169

B. Rondot, (ed.), *The St Cloud Manufactory ca.1690-1766* (New York, 1999)

H. Sandon, *The Illustrated Guide to Worcester Porcelain, 1751-1793* (London, 1980)

— *Coffee Pots and Teapots* (Edinburgh,1973)

— *Worcester Porcelain* (London, 1969)

J. Sandon, *The Dictionary of Worcester Porcelain 1751-1851* (Woodbridge, 1993)

G. Savage, *Eighteenth Century German Porcelain* (London, 1958)

— *Eighteenth Century English Porcelain* (London, 1952)

G. Savage, and H. Newman, *An Illustrated Dictionary of Ceramics* (London, 1974)

Sotheby's Auction Catalogue (27 April 1976)

S. Spero, *Exhibition Catalogues* (London, 1988 - 2004)

S. Spero, 'Vauxhall Porcelain. A Tentative Chronology', *ECC Transactions* Vol. 18, part 2, 2003, pp.349-372

— *The Bowles Collection of 18th-century English and French Porcelain* (San Francisco, 1995)

— *Twenty Five Years* (London, 1989)

— *A Taste Entirely New,* (Exhibition London, 1988)

— *Worcester Porcelain: The Klepser Collection* (Minneapolis and London, 1984)

S. Spero, and J. Sandon, *Worcester Porcelain, 1751-1790: The Zorensky Collection* (Woodbridge, 1996)

W.H. Tapp, *Jefferyes Hamett O'Neale* (London, 1938)

F. Tilley, *Teapots and Tea* (Newport, 1957)

P. Waldron, *The Price Guide to Antique Silver* (Woodbridge, 1982)

B. Watney, *Liverpool Porcelain of the Eighteenth Century* (London, 1997)

— *English Blue and White Porcelain of the 18th Century* (2nd edition, London, 1973)

— *Longton Hall Porcelain* (London, 1957)

B. Watney, and R. Charleston, 'Petitions for Patents concerning Porcelain, Glass and Enamels with special reference to Birmingham, "The Great Toyshop of Europe", *ECC Transactions* Vol. 6, part 2, 1966, pp.57-123

G. Wills *English Pottery and Porcelain* (London, 1969)

R.C. Yarborough, *Bow Porcelain and the London Theatre* (Hancock, 1996)

H. Young, *English Porcelain 1745-95* (London, 1999)

INDEX

References in bold are to catalogue numbers; references in roman are to page numbers

Index by Christine Shuttleworth